Miracle on Grass

DAVID FANUCCHI

Copyright © 2012 David Fanucchi

Editor: Sabrina Rood

Olympic game summary information provided by:

John Manuel – *Baseball America*

All rights reserved.

ISBN-10: 147835741X
ISBN-13: 978-1478357414

For my Dad, Larry, who instilled in me the work ethic that I needed to finish this project, and who has always been my biggest fan. You are my hero.

CONTENTS

	Foreword	1
1	July 26, 1999: Winnipeg, Canada	5
2	1998: Tucson, Arizona	10
3	The First Pro Team USA	25
4	1999 Pan Am Games	40
5	Olympic Baseball History	67
6	Dodger Blue	73
7	Watch List	82
8	Making the Team	96
9	Selecting Olympians	110
10	Gold Coast	130
11	Sydney	158
12	Pool Play	184
13	Building Momentum	215
14	Capturing the Gold	249
15	Returning Home Heroes	285
16	Since Winning it All	294
	Acknowledgments	316

FOREWORD

NBC network cameras moved down the medal podium in the Sydney Baseball Stadium while the American flag was raised and "The Star Spangled Banner" played. It was not much different than the other medal ceremonies held throughout the 2000 Olympic Games.

Until, that is, the focus tightened on the faces of the players who had just won Olympic gold. There were moist eyes. There was palpable emotion. When the camera reached Doug Mientkiewicz, whose career had been both reborn and launched in Sydney, tears streaked down his cheeks.

We often think of professional athletes as hardened, but in celebrating this gold-medal championship, their sheer joy and euphoria were apparent.

These men, along with all Olympians, experienced that deeper emotion. Wearing your country's name and colors carries immense pride. Hearing your national anthem and watching your flag ascend while wearing a gold medal brings grown men to tears.

Mientkiewicz's tears are my lasting vivid memory of that USA Baseball gold-medal victory. An improbable team captured America's attention. A collection of promising prospects like Ben Sheets and Roy Oswalt had their careers propelled, while those who never tasted success in the major leagues, like Mike Neill and John Cotton, enjoyed their greatest baseball moment.

Creating the team was a challenge for USA Baseball. Two premier executives, Sandy Alderson and Bob Watson, spent a year targeting players, cajoling major-league organizations into loaning top prospects for the month, and, in the waning years of pre-drug testing in MLB, ensuring all potential USA players could pass the stringent testing administered at the Olympic Games.

Once the team was formed, a manager was needed. Enter Tommy Lasorda.

The assembled team lacked even one name familiar to the casual American baseball fan, hence Lasorda became the face of Team USA. Over his decades with the Dodgers, Lasorda had become an ambassador for baseball second to none. Thus was the 2000 USA Olympic Baseball team born. Upon arrival in Sydney, rarely did anyone inquire about a player, but rather always asked about Lasorda. In the NBC broadcast compound, Team USA's games were coined "TommyBall."

Twelve years later, I remember with a smile Lasorda holding court in Sydney, never without his friend, USC coaching legend Rod Dedeaux. Lasorda gave Olympic Baseball spirit and credibility, and more importantly he commanded attention.

Team USA's journey in Sydney was colorful. They faced a young Japanese star named Daisuke Matsuzaka in the opening game. They needed heroics from Mientkiewicz twice against the same team (Korea) to reach the gold-medal game. Once there, they rebounded amazingly from a one-sided loss to the Cubans in pool play, thanks to the right arm of Ben Sheets.

The journey catapulted USA Baseball to a higher profile. NBC caught "TommyBall" fever, especially after Mientkiewicz won the semi-final game. Team USA battled Cuba for gold on live US television with extra equipment ordered specifically for the night.

Reflecting on that evening, the elevated attention was deserved. And during the medal ceremony, one other set of very moist eyes could be spotted. I will never forget Lasorda, who after learning that the Olympics only awarded medals to athletes, could be seen standing on the field wiping away tears, as the American flag flew in the Sydney night.

Baseball's exclusion from the Olympics may be permanent. If so, the 2000 USA Baseball Olympic Team will forever be the only American baseball players to win gold.

Dave Fanucchi was there to live the moments. His recollections ensure this story lives on.

Ted Robinson
NBC Sports Baseball Play-by-Play Announcer
2000 Olympic Games

Robinson (left) with NBC Sports baseball color commentator
Joe Magrane, in Sydney.

DAVID FANUCCHI

1

JULY 26, 1999: WINNIPEG, CANADA

It was a bright and sunny Monday afternoon—the third day of official competition in the 1999 Pan American Games. For Olympic athletes and teams that represented countries in North, Central, and South America, the Pan Ams would be serving as the qualifying event for the 2000 Summer Olympics that were to be held in Sydney, Australia in just over a year.

For the United States, they would be represented in the baseball tournament by the first-ever group of professional-level players to don the Team USA uniform. Players who were under contract with a major-league organization, but who at the time were on non-40-man rosters and playing in the minors, were being asked to represent their country for the first time in international competition. Only the top two teams out of the ten playing in Winnipeg would advance to Sydney.

In front of a capacity crowd of 6,140 at the small but cozy CanWest Global Stadium— home of the independent league Winnipeg Goldeyes—the 1999 Pan Am baseball tournament began. Team USA's opening-round contest had them pitted against the home team from Canada, as the event organizers saw this as a tremendous way to kick off the competition. The

Americans, who were one of the favorites coming into the event (along with the perennial powerhouse team from Cuba), would be facing a young but fairly experienced Canadian team that would be playing for pride in front of their home fans. Team USA found themselves in hostile territory right away.

The Americans jumped ahead in the top of the second inning with a pair of runs, and led 2-0 until Canada bounced back off USA starting pitcher John Patterson to tie the score 2-2. It stayed that way until the seventh inning, when Team USA shortstop Travis Dawkins—nicknamed "Gookie"—belted a solo home run to put the Americans back on top, 3-2. But Canada fought right back again and plated a run in the bottom half to knot the score at 3-3. They were in the game, the crowd was behind them, and the biggest problem for the Americans was that the Canadians now believed they could win.

"We were getting a big-time dose of what this international competition thing was going to be all about," said Team USA manager and former major-league All-Star Buddy Bell. "Three days earlier, we had demolished these Canadian kids in a practice game, but then when the money was on the line and it counted, they showed up ready to play, and they were giving us everything we could handle."

The game was pushed into extra innings tied at 3-3, and in the eleventh inning, Team USA finally broke through. St. Louis Cardinals prospect Adam Kennedy ripped a two-out, run-scoring double that gave them the lead, and when American utilityman Jason Hardtke followed with a blast over the fence, Team USA had gained a 6-3 advantage.

With just three outs needed for the victory, Team USA's closer Todd Williams was summoned from the bullpen. Williams, who had big-league experience for both the Dodgers and Reds and had posted 25 saves for the triple-A Indianapolis Indians earlier that season, easily got the first two outs. But then he walked a hitter.

Bell—not wanting anything to get out of hand—decided to play the odds and bring in Scott Stewart, the left-handed relief pitcher warming up in the bullpen, to face the next left-handed batter for Canada. With the entire crowd on their feet chanting "Can-a-da, Can-a-da," Stewart was immediately rattled and unprepared for the moment. Having trouble throwing strikes, he also walked the batter he was facing. Now, as the tying run strolled to the plate in the name of right-handed hitter Andy Stewart, the noise level in the tiny stadium was deafening.

Sure enough, when Scott grooved a fastball, Andy drove it deep over the left-field fence, tying the score at 6-6.

"The feeling I had at the moment that ball went over the fence is undescribable," said Bell. "We had that game won."

Following the chaos that had just occurred, there was no doubt that everyone involved with the American team was completely stunned, and the Canadians knew it. Team USA officials and coaches could not believe what they had just seen, and had to be thinking, "How could this be possible?"

Another walk and a hit batter later, Stewart still had not gotten out of the inning and was desperately trying to hang on to keep Team USA alive in the game. It had all happened so quickly that American pitching coach Marcel Lachemann didn't have enough time to get another reliever loose in the bullpen. Before you knew it, Canada's pesky leadoff hitter Stubby Clapp was at the plate, with the winning run at second base.

And with the crowd still on its feet while banging cowbells and drums, Clapp blooped a pitch into shallow left field. Converging on it were USA outfielder Shawn Gilbert and shortstop Dawkins, but miraculously, the ball fell between them both and onto the turf, giving the Canadians an improbable 7-6 victory.

In the locker room following the game, there was a "deer in the headlights" look in the American players' eyes. It was pure and utter shock.

"I wanted to throw up," said USA Baseball executive director Paul Seiler. "That was literally the feeling. For people who like to be in control, and I'm one of those people, that is the worst thing, to sit there and watch everything that you work for, end up in somebody else's hands. And the knot in your stomach just gets accentuated by the euphoria that's coming out of the opposing team's fans. As high as they're getting, you're getting as low and dark in the opposite direction. It was one of the worst feelings I've ever had."

The headline in the *Winnipeg Free Press* the next morning called it "The Miracle on Grass." Canada's upset win over Team USA in baseball was the talk of the entire country and the toast of the town. Every news channel had highlights of Andy Stewart's home run, and then Clapp's game-winning bloop single, along with the red-and-white on-field celebration that ensued.

"It took that opening loss for us to really realize that this wasn't going to be a cakewalk," said Williams. "It made us very aware that these games were all going to be close, even against the teams we thought we should beat up on. We found out right away that we were in for a dogfight and needed to figure this thing out."

In an event where the American team had such high expectations, they had put themselves behind the eight ball from the very beginning. It was going to be an uphill battle, just to get into a position where they might be able to qualify for the right to play in Sydney.

"Later that evening, after we'd lost that Canada game, I was walking through the lobby back at our team hotel," said Seiler. "I bumped into Buddy, who was standing there with his wife and daughter, and he had this lost look on his face. So I walked up to him and asked him if he was all right, and he said to me, 'What the hell happened?' I looked back and said, 'Hey, welcome to our world, my man. This is international baseball.' I knew that every game was going to be like this."

Bell, who had been around baseball for over 30 years, and who had a pedigree in the game at the highest level, found himself very quickly in a situation that he'd never faced before in the sport.

"That was the first time that I really felt the importance of what we were doing up there in Canada," said Bell. "Because now, all of a sudden, if we don't at least win a silver medal, Team USA's not going to the Olympics. So all these kids on our roster were going to be viewed as the reason why the United States is not playing in Sydney! More than that, though, was the fact that I had USA across my chest. You realized what you're playing for, nothing more than that, which was the most important thing. I really believe that our players didn't understand the significance of it until we lost that game to Canada. Suddenly, this tournament meant everything in the world to them."

The first-ever Olympic baseball competition with professional players was 15 months away, and the United States wasn't even going to be there? That would not only be an embarrassment to Major League Baseball and USA Baseball, but also a gigantic disappointment for both the International Olympic Committee and the Sydney Olympic Organizing Committee, who would be counting on Team USA as one of the main ticket draws of the baseball event. Failing to qualify for the Olympics was not an option, but Team USA already had lost their first game. They simply could not afford to lose another.

2

1998: TUCSON, ARIZONA

It was the Christmas holiday season of 1998, and the older, dilapidated office space located under the bleachers and behind home plate at Hi Corbett Field in Tucson, Arizona, was cold and dusty. No activity had taken place in the stadium for months. USA Baseball had just moved their headquarters into this Cactus League spring-training facility of the Colorado Rockies, which had also been utilized in the past as the home of the Tucson Toros, a triple-A affiliate of the Houston Astros that once played in the Pacific Coast League. But the city-owned stadium was probably more famously known as the site that was used for the spring-training scenes filmed in the movie *Major League* starring Charlie Sheen.

Since 1978, USA Baseball has been the National Governing Body (NGB) for amateur baseball. It represents the sport in the United States as a member of the U.S. Olympic Committee (USOC) and internationally as a member federation of the International Baseball Federation (IBAF). Nearly every major national amateur baseball organization in America—such as Little League, PONY, Babe Ruth, Dixie, and American Legion—is united as a National Member Organization. As a result, USA Baseball governs more than 12 million amateur players in ballparks and playgrounds across the country.

As the Commissioner's Office for amateur baseball, USA Baseball is a resource center for its various membership groups, fans, and players. USA Baseball is also responsible for promoting and developing the game of baseball on the grassroots level, both nationally and internationally. But at the heart of what they do is their responsibility to select the game's best amateur players who will get the right to represent their country and play for Team USA in international competitions, including the Olympic Games.

The USA Baseball executive director at the time was a longtime baseball executive named Dan O'Brien. O'Brien had been instrumental in the decision to move the governing body's offices to a baseball facility, away from the confines of an old two-story home in Trenton, New Jersey, where the organization had been formed in 1978. By the mid-'90s, O'Brien had seen the need for the organization to grow, add staff members, and be located at a facility that actually had baseball fields where they could host trials and Team USA exhibition games.

O'Brien had been in baseball for over 40 years and was nearing the end of his career. Once a general manager for the California Angels, O'Brien was well liked among pro baseball circles and respected by his major-league-level colleagues across the game. With his connections to civil leaders and baseball executives in Arizona, O'Brien had cut a deal with the city of Tucson for USA Baseball to utilize some extra office space at Hi Corbett. It would be a major upgrade to their location and give them a higher profile identity. But most importantly, it would give the governing body much better access to the professional game, as the Rockies and their staff would be in town for two months every year, working in the same facility. This was critical, because the International Olympic Committee had recently announced that professional baseball players would be allowed to participate in the Olympic Games for the first time, starting in 2000.

O'Brien had become much more familiar with the desert landscape back in 1993, when he had been placed in charge of MLB's brand-new prospect-training operation called the Arizona Fall League, based in Phoenix. In the league's second season, the AFL was put on the map when Michael Jordan decided to take a one-year hiatus from his NBA basketball career in 1994, and the Chicago White Sox sent him to play in the AFL after his minor-league stint with the double-A Birmingham Barons had ended. With the unexpected arrival of one of the biggest sports stars on the planet, O'Brien's office needed help handling the AFL's sudden crush of media attention and publicity.

I had been in my second season as the media relations assistant with the triple-A Phoenix Firebirds of the Pacific Coast League, the minor-league farm team of my beloved San Francisco Giants. The team played their games at Scottsdale Stadium, the spring-training site of the Giants and also one of the ballparks that was utilized in the Arizona Fall League.

When AFL Media Relations Director Steve Gilbert gave me a call, asking whether I would be able to assist him with the upcoming media attention the league was going to get upon Jordan's arrival, of course I was ready to do the job. It ended up being one of the craziest two months of my career and an experience I will never forget. It's also where I first met and worked with O'Brien.

Four years later, Dan was in a similar position, as USA Baseball now had a need for an extra publicity person with major-league experience. They now needed to begin interacting with all 30 major-league teams and selecting professional players. I had left Arizona and just finished two seasons in 1996 and 1997 as a media relations assistant with the St. Louis Cardinals. O'Brien was looking for someone to help handle communications and public relations at their new headquarters, and I was lucky enough to get a call from O'Brien with a job offer.

And so I began on the first business day of 1999. I walked into the somewhat renovated offices in the bowels of the facility with as much enthusiasm for my first full-time position in sports as I could possibly have. I was going to be working with the best players in baseball, and I would have the opportunity one day to possibly be a press officer for Team USA at the Olympics.

The staff of USA Baseball at that time consisted of just six people besides O'Brien, the most significant being a hockey enthusiast, former college soccer player, and New Jersey native named Paul Seiler. Seiler had joined USA Baseball in the early '80s in Trenton as one of the first staffers under the original executive director, Dick Case. Now newly married, he and his young wife, Wendi, had decided to make the move from the East Coast to the desert and start a new life together.

Seiler had been put in charge of selecting the USA National Team, made up of the best collegiate freshman and sophomore players in America. Each summer, Team USA would travel both throughout the U.S. and overseas to play exhibition games against the national teams of other countries, sometimes in organized IBAF-sanctioned world championship events, other times just as straight exhibition games. Their most important and competitive event each summer was the USA vs. Japan Collegiate All-Star Series: a series of five games played against the best Japanese players of the same age. Every year, the location of the series would rotate between the USA and Japan, and the home team almost always won the best of five matchups. Although it was often very competitive, the home crowd and the familiar surroundings usually gave one team the edge.

Seiler had also been heavily involved in the selection of the 1992 and 1996 USA Baseball Olympic Teams, because the collegiate National Team was the highest level team that USA Baseball would select each year, and therefore they would enter those amateur players as Team USA into the Olympics.

But with the IOC's decision to ramp the Olympic baseball competition up a notch to include professional players, 1996 would be the last time the amateurs would represent Team USA in the Games.

Another member of the USA Baseball staff in '99 was Steve Cohen, who was brought on to operate and select the Junior National Team, made up of the best high school (18 and under) players in the country. Cohen was a baseball dirtbag. He loved the game, was a diehard Minnesota Twins fan, and could never get enough baseball. A high school coach in the Twin Cities for years, he had led the USA Junior National Team to a gold-medal victory in the 1995 IBAF Junior World Championships, which happened to be played that summer in ballparks across Cape Cod on the eastern seaboard. For the gold-medal game, Team USA had earned the opportunity to play Korea at Fenway Park.

Two of the key players whom Cohen had selected to play on that team were a 17-year-old shortstop named Brent Abernathy from Marietta, Georgia and an 18-year-old outfielder and pitcher named Brad Wilkerson out of Owensboro, Kentucky.

"Not only were both of them outstanding high school players at the time, Brent and Brad both showed natural leadership abilities, on and off the field," said Cohen. "That's what I liked about them."

In nine games, Wilkerson became a star, both on the mound and with the bat. He went 3-0 with a 0.90 ERA in 20.0 innings pitched, allowing just two earned runs in the entire tournament. Offensively, he batted .360 with a team-high three home runs and collected eight RBIs. Abernathy batted .346 with a home run and five RBIs.

So as the winter of '99 turned to spring, the staff at USA Baseball was now in place to begin the selection process of their first-ever professional-level team, which in August would take on the task of competing in the 1999 Pan Am Games in Winnipeg, Canada: the qualifying event for the 2000 Olympics. Team USA would have to finish among the top two teams at the Pan Ams in order to make it to Sydney.

Knowing that the international baseball powerhouse from Cuba would also be in Winnipeg, along with a strong team from the host country of Canada and baseball-savvy Latin

American teams from Mexico, Venezuela, and the Dominican Republic, it was going to be a daunting task.

We were seven months away from the Olympic qualifying event, and about to embark on a journey where none of us knew what to expect.

When the IOC decided to allow the baseball governing bodies to bring professionals to the Olympics, they expected that each country would find a way to bring the very best 24 baseball players they had. So the first problem for USA Baseball was that every other country in the world was going to be able to come very close to doing that, but not the United States. We knew from the very beginning that there was no possible way we would ever get the greatest 24 living American baseball players to compete for us.

Why? Because those 24 players were earning millions of dollars playing games every day in the major leagues, and the Olympic Games are held during the summer at the exact same time. There would be no way that any major-league club would allow the likes of a Derek Jeter to step away from the Yankees for two weeks in August in order to compete for Team USA. Too much money was involved, and the major-league schedule is set in stone. Adjusting it to accommodate a two-week break so that players could play for their country was just not an option. Those factors would force USA Baseball to contain their requests for players to minor leaguers.

"Prior to the 1996 Olympics, the genesis of the pro idea for baseball was really a result of the success that the Dream Team in basketball had in 1992," said Seiler. "The Olympics had traditionally been the best amateur athletes in the world for many years, which was the Olympic ideal. But with the advent of the 1992 USA Basketball Dream Team featuring Michael Jordan, Larry Bird, and Patrick Ewing, and the high commercial success of that team, including merchandise and television ratings, it changed the face of the Olympic Games to some degree."

At the time, IOC President Juan Antonio Samaranch, in conversations with International Baseball Federation (IBAF) leadership, saw that success and, realizing that baseball was in a very similar position, suggested that the sport consider moving in that direction: incorporating professionals into the Olympic Games. Then began the conversation in and among the memberships of the countries of the IBAF to figure out what that meant moving forward. At that point, USA Baseball was led by their original executive director named Dick Case. Ultimately, in 1994 the IBAF ended up holding a vote among all member countries that led to the decision to begin using professional players at its highest level of international competition each year, whether that be the World Cup, Pan Am Games, or Olympic Games. The 1996 Games in Atlanta were already well into being scheduled and in the works, so the IBAF realized that the first opportunity to begin this transition would be after Atlanta.

"Samaranch had been talking to the IBAF and Major League Baseball about this, which by extension included conversations with the MLB Players Association as well," said Seiler. "But whomever the powers-that-be were that came together to have those conversations, I don't think at any time anyone from MLB or the union promised anything. I think the general desire was 'Yes, let's try to find a way to bring professionals into the game in some way.' I don't know if anybody ever promised the greatest living baseball players would be in the Olympics, but this was a chance to raise the level of play in the Olympic Games from what had been traditionally amateur/college players to a whole different level of player," said Seiler. "I find it hard to believe and I doubt highly that anybody from Major League Baseball and/or the Players Union sat in a meeting and promised something that they were not prepared to deliver." The nature of these conversations was political and historical. The thinking was "How do we position our sport in the right way to benefit baseball and to be a benefit to the Olympic Games?" But when it all shook out, the reality was very apparent. "The major-league season is what it is, and the financial impact of every game is incredible. The argument of closing down the

MLB season so that the All-Star players could play in the Olympics, while it may sound patriotic and it may sound idealistic, the reality is from a business perspective to do it you'd be looking at losing millions of revenue dollars."

But all initial indications were that this was a good thing. The level of play in the Olympics was going to rise, and that was the expectation. Japan was going to bring their best; Cuba was always going to bring their best; the other countries that qualify were going to be able to bring close to their best. And USA Baseball would be able to bring a roster of players that was far more experienced than any of their four previous USA Olympic teams.

Still, even asking the MLB teams for their minor leaguers presented its share of challenges. "We had no idea how each major-league general manager would react, when we inquired about the availability of some of their top prospects," said Seiler. "The reality for USA Baseball was, we were essentially asking them if we could 'borrow' some of their best American-born minor leaguers to play in a baseball tournament in Canada."

There were only two possible upsides for a major-league team to allow this to happen: 1) the player may gain valuable, high-quality experience playing in extreme pressure that normally does not occur during the minor-league season, which could help launch the player's confidence and lead him to bigger success; or 2) by being selected to play for Team USA, the player and his organization may receive media attention and publicity before and during the event.

On the contrary, the downsides were tremendous. The primary risk concern from the major-league GM's perspective was that their star future prospect—one whom they likely paid a high dollar signing bonus to and had big plans for in the future—could get injured while out of their own control and under the supervision of USA Baseball. That was an even bigger concern with the pitching prospects we were asking for, because MLB clubs are routinely strict on how often their pitchers work and are very protective of their throwing schedules. Once their pitchers left their control, these important factors would be out of the general managers' hands.

"We knew from the get-go that the most important aspect of this entire operation would be that we would need to build up the trust level of each and every general manager, in what we were doing with their players and how we would handle them," said Seiler.

So the first task was to figure out a way to begin having discussions with each MLB club's general manager about whether certain players in that team's system were "untouchable" and which ones they would consider allowing to play for Team USA. There was no sense wasting time and energy on a player if their organization was never going to allow them to do this in the first place. Unfortunately, for Team USA that happened to be the situation with many of the top marquee players who were in the minor leagues, because the clubs were simply not willing to allow their prized prospects to leave their control.

But to have those conversations, O'Brien knew he needed an experienced general manager who was well respected by his colleagues in baseball circles. He found that man in former Oakland A's GM Sandy Alderson, who had moved on from his team capacity in the San Francisco Bay Area and into an operations role in the MLB Commissioner's Office.

The son of an Air Force pilot, Alderson flew missions during World War II, Korea, and Vietnam, and attended Dartmouth College on an NROTC scholarship, graduating in 1969. He later graduated from Harvard Law School in 1976, and following law school, he worked for Farella Braun & Martel in San Francisco.

When one of the firm's partners left to become president of the Oakland Athletics when his father-in-law bought the team, Alderson joined the club to become the A's general counsel, and in 1983 he was named the team's general manager, a position he held through 1997. Under Alderson, the Athletics' minor-league system was rebuilt, which bore fruit later that decade as José Canseco (1986), Mark McGwire (1987), and Walt Weiss (1988) were chosen as American League Rookies of the Year. The Athletics won four division titles, three pennants, and the 1989 World Series during Alderson's tenure. In 1995, team owner Walter A. Haas, Jr. died and new owners Stephen Schott and Ken Hofmann ordered Alderson to slash payroll. As a result, Alderson began focusing on a system of sabermetric principles that he could use as a guide toward obtaining relatively undervalued players, and he became a mentor to his eventual successor, Billy Beane.

"At the time, I was responsible for all baseball operations and on-field activity for the Commissioner's Office, so international baseball fell within my realm," said Alderson. "But it was a natural extension of my role, and I thought we blended into what USA Baseball was doing fairly easily. We had access to the players, and they brought the international expertise. And we both had a common goal."

Seiler immediately took a liking to Alderson, as the two got to know one another and figured out the comfort zones of their new working relationship. "I knew my place and role was to guide our contingent through the ways that the United States Olympic Committee does things. I understood that exercise," said Seiler. "Major League Baseball does things their way, and that was separate. I didn't really know that world, but I knew I now had Sandy in my corner. My job was to help them understand the different hoops we had to jump through relative to the Olympic Committee exercise: why we had to be here and there at certain times. So it was as much about me being a conduit for MLB to understand the USOC operation, and to understand that we're not just a baseball team, we're part of the entire Team USA contingent that will compete in the Pan Am Games."

With this being a Pan Am team, everything was going to filter through the United States Olympic Committee. O'Brien didn't necessarily have the relationship with the USOC that Seiler did, because Seiler had been working with the organization for a much longer period of time and had been to other international events where the USOC was in control of Team USA. So Seiler brought the international USOC experience to the table, while O'Brien directed the organization into the world of MLB and brought the two entities together for the first time.

With Alderson serving as their conduit, Seiler led Alderson down the path to realize the timing and deadlines that were in place to put together a team, as Alderson began the process of identifying and ultimately selecting the players that would be on this club and determining how to get those players involved.

"Because I grew up in a family where my father was in the Marine Corps, that had been a part of my life forever. And Sandy was in the Marine Corps. So I realized that very quickly, and I really felt comfortable around his style. I was able to figure out how he operates," said Seiler. "Not really knowing how he had managed to have success with Oakland, all I knew was that this was a guy from the Commissioner's Office who didn't come in and say, 'What are we going to do here?' He comes in and says, 'Okay, listen. This is what we're going to do.' For me, looking back, that was great. Because again, we're venturing into a world of interaction with major-league clubs, professional athletes that had never been done before. I was wondering at the time, 'How are we going to evaluate these players? How do we actually select this team?' Sandy gave us those answers right away."

The first—and maybe the most important—team-related move made by Alderson was his hiring of a pair of longtime, highly regarded major-league-level baseball men with whom each MLB team would be comfortable working and communicating on behalf of USA Baseball.

The first was Pat Gillick, architect of the back-to-back World Series champion Toronto Blue Jays in 1992 and 1993. He later went on to become the general manager of the Baltimore Orioles and helped guide them to playoff appearances in 1996 and '97, before leaving after his contract expired in 1998. So in 1999 he was without a job in the major leagues and a perfect fit for what USA Baseball needed. He had a keen eye for talent and a great sense of what it takes to win baseball games. Gillick was named the Chairman of the USA Team Selection and Steering Committees.

"Sandy was in the Commissioner's Office at the time and called me one day to ask me if I'd be interested in getting involved with USA Baseball," said Gillick. "I'd just finished my contract with the Orioles after the '98 season and knew that we were pointing toward the Pan Am Games in the summer of '99. So I didn't plan to do anything that summer. I thought it would be a great challenge and a very unique opportunity to try and help our team qualify for the Olympics. It was going to be a challenge not only for USA Baseball, but for the United States in general.

"I knew a lot of the players in the minor leagues, and I thought we could put together a very respectable team. And the one thing about it is I had a committee of people who had a lot of scouting background. Consequently that didn't make it any easier, but it certainly expedited the way that we went about putting the team together."

Seiler and Alderson found another asset in Bob Watson, and named him Vice-Chairman under Gillick. Nicknamed "Bull," Watson spent 18 years playing in the big leagues for the Astros, Red Sox, Yankees, and Braves, from 1966-84. A two-time All-Star, Watson enjoyed a very successful career, hitting .295 with 184 home runs and 989 RBIs.

Maybe the most interesting fact about Watson's career was that he was credited with scoring the 1,000,000th run in major-league history on May 4, 1975 at 12:32 in the afternoon. While playing for the Astros, Watson scored from second base on a three-run homer by teammate Milt May at San Francisco's Candlestick Park. It was known that the 999,999th run had already scored, with sponsored updates being provided by and to every ballpark. Despite the lack of in-game urgency, Watson ran at full speed, reaching home plate approximately four seconds before Dave Concepción, who had just homered for the Reds in Cincinnati and was also racing around the base paths. "I never ran so fast in my entire life," said Concepción. But it was Watson who won $10,000 and one million Tootsie Rolls provided by the event's sponsor.

There were several other unique factors about Watson, the most Hollywood-like being the fact that he made a cameo appearance in the movie *The Bad News Bears in Breaking Training*, when the Bears played a game at the Astrodome in Houston. But after his playing days were over, Watson went on to several different jobs in the game and coached as well. Then in 1993 he was named general manager of the Astros, becoming the first African-American GM in MLB history.

Bull accomplished even more a few years later, when in 1996 he took over as GM of the New York Yankees and led the team to the World Series Championship and their first title since 1978. But two years later Watson reached a boiling point with then-owner of the Yankees George Steinbrenner.

"It had gotten to where my health wasn't the greatest, I was struggling physically, and George and I had one too many arguments, so the week before spring training started, I walked into Brian Cashman's office and told him that I had recommended him to be the new general manager of the Yankees," said Watson. "And here he is some 17 years later, still in that same role."

It was then that Watson got re-acquainted with his family, took some vacation time away from the game, got himself back into better shape, and traveled around the world with his wife. "I just really used the time to recharge my batteries and remove myself from baseball," said Watson. "But it was later on that off-season prior to '99, when Sandy called me. I didn't know much about USA Baseball at all, but I had begun to see what kind of jobs were out there to get back into the game. This one was certainly the most intriguing to me, so I went for it."

To USA Baseball, it was going to be critical to have men like Gillick and Watson calling their peers to talk about a business relationship, because that's essentially what it was. "When you ask a team for one of their prized prospects, you're talking about a business asset. I hate speaking in those terms because it depersonalizes the athlete, but at the end of the day, that's what we were talking about," said Seiler. "We were making an investment in these individuals, so we had to have someone on our end of the phone who had name recognition and respect. And I would venture to say that with any of the MLB club GMs who were in those roles in 1999, when Pat Gillick and Bob Watson called, there was total respect.

"Those were the two men we had representing USA Baseball and the United States of America, when that call was made that asked, 'Can we borrow your player?'" said Seiler. "A very critical aspect of how we were able to help those conversations have a positive outcome, meaning 'Yes, we'll make that player available to you.'"

So it would be left up to Watson and Gillick to begin the process of narrowing down the list of potential players whom Team USA would begin to monitor throughout the 1999 season. Considering the thousands of American-born minor-league players spread out across the country, it was going to be exhausting.

To help with the player-selection process, they created a committee of baseball front-office execs who would be able to give them input and opinions. The Selection Committee consisted of: Sal Artiaga of the Philadelphia Phillies, Roland Hemond of the Arizona Diamondbacks, Roger Jongwaard of the Seattle Mariners, Chuck Lamar of the Tampa Bay Devil Rays, Omar Minaya of the New York Mets, J. P. Ricciardi of the Oakland A's, Doc Rodgers of the Cincinnati Reds, Terry Ryan of the Minnesota Twins, Gary Sutherland of the Anaheim Angels, Steve Cobb of MLB's Arizona Fall League, and Seiler.

They also formed a Steering Committee that would assist in finding a coaching staff and the right people to serve in the team's administrative capacities, such as the trainer, physician, and equipment manager. The Steering Committee was made up of Gillick; Watson; O'Brien; Cobb; Hall of Famer Frank Robinson, who was working at the time for Major League Baseball; Bill Bavasi of the Anaheim Angels; Brian Cashman of the New York Yankees; Dave Dombrowski of the Florida Marlins; and Kevin Towers of the San Diego Padres.

With all of the key personnel now in place, it was time to begin the actual player-selection process. "I think Sandy really enjoyed it, because all of a sudden, he was able to put his GM hat back on, and went back to the point of team building, of building a club," said Seiler. "It gave him a nice break from his operations role at MLB, and I think he was excited about the work."

3

THE FIRST PRO TEAM USA

One of the first things Gillick and Watson did to prepare for the start of the 1999 season was to enlist the help of the Major League Baseball Scouting Bureau. Rather than relying on scouts from each of the major-league teams who might have biased opinions about certain players, the Bureau was a neutral scouting service that could inform USA Baseball about the true abilities of any player and give them scores in an unbiased rating system. Not only that, the Bureau had collected video footage of virtually every minor-league player, which was made available for Gillick and Watson to view. This was critical, because USA Baseball only had a limited amount of funding that could be tapped into for travel purposes, in order for Pat or Bob to see a player compete in person. Sophisticated video clips from baseball scouting services did not yet exist on the Internet, like those you would see today.

The three main scouts who the Bureau's executive director Frank Marcos assigned to work with Team USA were longtime baseball scouts Don Welke, Jim Walton, and Bart Johnson. They would be informing the USA Selection Committee about certain players, and in addition, when the competition began, they would be handling the advance intelligence work and putting together reports on the USA's opponents.

So as pitchers and catchers reported to spring training in both Florida and Arizona, little did most of them know that the first half of the minor-league season would become a virtual tryout for the United States Pan Am team. USA Baseball would be monitoring the statistics closer than ever before and would be cross-referencing that information with the reports that the Scouting Bureau would deliver.

"Not only were we looking for quality players on the field, but when you talk about representing your country, we had a certain quality of person we were looking for as well," said Seiler. "We wanted solid, hard-nosed players that the United States of America could be proud of."

Part of the director of communications' job was to organize the data of the ongoing season statistics for players on the early "watch" list, which contained over 250 players. This list consisted of not only the players whom the Scouting Bureau was recommending, but also a smaller group of individuals with whom USA Baseball was familiar. Many of the top collegiate and high-school level players who had come through their developmental system in the past had now moved on into their professional careers. Those were the players whom USA Baseball already knew something about, both in their personality and their character. They also knew whether that individual could handle the pressure of international competition.

Historically, USA Baseball had run an 18-under Junior National Team and a Collegiate National Team, and ideally those players would help create a pipeline to a pro team. If USA Baseball could take a player who had USA Baseball experience or international experience in the past, they of course would most likely choose that player over one who did not. But in this case, the pipeline was not going to be able to fill an entire 24-man roster. This team selection would create a break in that process.

"If a player came up in conversation, who had come through our National Team program, sure, we were going to have a different discussion about him, mostly because we probably knew something about that guy from spending weeks with him in the summer as a college player or a high school player," said Seiler. "But that was it. It was not like it is today, where we've got so many of our alumni at a very high pro level in the game. We just didn't have that depth yet."

As USA Baseball began to put together a team of 24 guys who had never played a game together, they knew they'd be facing the task of going up against a Cuban team that played together all the time with years of international experience. It was a bit of a concern.

"There was nothing we could do about that though," said Seiler. "Our confidence came from the fact that the United States had such a deep pool of baseball talent, and we understood that we were lucky and blessed to have that deep pool of talent in our country. So, although I did believe somewhat that we were at a slight disadvantage, the other side of that is, if we did our homework and had confidence and faith in our system, and if we vetted the players correctly as well as our coaching staff, we would be able to compete with any team in the world. When you have the right coaching staff, that's really where it started, the right manager and going on down the line from there."

So as the summer months approached, USA Baseball executives, Gillick, Watson, and Alderson were hard at work preparing to make 24 critical decisions on the ballplayers they would select to represent the United States at the 1999 Pan Am Games in Winnipeg, Manitoba, Canada.

Just before the player-selection process really began to get into full swing, a conference call was held about who Team USA should hire onto their coaching staff, including who might be the right man for this unique managerial experience that no other professional baseball skipper had ever handled before.

The Steering Committee agreed from the beginning that the

right person needed to have plenty of professional experience and that a college-level coach or a previous Team USA Olympic manager would not work well.

"Ideally, we were looking for someone that really understood how to handle and manage the everyday scenarios you deal with during a minor-league season, as well as someone who understood the mind-set of the typical professional ballplayer," said Seiler.

There were several names thrown into the hat by major-league clubs looking to have one of their up-and-coming minor-league managerial prospects land the opportunity. The teams saw this as a chance to have one of their own in control of the Team USA operation, so that they would feel much more comfortable if any of their players were chosen onto the roster.

But Watson and Gillick were hoping to land a big-name manager who possibly had major league–level experience, but who happened to be out of work at the moment. They found their man in Buddy Bell.

"I knew his background and he had plenty of major-league experience with the Tigers," said Gillick. "I knew Buddy well and I thought that he was the kind of guy that would not only relate to many of the high profile prospects we were going to have on the squad, but that he could also relate to some of those players that were more of the supporting role players we were expecting to have on the club."

Another critical aspect of the managerial decision was going to be finding a manager that the minor-league players would be excited about playing for. "I thought that another thing we had to do was attract the players, because it was very difficult, it was a changing terrain, a changing landscape all the time," said Gillick. "As players we were interested in got called up to the major leagues, then they were no longer available on our list. So consequently, we had to find substitutes. We needed a manager that was pretty flexible with who he was going to be given as a roster, and I thought Buddy was a very flexible guy. At the same time, he gave us good credibility with the major-league clubs: not only the farm directors, but the general managers as well."

David Gus "Buddy" Bell had spent 18 years playing in the major leagues, primarily as a third baseman for the Indians, Rangers, Reds, and Astros, and was a baseball lifer. His father Gus had also been a major-league outfielder in the 1950s and 60s with several clubs, and after Buddy's sons David and Mike reached the show in the early '90s, they became one of the only three-generation families in baseball history.

A five-time All-Star selection and a six-time Gold Glove Award winner, Bell knew the game inside and out. That is why after his playing career ended, he began working in the Reds' farm system as a coach until he was offered the managerial job for the Detroit Tigers in 1996. But over the next three seasons, Bell struggled to generate much success, as the Tigers failed to play .500 baseball.

He was let go by Detroit after the 1998 season and was working as the new farm director for the Cincinnati Reds.

"I had gotten a call from our GM (at the time) Jim Bowden and he explained to me that he had gotten a call from Pat Gillick, asking if I would be interested in managing the USA Pan American Team, and that I was a candidate for the job," said Bell. "At the time, I wasn't really interested at all in the opportunity, because I just had too much other stuff going on. But Pat called me directly one day and asked if he could come to my office to speak with me about it. I had known Pat for a long time, so out of respect for Pat, I agreed to the meeting, because I always liked seeing Pat anyway.

"He came in to talk with me and told me what it was all about. But even at that point in time, I wasn't even that much more interested. Then he essentially asked me if I would do it, and again, out of respect for Pat, I told him I would consider it. But at that point I was only a candidate, so I said to him that if I decided that I wanted to do it, I wanted the job: I didn't want to go through any sort of interview process," said Bell. "That's when he said that if I decided I wanted to do it, the job would be mine. So, I thought about it a couple of more days and again, out of my feelings for Pat, I took the job. Because I figured if Pat was going to be involved, then it was going to be done the right way. And when he mentioned some of the other people that were going to be involved like Bob Watson and Sandy Alderson, a lot of really good people that I had wanted to work with, that's what solidified the decision for me."

USA Baseball saw the opportunity to grab a manager who was well liked, as well as one who was open enough to deal with new challenges that he might not be used to handling. From there, Bell assembled a first class and highly experienced staff of assistant coaches who would end up heavily weighing in on whether Team USA was going to have any success. Former manager of the California Angels Marcel Lachemann was brought on as the pitching coach, former LA Dodgers All-Star Reggie Smith was named hitting coach, and former Oakland Athletics manager Jackie Moore was on board as an assistant bench coach to Bell.

"Our coaching staff was tremendous and we were fortunate to have all four of them. Buddy, Marcel, and Jackie had all managed in the big leagues, and Reggie had been a big-league hitting coach," said Gillick. "Most of the concern that the farm directors and the general managers had was about the pitching, and when we could say to them that Marcel Lachemann was going to be on our staff, and that they could be assured that he was going to do everything possible not only to develop a young pitcher, but at the same time look out for his well-being and not do anything that would injure him, I think that went a long way. Having Marcel on our staff gave us an inroad for our pitching, which was going to be very, very important. And then naturally Reggie and Jackie for our position players was a key component as well."

Moore had already had a long career in the game and was on the verge of retiring. But this was something he had yet to accomplish in baseball: a chance to wear the red, white, and blue uniform of Team USA.

"It was a really exciting chance for me to represent my

country, and be a part of the first professional American team," said Moore. "I knew right away I wanted to be involved."

So as the weekly conference calls with Alderson, Seiler, Gillick, Watson, the Selection Committee members, and the scouts began, and the player watch list was assembled, the date when the top 24 available players would report to training camp in Tucson was quickly approaching. The coaching staff was being brought up to speed on the rule differences of international baseball and the gravity of the circumstances surrounding this qualifying event.

For the Pan Am Games baseball tournament, the United States had landed in Pool A and would face the other four teams in their pool—Mexico, Canada, Cuba, and Brazil—one time each before the qualifying round. Pool B consisted of the Dominican Republic, Guatemala, Nicaragua, and Panama. Only the top-two finishers in the event would advance to the 2000 Olympic Games in Sydney. That meant that anything short of playing in the gold-medal game in Winnipeg would be a failure for the Americans.

"It started to sink in a little bit more when we began having the conference calls and were trying to put a team together," said Bell. "We wanted to get the best possible players, regardless of what level they were at. But we were actually having a little bit of a problem doing that, because the teams just didn't want to give us their best players, because of the liability. So, it wasn't an easy task at all, putting our team together to begin with."

In the midst of his full-time job with the Reds, and focusing on those responsibilities with his new organization, Bell had not even had time to think much about the concept that he was about to immerse himself squarely into the middle of a major international competition.

"I figured I'd be gone for three weeks or so, and then I'd be back doing my job," said Bell. "I hadn't thought about the USA across my chest or anything like that, at that particular time. Having watched the Olympics before, I think I understood what kids felt competing for their country. But until you're in the belly of all that, you just don't know. My lifelong dream was never to be an Olympic gold medalist—it was to play major-league baseball, and I had done that for many years. I just figured that everything was going to work out with this Team USA event."

As the weekly conference calls and the debates over which players should be invited to Tucson for the opportunity to try and make the final United States Pan Am roster continued, the task at hand was to determine which 24 American-born citizens would get that right.

By early May of 1999, USA Baseball had dwindled down the entire minor-league system of American-born players to a list of around 30 pitchers, 10 catchers, 20 infielders and utility players, and 10 outfielders. Approximately 70 players were left on the radar, and Gillick and Watson had gained clearance from each club to officially contact the players in their system who Team USA was interested in pursuing. Just because the club had given USA Baseball permission did not mean that the player would actually be interested in the opportunity, however.

Steve Cobb was in charge of sending the initial packets of information to the players, regarding the opportunity to play for Team USA, and coordinating the responses.

"The reality was, all 30 clubs were not 'all-in,' per se. All you had to do was look to see which clubs were active participants and which ones weren't. We did have support, but it wasn't industry-wide support," said Cobb. "So as we were getting responses from players, whether it was their personal choice not to play or their club suggesting to them that they would prefer the player not participate—even though the club had already done the politically correct thing in allowing us to contact the player—we were sort of fighting an internal lack of cooperation. We weren't going to call any of the organizations out on it. But the public perception was 'Team USA is going to win' and meanwhile, we were feeling more and more pressure from an administrative standpoint, just trying to put this team together. Identifying the players was the easy part; getting them onto the team was another story. There weren't a lot of organizations coming to us and asking for their player to be on the team."

In a breakdown of the estimated 70 players that USA Baseball had to choose from, 28 of the 30 organizations had at least one player on the list, the only exceptions being the San Diego Padres and Texas Rangers. Either the Padres and Rangers refused to grant permission for any of their players to participate, or USA Baseball had not asked permission to speak with any of the players within those two farm systems. More than likely it was the latter, because every major-league club was being approached for access to their players, not just by Team USA, but by other countries participating in the Pan Ams as well, such as Canada, the Dominican Republic, Mexico, and Venezuela. Those teams also had minor-league players that were native born to those countries, and would be participating in the Pan Am Games as well. So, it was going to be virtually impossible for a major-league general manager to completely shut off access to his entire farm system.

Of the 30 MLB teams, seven other clubs had granted Team USA permission to contact only one of their players. Meanwhile, the Tampa Bay Devil Rays had seven players on the American list, while the Oakland A's and St. Louis Cardinals each had four.

After nine of the contacted players responded with a "not interested," the USA Baseball Selection Committee was left with a working list of 60 players to make their final selections from. Those 60 players were put on the daily radar and were monitored on a nightly basis, as the Committee scrutinized their minor-league game performances.

"What we realized was and what we were willing to do going into this, was start to examine which players were really performing well leading up to the Pan Am Games that summer," said Cobb. "It was not going to be about selecting the biggest prospects or high-round draft picks to be on our team. It had to be more about who has the experience, who was playing great baseball right now, who is performing well. If he wasn't performing well enough that season, but was going to be a top player two or three years from now, we didn't care."

USA Baseball had started out by focusing on the rising stars of the game and in particular, they put a premium on the starting pitching arms that might be available. But the Committee quickly realized that experience under pressure and current ability were much more important in a two-week tournament.

Finally, after every argument was made and every debate was hashed out, USA Baseball began the process of officially inviting the players they had selected, by informing each team's general manager. After all, it was each GM that would be giving Team USA the final permission to "borrow" that asset.

When the 24 players finally arrived at the USA Baseball training facility in Tucson for what would be a final live warm-up session before the team headed to Canada, it was an incredibly exciting and emotional time around the USA Baseball office. The week-long practice was a chance for the group to get to know one another and for the coaching staff to evaluate what kind of talent they had to work with. But almost immediately, things did not go as smoothly as they had hoped.

On July 15, 1999, the 24 selected players from around the country made their way to Tucson for a week-long Team USA training camp. But by the time a young outfielder named Lance Berkman stepped off the airplane in Arizona, USA Baseball had already received a message that the Astros were calling him up to the majors.

"I was in Pat Gillick's suite at our team hotel, and we were watching ESPN," said Seiler. "All of the sudden Pat turns to me and says, 'Whatever you do, don't answer the phone.' And I'm like, 'What are you talking about?'" Astros outfielder Carl Everett had just gotten injured trying to make a catch in center field, and Houston's best prospect was Berkman. Gillick knew that his chances of staying with Team USA were not good. By the time Cobb had picked up Berkman at the Tucson Airport and brought him to Hi Corbett Field clubhouse, his call-up to the major leagues was already in the works. "Lance had already gotten his meal money from us, the whole nine yards. We started to fit him into his uniform, and Pat gets the call while we're standing in the clubhouse from Astros GM Gerry Hunsicker. The next thing you know, Lance is shaking hands and saying goodbye, and he went to the big leagues and never looked back."

Berkman was slated to be the Team USA switch-hitting cleanup hitter, and it was a significant loss. The circumstances had changed so quickly—his name had actually been printed on the official Team USA roster that had been released to the media the previous day—it left team officials scrambling to find his replacement and to make arrangements for the new player to get to Tucson as quickly as possible.

"That is exactly what we had decided to name a list of alternate players for," said Seiler. "In case something changed or a player got injured severely enough during practice where it would prevent him from participating, we had a backup plan."

That backup plan for Berkman's outfield spot consisted of a 30-year-old left-handed hitting minor leaguer in the Oakland A's farm system named Mike Neill, who originally hailed from Seaford, Delaware. Neill had just five games of major-league experience and was currently playing for the triple-A Vancouver Canadians in the Pacific Coast League.

Neill's career path to the major leagues had taken an unexpected turn one year earlier, during his initial stint in the big leagues with the A's, when he was sidelined by an injury. After being drafted out of Villanova University in 1991 by Alderson, who at that time was the Oakland general manager, Neill's career had been on a steady climb, and he found himself in the majors during a call-up in the summer of '98.

But during his first week in the show, he was in left field playing in a game in Oakland against the Cleveland Indians. When a fly ball was lifted into shallow outfield, he and Miguel Tejada converged on the ball together but collided, and Neill separated his shoulder on the play. He was placed on the disabled list and never returned to the A's lineup the rest of the year.

"You can imagine how disappointing it was, having worked so hard for this opportunity the A's were giving me," said Neill. "Art Howe had been playing me more than I thought he would that first week, and I actually had two hits and reached base four times in a game against the Red Sox, so I was really feeling good about myself. The injury was extremely frustrating, especially because that afternoon Art had told me I would be starting the next day against the Yankees."

Following the 1998 season, after he had fully recovered from the shoulder problem, Neill was having a solid year in the PCL.

"I remember early in the season, my obvious goal had been to get back to the majors, and I got off to a pretty good start. But it became clear by mid-season that I wasn't going to be in a position to get a call-up again, as we had some other very good prospects in the outfield at the time," said Neill. "Then, I received a letter from USA Baseball asking me about my interest in playing for the USA Pan Am team, and that immediately changed my focus. I knew if given that chance, I would definitely want to be a part of that team."

Later on, as team officials kept the players on the watch list informed of their status, Neill kept pressing on in Vancouver. In the end, he was chosen as an alternate, but was told to stay "ready" in case something happened.

"I was pretty disappointed to have come so close," said Neill. "I think it was about four or five days until I got another call from Mr. Gillick that Berkman had been called up, and that I needed to get on a plane to Tucson. It was a huge break and a great feeling. I was just very excited to be a part of it."

Just a few hours after Berkman had been suddenly removed from the Team USA roster, Gillick and Watson encountered their second player availability issue. Double-A Chicago Cubs pitching prospect Steve Rain, who had also already made the trip from West Tennessee to Tucson, was being called up to the majors by the Cubs to replace an injured reliever.

Gillick and Watson quickly moved to the phones to find Rain's replacement and ended up securing Seattle Mariners prospect Ryan Anderson, who actually wasn't even listed as an alternate on the roster.

"I think that was a lot due to the fact that Roger Jongwaard of the Mariners was one of our Selection Committee members, so I called Roger and told him that at the last minute we had lost Rain, and we needed another pitcher," said Gillick. "He offered us Ryan Anderson, and that gave us four left-handed pitchers, which turned out to be great."

A 6-foot-10, 20-year-old left-hander was the Mariners' first-round draft pick in 1997 and had a high ceiling. Very tall and lanky, he threw a fastball in the upper 90's and was working on perfecting his breaking ball, but he would end up being the USA Pan Am Team's youngest member.

As the team came together that first day, Bell and his staff wasted no time trying to get the players acclimated to their new surroundings and the group of men who would be their teammates for the next three weeks. On the morning of the team's first workout, Seiler remembers well the attitude that most of the players had when they gathered in the clubhouse. As he tried to prepare them for what to expect in an international competition, he got the feeling like the message wasn't sinking in.

"These guys were sitting there in the locker room with years of experience, some of them had even been in the major leagues," Seiler told *Baseball America*. "I was giving them my 'This is what you're in for' speech, and you could tell the look in their eyes was, 'What do you mean? Can we go out and play some baseball now?'"

USA Baseball had arranged a four-game exhibition schedule in Tucson for Team USA to take on the Pan Am teams that had formed from Nicaragua and the Dominican Republic, that would also need to travel to Winnipeg and were on a similar schedule. This worked out conveniently for all three teams: They all needed some time to compete together and evaluate the rosters they had been offered by the pro ranks.

Bell's squad won three of the four exhibition games, with only a 10-3 loss to the Dominicans causing a slight concern.

As the Team USA players, coaching staff, and administration boarded a bus on July 20 and headed to the Tucson Airport, the feeling was one of great anticipation. Bell was beginning to get a feel for his lineup, where his players were most comfortable on defense and what kind of flexibility he had with certain positions.

When the dust settled, here is the official 24-man roster that became the first-ever professional team in USA Baseball history:

Starting Pitchers
LHP Ryan Anderson – Seattle Mariners – Southfield, MI
LHP Mark Mulder – Oakland A's – South Holland, IL
RHP John Patterson – Arizona Diamondbacks – Orange, TX
RHP Brad Penny – Florida Marlins – Broken Arrow, OK

Relief Pitchers
RHP David Holdridge – Seattle Mariners – Wayne, MI
LHP J.C. Romero – Minnesota Twins – Rio Piedras, PR
LHP Bobby Seay – Tampa Bay Devil Rays – Sarasota, FL
LHP Scott Stewart – New York Mets – Stanley, NC
RHP Derek Wallace – New York Mets – Oxnard, CA
RHP Todd Williams – Cincinnati Reds – Syracuse, NY
RHP Dan Wheeler – Tampa Bay Devil Rays – Warwick, RI

Catchers
Charlie Greene – Milwaukee Brewers – Miami, FL
Marcus Jensen – St. Louis Cardinals – Scottsdale, AZ
Matt LeCroy – Minnesota Twins – Belton, SC

Infielders
SS Travis Dawkins – Cincinnati Reds – Chappells, SC
IF Shawn Gilbert – Los Angeles Dodgers – Glendale, AZ
IF Jason Hardtke – Cincinnati Reds – Port Washington, NY
2B Adam Kennedy – St. Louis Cardinals – Riverside, CA

3B Craig Paquette – New York Mets – Tempe, AZ
1B Jon Zuber – Philadelphia Phillies – Moraga, CA

<u>Outfielders</u>
CF Peter Bergeron – Montreal Expos – Greenfield, MA
RF Milton Bradley – Montreal Expos – Long Beach, CA
LF Mike Neill – Oakland A's – Seaford, DE
OF Dave Roberts – Cleveland Indians – Oceanside, CA

"I liked our outfield a lot, with Roberts, Bradley, and Bergeron from a speed standpoint, and Neill from a power standpoint," said Gillick. "They were aggressive and weren't afraid to take extra bases, and they could all play defense. I liked our infield and thought we had good power at third base with Paquette, and Zuber was solid at first base, Kennedy would do a good job at second, and Dawkins could fill in well. So overall, I thought we had a well-balanced club. We had speed at the top of the order, we had a little power, and we were hoping to get some timely hitting out of guys like Zuber and Kennedy. So I was happy with the roster we created and thought we had a great chance to qualify for the Olympics."

4

1999 PAN AM GAMES

One big advantage for the Americans of the Pan Am Games being held just across the border in Canada was that the travel would be fairly easy and the normal, everyday comforts of life that our players were used to in the States wouldn't be that much different in Winnipeg. People would be speaking English, while the food and culture would be similar to life in a lot of minor-league cities.

"But still, we had no idea what we were about to get into," said Todd Williams, who was pegged as the team's closer. "We were all looking forward to the experience, and we knew what we had to do. There was somewhat of a sense when we gathered in Arizona that this was no ordinary baseball situation, and that the intensity of these games was going to be ramped up a notch, compared to the minor-league games we'd just come from. We just had no idea how big that notch was going to be."

Back in early February, Seiler, Cobb, Gillick, and a liaison from the United States Olympic Committee named Greg Farney flew to Fargo, North Dakota in order to do a site-inspection visit to Winnipeg, where the Pan Am Games would be held. "We crossed the border in just absolutely hellacious snowy conditions, and I remember seeing the main baseball stadium for the first time," said Seiler. "It was covered in snow, but from what we could tell, it was going to be a nice venue."

Cobb, who would be serving as Team USA's quasi-traveling secretary, had a different impression. "The Canadian host committee took us out on this tour of the facilities that were going to be used, and they did their best to show them to us, but everything was covered in snow. You couldn't see a thing; it was like a white-out and it was about 20 degrees below outside! In retrospect, it was a waste of time, but it was one of those things that they made us do. I remember looking at Pat and saying, 'Looks good to me!' and we both started laughing."

Now Team USA was ready to get to Canada and play some baseball. To get there from Tucson, USA Baseball had rented a charter plane that would take Team USA and Panama up to Fargo, where they would go through USOC Team Processing, and then a bus from Fargo up to Winnipeg.

In charge of all travel and logistics was Cobb, who had served as the Cincinnati Reds traveling secretary for several years in the late '70s and early '80s. In this instance, though, for the charter flight, he was very concerned about where everybody sat on the plane. He had a particular order that he had wanted to implement, with team officials and administrators up front, the American players in the middle, and the Panamanian players in the back. "When the Panamanians got on the plane first, Cobb began to get a little upset," said Seiler. "So Pat says to him, 'Hey Steve, don't worry about it. Have you ever heard of a plane backing into a mountain? Hey, if we go into a mountain, they're going to get killed first, right?' It was a funny moment and helped us all relax and not take any of the travel hassles too seriously. Because the players, coaches, and almost everybody involved were all about to go through something they had never done before."

After the charter plane touched down in North Dakota, the

group would spend the night in Fargo, where the United States Olympic Committee had set up the Team USA processing center at a local college. USOC Team Processing is the check-in center where everything takes place prior to an international competition, for every athlete, coach, and administrator in the American delegation. Every person gets their photo taken and receives their official ID badge, so that when they arrive on-site at the Games, he or she is cleared for the security access needed.

Another critical part of processing is the fitting of each person with the officially licensed uniform and gear of that year's United States team. In this case, it required that every person pushed a large shopping cart one by one through a line where you had to select your size for a laundry list of clothing items, athletic uniforms, jackets, shoes, hats, and luggage. When you watch the Opening Ceremonies on TV, this is how the United States delegation gets to be all dressed in the exact same way when they walk into the arena or stadium.

Other things that needed to occur at processing were a team photo, a seminar on how the drug-testing procedures would work, and a welcome speech from the United States delegation leader, who would explain to the athletes what the expectations were for their personal behavior in a foreign country. It was made very clear to everyone involved that in this circumstance, you are not just representing yourself or your team, but the entire United States of America, and to take pride in that. The last thing that the USOC wants to deal with when in a foreign country is a PR nightmare over one of their athletes acting like an "ugly American."

The following day, two buses for Team USA headed north from Fargo across the border and into Winnipeg. Major League Baseball had decided that it would be best to keep the entire team and staff, including the players, together in one hotel, rather than splitting up the coaches at a hotel and putting the players in the Pan Am Athletes Village.

That hotel ended up being the Fort Garry, one of Winnipeg's most famous and historic properties. Built in 1913 as one of Canada's Grand Railway hotels, it was located just one block from Union Station and about four blocks from the main baseball stadium that would be used for the Pan Am Games: Canwest Global Park. It was the home of the independent Winnipeg Goldeyes of the Northern League.

"The thinking behind that was, first of all we wanted to be successful. That was first and foremost: qualify for the Olympics. But secondary to that, we wanted to make this an experience for these players that will give them a positive disruption to their ordinary double-A or triple-A lives," said Cobb. "So we upgraded the hotel, because we wanted them to stay in a big-league type of hotel. We gave them major-league meal money and wanted to create the feeling like this was something special to be a part of, not just another road trip in the minor leagues.

"The hope was that with the recruitment of this class of players, hopefully there would be some carry-over, and that those guys were going to go back into the minor-league system when this event was over with and we could have them basically be walking billboards for us. The hope was that when other players asked them about what it was like to play for Team USA, they would say that if you ever get the opportunity, you needed to take it, that USA Baseball treated us well, we had a lot of fun, and we were successful," said Seiler. "So we wanted it to register, we wanted it to resonate. So that was the recruitment part, to use these players in a positive way to hopefully improve the quality of player we might get for the 2000 Olympic team. So Cobb's job was to try to streamline that process, try to take care of the players as much as we could, to make it a positive experience. The cost was what it was."

The players took notice right away, as apparently the plan worked. "It was a very nice location and a great property, first-class all the way," said Neill. "USA Baseball had spared no expense, and they were treating us like we were in the major leagues. We all had our own rooms and were getting a nice per diem. There were restaurants within walking distance, and I think it helped us players feel like this was more like a big-league call-up than a strange international sporting event that we were participating in."

First up on the main agenda was a pair of practice exhibition games against the host country from Canada. These would end up being the final tune-up sessions for Bell and his staff to decide who their starting position players would be and to set up their pitching rotation. With the Opening Ceremonies just 48 hours away, and Team USA's first official competition a few days later, the American lineup was beginning to take shape.

But in order for the two teams to scrimmage against one another, organizers had to reserve a remote practice field at a local park in Winnipeg that was not an official venue of the games, because both of the baseball diamonds and facilities that would be used for the tournament were getting the final prep work they needed done.

"I had chartered a local bus company to move our team around Winnipeg for the first week or so, and they dropped us off at this remote field, and I gave them a time that I expected them to be back, because they had some other runs they needed to make," said Cobb. "Well, there must have been a lot going on that day, because they never returned. We were out there in this isolated location after practice, with no way for the team to get back to the hotel. I was about to blow a gasket when they told me they couldn't get a bus out to us. They gave me another number to call, to do whatever I had to do. And an hour later, this double-decker bus comes pulling up, the only bus they had available, and everybody got a kick out of that! Buddy Bell and the whole team was making fun of the situation, but the guys got on and they started having so much fun on the ride back. It turned out to be a great moment, as it kind of loosened the club up right before the games were about to start."

With neither side caring much about the results or the score, and both concentrating on fine-tuning their pitchers and hitters, Team USA easily rolled to victories in both practice games and looked to be ready to go.

"I wasn't getting much playing time, so it was a little frustrating at that point," said Neill. "Buddy had told me that they were going with a starting outfield of Roberts, Bergeron, and Bradley, so my role was going to be more of a left-handed bat off the bench. But he wanted me to be ready to play at all times. I had been used to starting at Vancouver all season, so it was a bit of an adjustment for me."

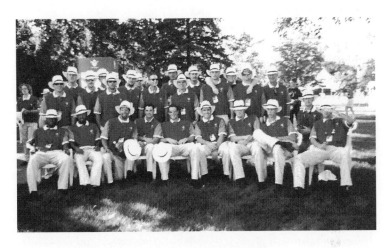

The 1999 USA Baseball Pan Am Team, just prior to the Opening Ceremonies in Winnipeg, Canada.

Team USA enters the stadium during the Opening Ceremonies of the 1999 Pan Am Games, as an American flag waves in the crowd.

GAME ONE: USA (0-0) vs. CANADA (0-0)

So on a clear blue sky day, Monday, July 26, 1999, Team USA would take the field for the very first time with professional players in uniform during an official International Baseball Federation (IBAF)-sanctioned competition.

Bell and Lachemann had decided to hand the ball in the team's opener vs. Canada to a young, highly touted prospect in the Arizona Diamondbacks organization named John Patterson. Originally taken by the Montreal Expos with the fifth pick overall in the 1996 draft, Patterson did not sign with the Expos but instead waited a year and became a free agent. He then reached a deal with the Diamondbacks, agreeing to a deal with a multi-million-dollar signing bonus, one of the largest in baseball history at the time.

The matchup of Team USA and Canada was being talked about in Winnipeg as a David vs. Goliath story. The Americans were viewed as huge favorites, with a roster full of triple-A players with major-league experience, prospects at every position, pitchers who threw extremely hard, and a coaching staff that was second to none. On the other hand, there was little to no history of baseball success for the Canadian national team. Although many of their players were playing professionally in the minor leagues, the majority of them were floundering at the single- and double-A level. The ones who weren't pros yet had just finished playing college baseball either in the States or in Canada.

In the dugout for Canada was a name that the entire country would recognize, one that epitomizes Canadian baseball. It was also one that the Americans would be familiar with as well: Ernie Whitt. A 12-year starting catcher for the Toronto Blue Jays, Whitt joined the team when they began in 1977 and was the last remaining member of the original Blue Jays when he left the squad in 1989. He gave the Canadians a high profile voice that helped spark interest in his team, and both the city of Winnipeg and the entire country were excited to see what their young group of ballplayers might be able to accomplish against the shiny roster of the Red, White, and Blue.

In front of a sold-out crowd in what felt like a pressure cooker of a ballpark, the Canadians rose to the occasion and gave the Americans everything they could handle. The game went into extra innings, and when Canada's Stubby Clapp hit a game-ending, walk-off base hit in the bottom of the 11th, Team USA immediately found themselves in a deep hole they did not desire to be in.

In the locker room following the game, several American players were upset with relief pitcher Scott Stewart, who had not performed well, wasn't ready for the moment, and had irked team officials earlier in the week by being late for several buses. "The thought was that if you were going to start to rub people the wrong way and act up, that you had better be damn good on the field," said Neill. "None of us knew much about Scott, so when he was starting to step out of bounds with team rules, and then he went out and completely blew that first game, it didn't go over well at all. Most of us were pissed off with his act."

The role of the official Team USA press officer was to coordinate the players who would be brought into the media "pool area, so that reporters from around the world who were covering the game could ask questions. Then, once the questions were answered, they could be translated into other languages by the event services media operations staff and documented. Team USA officials and Bell decided that the story of the game was the Canadian team, and that the media should be focused on them and their heroic effort, not the failures of the American players. The last thing USA Baseball wanted to do was to subject the USA players to a rash of harsh media questions about how they had blown such a big game and have it affect their confidence. After all, this was the very first game of the event, and there were many more to be played. There was a more important goal still at hand, and Bell was protecting his troops. He was the only person brought into the media pool, and he answered all of the questions on behalf of his team.

The headline on the front page of the Winnipeg *Free Press* the next morning called it the "Miracle on Grass." Canada's upset win over Team USA in baseball was the talk of the entire country and the toast of the town. Every news channel had highlights of Andy Stewart's home run and then Clapp's game-winning blooper, along with the celebration that ensued.

GAME TWO: USA (0-1) vs. MEXICO (0-1)

Fortunately for Team USA, they didn't have much time to dwell on what happened against Canada, because their second game against Mexico would be the very next day. Depending on how you looked at it, it was either a blessing in disguise or much too early of a wake-up call, because the game was scheduled for a 9:00 a.m. first pitch. Nobody on the Team USA roster—including the coaches or the administration—had woken up so early in the morning to put on their cleats and play a baseball game, probably since their Little League days.

"It really did turn out to be a blessing," said Seiler. "We were all forced to forget about the loss to Canada, and had to immediately focus on what was next. Even though it was early in the morning, it was better than having to sit around all day and wait to play a night game."

Taking the ball that morning for the Americans would be left-hander Mark Mulder, the second overall pick in the 1998 draft out of Michigan State by the Oakland A's. He did exactly what Bell and company needed to get Team USA back on track, as he limited a very experienced Mexican National Team to just one run on six hits, in 6.2 innings of work.

"Mark had been pitching like that all year for us at Vancouver," said Neill. "He was a stud that day, and came through with a clutch performance."

That one run allowed occurred in the top of the fourth, and it gave Mexico a brief 1-0 lead. But after a pair of singles by Milton Bradley and Jon Zuber, Marcus Jensen connected on a three-run, opposite-field homer in the fifth off Mexican starter Jesus Rios, who had held Team USA scoreless on one hit through the first four innings.

Jensen later gave the Americans some insurance in the seventh, when he tagged Mexican reliever Eduardo Neri for a two-run shot after Craig Paquette had reached on a walk. It gave Team USA a 5-1 lead, and the USA bullpen made that score hold up.

"I remember before the game that morning, before we got dressed and went to the ballpark, I called Dave Roberts and Shawn Gilbert up to my room," recalled Bell. "I basically explained that this thing had gotten important really quickly overnight, and is pretty serious. I was trying to convey somehow that I needed them to make sure everybody knew that, and they did a great job getting that point across to the rest of the team, apparently. Because from then on, we played solid baseball: It was all business."

The first Pan Am victory for Team USA was a big one, as it was also a solid comeback after such a devastating defeat the previous day and got them back on track. But there was no time to rest. They would be facing the top-ranked international baseball team in the world—the Cuban National Team—at 2:00 p.m. the next afternoon.

GAME THREE: USA (1-1) vs. CUBA (2-0)

When the United States and Cuba get together to play a baseball game, it's a one-of-a-kind event. The entire baseball world, from the pro leagues of Japan to the major leagues in Wrigley Field and Fenway Park, stops what they are doing to pay attention. It's a heavyweight fight.

Our country considers itself to be the founding fathers of the game, where baseball was invented. Americans have long cherished the game as our "national pastime." Our heroes are Babe Ruth, Jackie Robinson, Willie Mays, and Mickey Mantle. Our favorite teams play in baseball shrines all across the country, while fathers and sons play catch in the yard and listen to games on the radio.

Somewhere along the way, Cuban kids began to play the game in the dirt fields all across this tiny island nation, and they have played it extremely well for many years, so much so that the entire country has become so passionate about baseball that their star players have been given hero status. They have produced some of the greatest Latin American players the game has ever seen. But because the Cuban government understands that defections from the team are always a threat when they travel to play outside of their homeland, there is a certain mystique surrounding the Cuban National Team. Many of their top players long for the opportunity to compete and rise to fame and fortune in the American major leagues, and when those players have left the Cuban borders to play in an international baseball tournament, there is always the chance that one or more of them may disappear out of the grasp of Cuban team officials.

Even with that constant threat to their stability, no team, including the United States, has dominated internationally more than Cuba since the era of organized IBAF competitions began in the '50s.

In the late '80s and early '90s, Cuba was literally unbeatable. The machine went 18-0 across the span of two Olympic Games (1992 in Barcelona and 1996 in Atlanta), and from 1984 to 1999, the Cubans captured seven straight World Cup titles.

Cuba entered the 1999 Pan Am Games having won the event in nine of the 12 years it had been played dating back to 1951, including each of the last seven Pan Am championships in a row. Meanwhile, the United States had not won Pan Am gold since 1967—beating Cuba in the finals—when ironically, the event was held in Winnipeg. It was the only gold medal for Team USA in Pan Am history, USA having earned six silvers and three bronze.

"It's the Yankees vs. the Red Sox—the two biggest kids on the block, who want to go toe to toe to see who's the better kid, the better athlete," said Seiler. "So for us, we are their barometer, and they are our barometer, when it comes to international baseball. And that's all you have to say. That doesn't mean we don't respect Japan and Korea and all of the other countries who have a ton of success to their credit. But at the end of the day, if you ask anybody in the international baseball world, 'Give us the dream matchup,' it's the USA vs. Cuba, because of everything that we both stand for in the sport and the religious element of baseball in our countries. Every time we go to an event, we look at a schedule to see when we're playing Cuba and to start thinking about who you want to have on the mound that day. And they do the exact same thing for us. There's no doubt about it."

The Cuban team who had shown up in Winnipeg this time was beginning to show a slight sign of a crack in the armor. This roster of loyal players had been together for over 10 years, and their air of invincibility had been erased when they had lost the 1997 Intercontinental Cup crown to Japan.

But even in their current form, they were still a force to be reckoned with, and the clear favorite to take the gold home from Canada. Stars Omar Linares, Orestes Kindelan, German Mesa, and Antonio Pacheco had first played together on the team in 1989, and they had a very long and distinguished track record of success. Even though they would be the oldest team that Cuba had ever sent to a major international competition, they were perceived to be very loyal to the government and much less likely to defect. And because of their ages, they would draw less interest from MLB scouts.

This matchup between the USA and Cuba in front of a sold-out stadium was being shown on national TV in Canada, but was nowhere to be found on satellite signals in the USA. Gillick and Seiler—using late '90s cell-phone technology—would end up reporting a scoring update every couple of innings, back to all of the MLB executives through the Commissioner's Office in New York City.

Team USA leadoff hitter Dave Roberts takes the first pitch of the game vs. Cuba, at CanWest Global Park.

As the visiting team, the red, white, and blue got on the scoreboard in the second inning, when they plated a pair of runs to take a 2-0 lead. American Brad Penny of the Florida Marlins—a 6-4, hard-throwing right hander from Oklahoma—had started on the mound for Team USA, but got touched for three in the bottom of the second and got knocked out of the game early.

"They had the best players in the tournament by far, and I was really impressed by the way they played the game. They played at a different speed than the rest of us," said Bell. "Brad was pretty fired up to pitch against them, and we wanted him to throw that game, just because he was made that way. But he only ended up lasting three innings, because he spent up all his energy out there."

"We all knew the history of the Cuban team, and that they were the heavy favorites coming in," said Neill. "But I couldn't believe how hard Penny was throwing that day, I mean 96-98 fastballs and they were turning them around and hitting him. I hadn't seen anyone throw that hard all season at Triple A, but Cuba handled it without a problem. It was impressive." After Penny only lasted a couple of innings, Bell and Lachemann turned to a virtually unknown relief pitcher from Rhode Island named Dan Wheeler.

"I had worked very hard the off-season prior to 1999 to put myself into a much better position to succeed, and I was having a good season that year, so my confidence was pretty high going to Winnipeg," said Wheeler, who had been an unexpected surprise out of spring training for the Devil Rays. "But nothing prepared me for the pressure that I felt in the Pan Ams. Against Cuba, I was trying my best to keep us in that game." Wheeler did just that, tossing 5.1 shutout innings of relief.

In the top of the seventh, Paquette belted a go-ahead, two-run homer that gave the USA a 4-3 lead. They tacked on another run in the eighth, and led 5-3 until Cuban outfielder Isaac Martinez smoked a line drive, two-run homer over the right-field wall to knot the score at 5-5. Lefty J. C. Romero then came on in relief of Wheeler to get the final two outs of the eighth, but Wheeler's performance certainly opened some eyes among baseball scouting circles.

In the ninth inning of a tie game, Jensen again stepped up to the plate in a crucial situation and came through. The switch-hitting catcher launched a three-run shot to put Team

USA back on top 8-5, and with the momentum they stunned the heavily favored Cubans for two more runs to win the game, 10-5. It was Jensen's third homer in as many games, and the Americans had rapped out 19 hits off the Cuban pitching staff, including four by leadoff man Dave Roberts. Adam Kennedy went 3-for-6 with two RBIs, and Romero was credited as the winning pitcher, even though it was Wheeler who had kept the Cuban bats at bay.

"That was a really exciting game, a fun game," said Jensen. "The crowd was into it, and for most of us, it was our first exposure to international baseball outside of playing winter ball. The energy in the stadium that day was incredible, and for me to get a hit like that, late in the game with that type of pressure, that's what it was all about. It was so great."

"It's hard to explain the excitement, I think, in beating Cuba," said Gillick. "We—the United States—hadn't beaten Cuba for a long period of time in those tournaments, so to beat them and to get our way back into a position to go to the Olympics, it was fantastic. It's something that I'll never forget, the thrill of winning that game."

The victory was the first for Team USA over Cuba in a major international competition since 1987, when lefty Jim Abbott pitched the Americans to a 6-4 win at the Pan Am Games in Indianapolis, Indiana.

"That was a big day for our team, and for USA Baseball in general," said Seiler. "It showed us that Cuba was beatable, and I think it gave us as team officials a lot of confidence that what we were doing was working, and that our player-selection process was solid."

Following Bell and company's dramatic triumph over the favored Cubans in pool play, Team USA was left with one more opponent to face before the medal round began: Brazil. After each of the four teams in both Pool A and Pool B had played one another, seeding would be drawn and the do-or-die elimination round would commence.

One interesting scenario that was taking place behind the scenes for Team USA centered around the professional medical and training staff that USA Baseball and MLB had hired to travel with the team to Winnipeg. They wanted to be extra sure that the American players were well informed about the anti-doping rules that were in place for this international competition, which could be very different from those MLB had in place for minor leaguers at the time. Any infraction caused by a cold remedy or any other type of over-the-counter medication that a player took could cause the USA to be disqualified from the Pan Am Games, ending their chances at an Olympic berth.

Because these American players were heavily valued by their respective organizations, MLB also wanted to have their own doctors on hand to manage any injuries, as well as an experienced team trainer who knew how to treat baseball-related muscle tweaks and soreness as well as the arms of the USA pitchers, both pre- and post-game.

By way of Steve Cobb's office in the Arizona Fall League, Drs. Angelo Mattalino and Fred Dicke were added onto the USA Baseball staff, and John Fierro was named the Team USA trainer and equipment manager. Both Mattalino and Dicke had their own practices in Scottsdale, Arizona, as well as several years of experience treating baseball injuries for players living in the Valley of the Sun. Mattalino had worked for the Milwaukee Brewers in the past, while Dicke had been with the Anaheim Angels. Fierro had been a longtime trainer with the Chicago Cubs and was at the time operating his own business in the Phoenix area.

During the Pan Am Games, each team was only allowed to have a certain number of players, coaches, and team officials "credentialed" for access to the field and locker rooms or competition areas. In this case, with the 24 players, four coaches, and other MLB and USA Baseball officials, Fierro, Dicke, and Mattalino had not made the initial list that was submitted.

"When we arrived in Canada, the Pan Am officials didn't have us listed as being with the USA Baseball team in any way," said Mattalino. "We were basically strangers, and not welcomed whatsoever."

As part of the United States Olympic Committee's delegation, the American baseball players were thought to be a regular part of the entire group of athletes who would be covered medically by the professionally trained staff brought to Canada by the USOC. That is where the confusion began: The USOC and the Pan Am Games Committee did not understand why USA Baseball would need their own doctors on hand when medical staff was already provided for athletes.

"The medical people at the USOC at the time were very hard to deal with, because they were very headstrong," said Dicke. "They had had some problems with the trainers from another professional sport that had been introduced to the Olympic world, so I think there was fear there, and their guard was up. I don't think it was anything personal against us, but they had their defenses up. We didn't want to say it, but we think that's what it was."

Even after Seiler and Alderson pulled some strings with the USOC to get some Team USA identification credentials around the necks of Mattalino, Dicke, and Fierro that would allow them into the games, the situation still was not ideal.

"We of course were used to treating our players in the locker room and the dugouts, yet we still could not get access," said Fierro. "During games, we would sit in the stands and watch from behind home plate, in the scouting seats. I think after the third game, I was finally able to convince the security guard by the locker-room door to let me in, only because he recognized me as a former Cubs trainer and he was a huge Cubs fan. That's the only way I was able to get into the dugout."

GAME FOUR: USA (2-1) vs. BRAZIL (0-3)

With the medical training issue being worked out somewhat, and with a 2-1 record, the Americans would send lefty Ryan Anderson to the mound against a Brazilian team made up mostly of the sons of Japanese auto dealers and builders who lived in Brazil and were now citizens. Their roster was scattered with Japanese-named players who had immigrated to the heavily populated South American country.

Because the game was not seen as a huge ticket draw, and because the host country Canada was playing against Cuba in the main stadium, the USA-Brazil game was contested at the secondary facility being used, called Stonewall. In reality, it was the equivalent of any average Midwestern city's high school baseball field found across America. It had a nice grass field, metal bleachers down each line above the dugouts, and a tiny press box.

Whether it was the unimportant feel of playing in such a small venue or the fact that they were coming off the high of beating Cuba, Team USA played down to their competition. Jason Hardtke got the Americans on the board with a first-inning solo home run, before Brazil tallied twice off Anderson in the second to grab a brief 2-1 lead. Mike Neill then hit a one-out double in the bottom of the second and later scored on an error by Brazilian starting pitcher Douglas Assada.

It stayed that way until the fifth, when Team USA took the lead for good on a bases-loaded fielder's choice by Neill that drove home Hardtke, who had singled. With a 3-2 advantage, Anderson was able to complete 6.0 innings and allowed only three hits while fanning nine. Bell then brought on American left-handed reliever Bobby Seay, who pitched the final three frames to earn the save, but it was not without a scare.

"They (Brazil) had a runner on first base and two outs in the top of the eighth, and we were holding onto that one-run lead," said Seiler. "And I don't recall the kid's name, but their batter hit a line drive off the top of the fence in left field that missed going over the wall by about two feet. We got it back into the infield so quickly that their runner was held at third base, and Bobby got the next out. But that was way too close: I almost had a heart attack when that ball was in the air."

Although the third win was more uncomfortable than they would have wanted, Team USA was able to secure the second seed in Pool A with a 3-1 record. That's because on the same day, the Canadians—playing inspired baseball after their miracle against the USA—continued their momentum and shocked Cuba by a score of 8-1. The home team from Canada had run the table in pool play with a 4-0 record, while Cuba finished 2-2 and Mexico ended up 1-3. Brazil went 0-4 and was eliminated.

In Pool B, Nicaragua, the Dominican Republic, and Panama all finished with identical 2-1 records, while Guatemala went 0-3 (there were only four teams in Pool B). Based on tie-breaking rules, Nicaragua was awarded the top seed, followed by the Dominicans and then Panama. So here were the final pool-play standings in the 1999 Pan Am Games baseball qualifying event:

Pool A		Pool B	
Canada	4-0	Nicaragua	2-1
USA	3-1	Dominican Republic	2-1
Cuba	2-2	Panama	2-1
Mexico	1-3	Guatemala	0-3
Brazil	0-4		

In this event format, the quarterfinal game matchups would be determined by crossing over to the other pool, where #1 would face #4, and #2 would meet #3. That meant the quarterfinals looked like this:

Canada vs. Guatemala
USA vs. Panama
Cuba vs. Dominican Republic
Mexico vs. Nicaragua

These games would be elimination games, meaning that if you lost, your bid for an Olympic berth was over. There were only two bids up for grabs in Winnipeg, meaning that only the two teams playing for the gold medal would advance to Sydney. That, in essence, made the semifinal games the two most important games of the entire event.

QUARTERFINALS: USA (3-1) vs. PANAMA (2-1)

It was back to the top of the rotation for Team USA, as they gave the ball back to John Patterson. He had pitched fairly well against Canada in the opening game, but was not involved in the decision of that contest. But on this night he was on, as he carried a no-hitter into the sixth inning and limited Panama to just two hits over eight frames.

The American offense gave Patterson an early lead to work with when they scored four times in the third off Panamanian starter Lenin Picota. Adam Kennedy smashed a run-scoring double to bring home Dave Roberts, and Jason Hardtke followed with a single to left that scored Kennedy. Jon Zuber then added a two-run double to make it 4-0.

Craig Paquette tacked on a solo homer in the fifth before Patterson's no-hit bid ended with two outs in the sixth when DeLeon Flores touched him for a two-run homer to right field. Todd Williams came on to notch the save, as Team USA advanced with a 5-2 triumph.

"John did a very nice job of keeping the suspense to a minimum that night, as we won the game fairly easily," said Gillick. "He kept it low-scoring, and for the amount of pressure that everybody felt in that situation, he was outstanding."

With Canada riding the wave and easily rolling past Guatemala 12-2, Cuba advanced with a 3-1 win over the Dominicans and Mexico held off Nicaragua, 5-1. That gave all four Pool A contenders the chance to play for an Olympic berth, with the USA matched up against Mexico and Canada facing Cuba.

"It worked out extremely well for us, because we didn't have to face the hottest team in the tournament (Canada) on their own field, nor did we have to face Cuba in a do-or-die game," said Gillick. "The draw couldn't have worked out better, but we knew it wasn't going to be a cakewalk against Mexico either."

SEMIFINALS: USA (4-1) vs. MEXICO (2-3)

Even though Team USA had beaten Mexico earlier in the event, everyone in the American contingent knew that this game was going to carry an extreme amount of pressure. Win and you're in, lose and you go home.

It was Mark Mulder's turn to pitch.

"I absolutely knew what the consequences of that game were, but USA Baseball had done a very good job of trying to shelter us from feeling and really knowing how big of a game that actually was," said Mulder. "I did not have my best stuff that night, but I was doing everything I could to try and make good pitches and get outs. Looking back on it, I probably should have been more nervous than I was. I just felt like we had been playing well, and were going to win the game."

For Mexico, Jesus Rios got the nod again, as he did when the two teams met in pool play. In that contest, Rios was solid, as he had limited Team USA to just one hit through four innings before being tagged for three runs in the fifth.

With semifinal tension in the air and both sides feeling it, the pitching again dominated the hitting early, as the game was scoreless through three. But Mexico broke through with a run in the bottom of the fourth and held a 1-0 lead into the sixth.

"Well, I have played in a lot of major-league games, and I've managed them too, but because of what was at stake, it was as much pressure as any of us had ever been through," said Bell. "It really brought you back to your roots in the game, it was only about baseball and trying to win. I tried not to think about what was on the line that night, because it always brought you back to having the weight of our entire country on our shoulders, and you had to focus on the game at hand."

As the man in charge of USA Baseball, Seiler was having an extremely difficult time watching, as years of work had boiled down to two hours in a small Canadian ballpark.

"I was moving around the stadium—I couldn't sit still—as

I was trying to find that place to stand where we were going to get some good results," said Seiler, who doesn't shy away from his superstitions. "At one point, I remember seeing Sandy Alderson and Pat Gillick, both of them who had seen so much in this game, they were so tight watching us play that night that they were literally on the verge of being sick. It was hard to breathe."

Seiler must have found a lucky spot, as the Americans were finally able to tie the score at 1-1 in the top of the sixth, when Peter Bergeron led off with a walk and came around to score on a base hit by Adam Kennedy. But that was it for Mulder, as Bell and Latch went to reliever Dan Wheeler out of the bullpen, who had pitched so well against the Cubans.

A coin flip had given Mexico last licks as the home team, so the Americans knew they would have to win the game with their pitching. And Wheeler was again lights out. After Team USA failed to take a lead in the top of the seventh, he retired all three Mexican hitters in the bottom half. That scenario repeated itself in the eighth inning, and when Team USA once again failed to score in the top of the ninth, their Olympic bid was in the hands of Wheeler, who needed to get three more outs just to give the Americans another chance.

"Every batter that came to the plate for Mexico those last three innings, you were just praying that one of them didn't connect on a fastball and put it over the fence," said Seiler. "But Dan was unbelievable. You want to talk about shutting the door? It was just incredible. Every inning, he went out there and got better and better. It was really impressive."

Wheeler retired the side in order in the ninth, and Team USA had another life to try and score a run. And this time, they took advantage of it. Marcus Jensen, who had already supplied the American offense with several key hits in the tournament, hammered a one-out double into the gap and was then lifted for pinch-runner Shawn Gilbert.

With Mexican right-handed reliever Vicente Palacios on the mound, Bell called for his left-handed bat off the bench Mike Neill to head out into the on-deck circle.

"Buddy had told me before the game that he was going with the other three outfielders that night, so I told him that if he needed me to hit, I'd be ready," said Neill. "As I watched the game and saw how things were developing, I'd just tried to stay as ready as I could. It was such a struggle to score that night, and since we had a guy on second base, I knew this was going to be a big moment."

It was a moment that Neill and the rest of the Team USA contingent would never forget. "I thought that with a base open, Palacios might try to pitch around me, so as I walked to the plate, I was thinking to be patient. Seeing how nervous the coaches were and all of us, it was tough not playing in the game, and I hadn't done that a whole lot in my career, being a pinch-hitter. But I certainly knew how big a deal this was," said Neill.

Neill's hunch was right, as Palacios tried to get him to chase a bad pitch. Neill didn't bite and got ahead in the count 3-0. He took a strike, and with the count 3-1, he planned on being aggressive if he got a pitch he liked. But Palacios painted the outside corner with a fastball to make the count full.

"I thought maybe he would go back outside again on that corner, but instead of going outside, he came inside on me with the 3-2 pitch. I just tried to fight it off, and that's all that happened. I got enough off of it to reach the outfield for a base hit."

Neill's two-out, broken-bat looping liner had just enough to carry over the glove of the second baseman and landed on the turf in shallow center field, and with Gilbert running on the pitch, Team USA had their first lead of the game, 2-1.

"To be a part of that team, to be able to contribute like that, and to get a hit that put us ahead, was something that I knew I would never forget the rest of my life," said Neill.

But the game wasn't over. There was no question in Bell's mind who would pitch the bottom of the 10th to try and send Team USA to Australia: Dan Wheeler.

At that point, both Alderson and Gillick—arguably the two men who had watched more baseball and been through more intense situations with their teams during the major-league postseason and World Series than anyone else in the stadium—had decided they had seen enough. "Well, it's funny. We didn't watch the bottom of the tenth inning," said Gillick. "Sandy and I were sitting in the stands the whole game, and all of a sudden after we took the lead, he said, 'Let's go.' And I said, 'What do you mean, let's go?' And he said, 'Let's get out of here. I don't know if I can watch the end of this. We'll be able to tell by the sound of the crowd what happens.' So we actually left the park, and started to walk down the street back to the hotel, and I think Sandy was accustomed to this, not being able to watch tight games to the end."

As Wheeler put the final touch on his performance by nailing down the final three outs, Gillick and Alderson heard three cheers from the crowd and knew their assignment was complete: The United States would be playing in the 2000 Olympic Games in the sport of baseball.

Wheeler had faced 12 batters in the game, and retired them all under gut-wrenching circumstances. "The intensity of that game was just awesome. It was everything you could ask for as a baseball player, and it was what you had been practicing for and playing for your whole life," said Wheeler. "To be put in that kind of situation, and to be able to successfully focus on making great pitches, that experience in itself gave me so much confidence, and really helped launch me into the major leagues. When we finally scored that run, there was no way I was going to let them get one back on us. It was one of the greatest moments of my baseball career."

"I don't think I fully appreciated the impact and intensity of that game right away," said Alderson. "I think we all understood the magnitude of it at the time, but it wasn't until four years later, when we lost a similar game to Mexico and failed to get into the 2004 Olympics, did I realize how critical that night in Winnipeg was."

And for Seiler, it was pure relief more than anything. "The euphoria of winning is sometimes overshadowed by the relief of winning," said Seiler. "In our country,, there's an expectation level that we're going to do well in everything that we do. And specifically to the sport of baseball internationally, that means we're going to be in contention to win gold medals. So if we had not qualified for the Olympic Games, there's a level of shame and embarrassment with that failure. Winning that game was as much about the relief of not having to face failure as it was about the joy of qualifying for the Olympics."

Unfortunately for the host country of Canada, they ran into the Cuban powerhouse at the wrong time. The veteran-laden club picked up their play when they needed to, and handed the upstart Canadians their only loss of the event in the second semifinal earlier that day, 3-2. Which meant that the United States and Cuba would be playing for the Pan Am gold medal. This was the perfect matchup for international baseball, but the fans in Winnipeg were disappointed that Canada had not only failed to qualify for Sydney, but that they'd only be playing for a Pan Am bronze medal. Canada won that bronze medal with a 9-2 win over a Mexican team that had spent itself trying to shock the Americans the night before.

GOLD-MEDAL GAME: USA (5-1) vs. CUBA (4-2)

Team USA sent Brad Penny back to the mound against Cuban right hander Jose Contreras, who later in his career would defect from Cuba and go on to spend 10 years in the major leagues for the Yankees, White Sox, Rockies, and Phillies, winning a World Series title with Chicago in 2006.

Contreras had long been the ace of the Cuban pitching staff and in 1999 was pitching better than he ever had. In the gold-medal game, he overpowered the Team USA lineup, striking out 13 in eight dominant innings while allowing only four hits, as Cuba took home the gold with a 5-1 victory. Cuban slugger Orestes Kindelan belted a pair of home runs while Daniel Lazo also went deep off Penny.

"We understood our team's mentality that day going into it was that it would have been nice to win—we had already beaten these guys once in the event—so it was going to be very hard to get them again. They threw their ace at us, but we as an organization and a team knew that our goal had already been accomplished. So I think we played pretty relaxed and without a sense of urgency, and just didn't win the game," said Seiler. "The hangover of all of the emotion and energy we had put into that event, and with the tense, extra innings the night before, there wasn't much left in the tank to come back and play the Cubans the next day. Especially when we knew that there was nothing at stake other than pride."

Ultimately, the 1999 USA Baseball silver-medal-winning Pan Am Team will be remembered for what they accomplished under extreme pressure. They played winning baseball against tough competition, when everything was on the line. They represented their country extremely well and left the field proud of what they had done.

"You lose one game and you're behind the eight-ball right away, and it's not like playing a seven-game series and coming back to win four games to three or anything like that," said Gillick. "So consequently I think the biggest thing we were able to do was getting over to the players how much every game meant, how much every game counted. There were no games where you could take any chance of losing, because there might not be a tomorrow where you could come back. You had to concentrate, and there was pressure on every game. And a lot of our players, I don't think, had experienced that kind of pressure of having to win every game to be successful. So that was the one thing that Buddy and the staff did an incredible job of impressing upon them: how important every game was, no matter who we were playing."

And there's no doubt that it was a baseball experience that changed every person involved.

"It ranks right up there at the top for me, right with the World Series Championships," said Gillick. "I've been fortunate enough to be on an NCAA championship team over 50 years ago in 1958, with USC, but certainly that Team USA silver medal and qualify for the Olympics ranks right up there. Because really, I wasn't doing it for the university, or for the particular city that I was representing in the professional ranks, be it Toronto or Philadelphia. I was doing it for the country, and if we were successful, we were going to represent the United States in the Olympic Games. So it was something very special to me in my career, where I had a chance to impact our entire country."

The medal ceremony in Winnipeg had Cuba (middle) on the gold-medal stand, but Team USA (left) got the job done with a silver-medal finish, to secure a berth in the 2000 Olympic Games.

5

OLYMPIC BASEBALL HISTORY

With USA Baseball now knowing that they had another opportunity to prepare a professional team once again, to compete as one of eight teams in the 2000 Olympic Games baseball event, Seiler, Cohen, and the entire USA Baseball staff went straight into preparation mode. When you work for one of the national governing bodies (NGB) of a sport, the Olympics are your World Series, your Super Bowl, your ultimate. The role of an NGB is to prepare athletes for that level of competition: to compete against the best in the world. Everything that you do in the years in between the Games is supposed to culminate at the Olympics, with your premier athletes peaking at just the right time.

Most other NGBs have the luxury of training their athletes on a year-round basis, and some Americans even have the opportunity to live in corporate-sponsored housing at the USOC headquarters in Colorado Springs, Colorado, where their Athletic Training Center is located. Sports such as swimming, diving, skiing, and speed skating take advantage of those facilities.

For obvious reasons, USA Baseball was not one of those

types of NGBs. There was no way to internally train baseball players year-round, so they were always forced to choose the best players they could find at any given age level in order to form a roster, whether it be high school, college, or pro. The upside is that over time, many players end up getting the chance to wear the Team USA uniform. The downside is that it does not generate a solid concentration of players who are gaining international experience that USA Baseball could go back to and draw from. At least half of the players, if not more, on every team they formed had no international experience whatsoever.

"There's nothing we can do about that, but our confidence comes from the fact we have a deep pool of baseball talent here in the United States, and we understand that we're lucky to have that kind of talent in our country," said Seiler. "So I believe, that is we do our homework, and players are vetted correctly by our staff, and we have the right coaches in place, you're going to be OK. Over the course of the past 20 years, you look at our international record, and it's been very, very successful. That's a tribute to the depth of talent that we have in the USA. And if we do things the right way, we usually do pretty well in terms of being competitive internationally, and we always believe we have a great shot at winning a gold medal."

Prior to 2000, USA Baseball's history of selecting its first four Olympic teams and competing in the Games had been a bag of mixed results. Starting with baseball's first opportunity to be played as a demonstration sport in 1984 in Los Angeles, and up through the 1996 Games in Atlanta, Team USA had collected an overall record of 20 wins and 8 losses. They had earned one official Olympic team medal: a bronze in Atlanta just four years prior, when a group of all-star college players came back to beat Nicaragua 10-3, after losing badly to Japan in the semifinals by an 11-2 score. And in 1992 in Barcelona, Team USA failed to medal completely, when they ended up on the wrong side of the draw after pool play, losing to Cuba in the semifinals and Japan in the bronze-medal game.

Cuba had chosen to participate only in each of those previous two Olympic Games (1992 and 1996), because baseball had earned official medal status. That was only after it had passed the test of the International Olympic Committee as a demonstration event in both 1984 in Los Angeles and in 1988 in Seoul, South Korea. And in all four of these Olympics, only amateur players were allowed to participate, meaning that for the past 16 years, USA Baseball had been selecting their Olympic rosters from the collegiate ranks.

The 1984 USA Team, led by legendary University of Southern California head baseball coach Rod Dedeaux, had become the most famous and well-recognized roster of players in the history of the organization. With the baseball event played at Dodger Stadium, Dedeaux's squad had earned a silver medal and had become the darlings of baseball that year. Names like USC's Mark McGwire, Mississippi State's Will Clark, and recently named Hall of Famer Barry Larkin of Michigan led a star-studded roster that was popularized when the baseball trading-card company Topps gave each player his own card donning the red, white, and blue uniform of Team USA and mixed them all into the packs of traditional cards of major-league players.

That group of unknown-at-the-time 20-year-olds almost pulled off a start to American Olympic baseball history that would have been hard to top. Having won each of their first four games, and leading Japan early in the gold-medal final in front of over 55,000 screaming American fans, they weren't able to contain the precision and power of the very experienced Japanese team, falling 6-3.

Still, the silver-medal finish was something to be proud of and to build upon going into the 1988 Games in Korea. With 10 players returning from the USA's 1987 Pan Am Team, this USA squad went overseas on a mission: to get the gold that had eluded the '84 team.

It was Stanford University head coach Mark Marquess who guided another roster of collegiate stars—one that included the likes of Tino Martinez of Tampa, Robin Ventura of Oklahoma

State, Ben McDonald of LSU, Andy Benes of Creighton, and Jim Abbott of Michigan—into a gold-medal rematch with Japan. And this time, it was the Americans who came out on top behind the arm of Abbott, who tossed a complete-game 5-3 victory, and the bat of Martinez, who connected on a pair of homers in the win.

Abbott's Olympic heroics in Seoul helped launch him into a very successful career in the major leagues, one that was capped when he threw a no-hitter for the Yankees in 1993. But before he had ever played for Team USA, the youngster from Flint, Michigan had inspired millions of people with his personal story, not his pitching performances. Born without a right hand, he had become a star at the University of Michigan, carried the American flag at the opening ceremonies of the 1987 Pan Am Games, and was given the '87 James E. Sullivan Award as the nation's top amateur athlete.

Finally, after many years of dedicated effort by the IBAF, baseball was given official medal status for the 1992 Games in Barcelona, Spain. USA Baseball went with a collegiate head coach named Ron Fraser, who at the time was one of the winningest coaches in college baseball and in the middle of a storied career at the University of Miami-Florida.

His roster was filled with many of the top sophomores and juniors in the college ranks: infielders Nomar Garciaparra of Georgia Tech, Jason Giambi of Long Beach State, and Phil Nevin of Cal State Fullerton; outfielders Jeffrey Hammonds of Stanford, Calvin Murray of Texas, and Michael Tucker of Longwood College; catchers Charles Johnson of Miami and Jason Varitek of Georgia Tech; and a pitching staff that included Willie Adams of Stanford, Jeff Alkire of Miami, Darren Dreifort of Wichita State, Rick Greene of LSU, Rick Helling of Stanford, and Ron Villone of Mississippi State.

Team USA fared well in the round-robin portion of the '92 Games, going 5-2 to earn a berth in the medal round. However, the two losses to Cuba and Japan were early premonitions of what was to come. Drawn into the semifinals against Cuba, Osvaldo Fernandez, who would later defect from

Cuba to sign a lucrative contract with the San Francisco Giants, pitched 5.2 innings, allowing only five hits to lead the Cubans to a 6-1 triumph. Cuban star Omar Linares went 3-for-3 and scored a pair of runs, while Victor Mesa added a home run and four RBIs, as American starter Rick Helling suffered the defeat.

After Chinese Taipei (Taiwan) stunned the Japanese 5-2 in the second semifinal, Team USA was unable to muster enough to earn an official medal, losing the bronze-medal game to Japan 8-3. And the Cubans went on to capture the first official Olympic gold medal in baseball history, with a 11-1 whitewash over Taipei.

Four years later, USA Baseball had a second chance and a golden opportunity to finally reach the pinnacle of international baseball. The Games were to be played in Atlanta, Georgia in the home stadium of the Atlanta Braves: Fulton County Stadium.

One of college baseball's great leaders and motivators, Skip Bertman of Louisiana State University was named the Team USA head coach. He was given a roster of what he called "the best offensive team ever assembled by USA Baseball" and the group had visions of gold, with the home-field advantage on their side.

Offensively, Team USA was led by Jacque Jones of USC, Troy Glaus of UCLA, Mark Kotsay of Cal State Fullerton, Travis Lee of San Diego State, A.J. Hinch of Stanford, and Warren Morris of LSU. On the mound, they could rely on arms such as Braden Looper of Wichita State, Kris Benson and Billy Koch of Clemson, Jeff Weaver of Fresno State, and R.A. Dickey of Tennessee.

With metal bats still in play (they had been used in every Olympic baseball event until this point), the USA lineup had firepower like never before, and in the hot summer air of Georgia, the ball was flying out of the park. The Americans pounded out 32 home runs and averaged more than 10 runs per game. But the highly anticipated matchup against Cuba once again failed to occur. The Cubans held up their end of the bargain by defeating Nicaragua in the semifinals 8-1. On the other hand, Bertman's squad was stymied by Japan in the semifinals, 11-2. The Japanese played long ball on that night, smashing five home runs while shutting down the USA attack on just six hits.

In the gold-medal game, Cuba retained its title as Olympic Champion with a 13-9 win over Japan, and reaffirmed its status going into the Sydney Games as the ruler of the international baseball world.

And although the USA didn't achieve its ultimate goal, the young collegians brought back the first ever official medal in baseball history by beating Nicaragua 10-3 for the bronze. So after finishing with gold ('88) and silver ('84) demonstration medals, and one official bronze ('96), USA Baseball officials were eager to see how they might fare against the Cubans and Japanese when they would have the opportunity to compete with a more experienced level of player, wooden bats instead of metal, and a roster that they could call professional.

6

DODGER BLUE

Suddenly in February of 2000, the USA Baseball Board of Directors decided to remove Dan O'Brien from his role as executive director and handed the reins of the organization over to Paul Seiler, naming him the interim executive director. It was a move that stunned the entire staff, but Seiler immediately had the instincts to shore up some areas of the internal operation that had begun to fall to the wayside, removed several staffers that were not carrying their weight, and added others to his team whom he could rely on for more efficient work.

"I wasn't chasing the executive directorship, but I considered myself a big part of the organization, a member of the team, and I was someone that had a lot of institutional knowledge," said Seiler. "I'd been with a number of our National teams and I'd been working heavily with MLB for the past 24 months, so as the Board moved forward and we had a change, it was a transitional period, and I don't think they wanted to bring in somebody new after we had just qualified for the Olympics."

For Seiler, it was an opportunity to keep the ship pointed in the right direction and show that he was capable of leading the organization. "I was hoping that they realized after a while that they had somebody already on staff that can be their next executive director. But at that point, there was so much going on, that I couldn't focus everything on myself. It was about our team, the Olympics, and trying to do a great job putting that together, to give us the best shot at a gold medal. There were some staff decisions that had to be made, and I made those decisions based upon what I thought was right, in the best interest of the organization. Those were hard decisions and they were tough things, but ultimately looking back, hopefully they were the correct decisions."

Over the offseason, Gillick—following his successful maneuvering that helped qualify the United States for the Sydney Games—signed on with the Seattle Mariners as their new general manager. That immediately took him out of the running to remain as the leading voice in player selection for the USA Baseball Olympic Team in 2000. So Seiler and Alderson decided to make Bob Watson the team's co-general manager, and added Bill Bavasi for Watson to partner with, moving him up from his role on the '99 Pan Am Team Selection Committee.

Having just recently resigned from his role as GM of the Angels at the end of the '99 season, Bavasi was working on several different new baseball projects, when he got a call from Alderson.

"I had started working with Peter Ueberroth brokering player acquisitions for one of the professional Japanese League teams," said Bavasi. "So when Sandy called and asked me if I'd be interested in helping put together the Olympic team, I wanted to do that, but I knew that I probably wouldn't be able to travel with the club to Australia, because I was committed to some other things." Bavasi had also just gotten involved with the Inside Edge, an independent advance scouting service, as a part owner, so he was not really sure where they might need him to be when the summer rolled around.

"So I told Sandy that I was committed to my other

opportunities, but not so much that I couldn't help USA Baseball as well," said Bavasi. "Because in an effort to find the right guys for the Japanese clubs in the future, I was going to be scouting four-A players anyways. I'll be out there looking at teams and looking at players, and that it could be a real good match. But I just wasn't sure I could commit to spending a month in Australia."

Alderson didn't see any problem with that scenario, as his only need was to have Bavasi assist Watson in putting together the right club.

"Looking back on it, I'll forever be indebted to Sandy for giving me the chance, because people don't understand what a great opportunity it was for Pat, Bob, and I to be involved with USA Baseball. It was just a great opportunity: I was so lucky to get it."

Both Seiler and Alderson were ecstatic with the two leaders they had in place and glad to have Bavasi back on board. "It just made a lot of sense for us to keep Bob in the mix, and bring up Bill from the Committee into a more official capacity," said Seiler. "They both knew very well what type of players we needed, and the MLB general managers were comfortable working with both of them."

So once the structure was in place of who would be making final player-personnel decisions and the workload was spread out between Watson and Bavasi, it was time to get back to the statistics and analyzing the data on who the best players from across the land were going to be. To do that, they once again were going to rely on a staff of experienced scouting department personnel from across Major League Baseball teams.

Five members of the 1999 Pan Am Team Selection Committee were asked to return in 2000 and accepted the opportunity: Roger Jongewaard (Seattle), Chuck Lamar (Tampa Bay), Omar Minaya (New York Mets), J.P. Ricciardi (Oakland), and Gary Sutherland (Anaheim). And nine new members were then added to the 2000 USA Baseball Olympic Team Selection Committee: Allard Baird (Kansas City), Pat Daugherty

(Colorado), Gary Hughes (Cincinnati), Sandy Johnson (Arizona), Bill LaJoie (Atlanta), Gary Nickels (San Diego), Paul Ricciarini (Houston), Don Welke (Los Angeles), and Dave Wilder (Milwaukee).

As spring-training camps opened up and the baseball world began its business again for the 2000 season, the Committee's first order of business was to figure out who would manage Team USA in Sydney. It was going to be a high-profile job, one that would gain quite a bit of media attention. It would also be critical that this person could handle the grueling trip to a foreign country that was halfway around the world and also take on a baseball experience like nothing he would have ever been accustomed to seeing.

Buddy Bell was out of the mix, after he had accepted the managerial job in the offseason with the Colorado Rockies. That left Watson, Bavasi, and the Selection Committee with a very short list of candidates on their first conference call that March.

Terry Collins was a career minor-league infielder who had played in both the Dodgers' and Pirates' farm systems in the 1970s and early '80s. By the early '90s, he had begun to rise as a managerial prospect and was promoted to the coaching staff in Pittsburgh in 1992 as a bullpen coach. When Watson was still the general manager in Houston and needed a new field manager after he had fired Art Howe in 1993, he brought in Collins and gave him his first managerial job in the big leagues.

Collins lasted three seasons in Houston, finishing second all three years. Less than a month after being let go by the Astros, Collins resurfaced in Anaheim and took over as manager of the Angels in 1997. His first two years with the Angels also produced winning records and second-place finishes. But in 1999, the Angels were hampered by injuries and Collins resigned with 29 games left in the season, handing in his walking papers to then-Angels GM Bill Bavasi. So Watson and Bavasi both had a strong history with Collins, knew him well, and thought he would provide a great motivating presence for the young minor-league players he could potentially be handling for Team USA.

Jim Lefebvre is a former major-league infielder and was named the 1965 National League Rookie of the Year with the Los Angeles Dodgers, when he hit .250 with 12 home runs and 69 RBIs. A National League All-Star in 1966, Lefebvre also played four seasons in Japan, from 1973 until 1976, for the Lotte Orions. He then moved into managing, started in the minors, and worked his way up into his first job in the big leagues with the Seattle Mariners in 1989, where he lasted three seasons. He moved to the Chicago Cubs in 1992 and spent two years there, coached in the minors for several more seasons, and then spent his final year managing at the major-league level with the Milwaukee Brewers in 1999.

With a long history and a very unique perspective on the game, including some international experience, Lefebvre was also a viable candidate to manage Team USA.

The third and final name being discussed was Tommy Lasorda.

After a brief career in the 1950s as a left-handed pitcher for both the Brooklyn Dodgers and the Kansas City Athletics, the Pennsylvania native became one of the most enthusiastic and successful managers in baseball history. Known for his fondness of pasta and pitching, the jovial Lasorda led the Los Angeles Dodgers to eight division titles and two World Championships in 21 seasons as manager. After suffering a mild heart attack in 1995, Lasorda retired from the dugout and moved into the Dodgers front office. His association with the club has spanned seven decades, and he was inducted into the Baseball Hall of Fame in 1997. Also known for his passion for everything about the Dodgers, he remains one of the most charismatic and famous baseball people on the planet.

There was no question: Lasorda would draw an incredible amount of attention if he was to be named the manager of Team USA. But the first concern that both Alderson and Seiler had was that at the time in 2000, Lasorda was 73 years old.

"The Lasorda conversation actually came up in '99 as well,

because we had gotten word that Tommy had an interest in managing Team USA," said Seiler. "But the thought was that a guy like Tommy is so high profile that if we were going to go that route, it would have to be with the Olympic Team, and not the '99 qualifying team. We had to get to the Olympics first, before we could even consider utilizing a manager like Tommy Lasorda. So, once we then began to seriously take him into consideration for the Sydney job, here was a guy who wanted to do it, which was half the battle right there. Not only did he want to do it, he embraced it, he had passion for it, and we knew that his passion was going to help us recruit players. When we looked at the available people at that point, how could you not help but be excited about a Hall of Famer managing your Olympic team?"

Alderson had a slightly different view of the situation. Lasorda had been politicking MLB Commissioner Bud Selig for over a year about giving him the Team USA job and had mentioned it to Selig again during March of 2000, when both Tommy and Bud were in Japan together for the start of the MLB season for games being played in Tokyo between the New York Mets and Chicago Cubs.

"I told my wife, because she started to ask me, 'Tommy, why do you want to do this?' and I told her because 25 years from now, there's going to be a quiz: 'Who's the only manager to ever win a World Series and an Olympic gold medal?' and I told her that was going to be me," said Lasorda. "And she said, 'Well, you don't even know who your players are,' and I said, 'I don't care, I just need them to be alive.' That's all I cared about. I just felt like I wanted to take this team, because everybody was saying that we couldn't beat the Cubans. That was the main topic of conversation about the Olympics; the Cuban team had won every existing tournament that they participated in. So all I asked was 'Did they ever lose one game?' and of course they had, so I said, 'Well then, they'll lose another one when we get to them.' That was primary motivation and my purpose in wanting to be the manager of the USA Olympic team, was to beat Cuba."

Despite his motivation and well-known enthusiasm for the opportunity, it was still not a lock that Lasorda would be given the job. At least not in Alderson's mind.

"There was a lot of discussion among the Committee about who should manage the club, and there were two schools of thought," said Alderson. "The first was that it needed to be a solid, salt-of-the-earth baseball guy, and the second category was somebody like Tommy, who was very solid baseball-wise, but also brought a higher profile and a higher level of interest to the team and the baseball event itself. At the time, Tommy had been retired for over five years, and there were quite a few on the Committee who thought we needed to go with somebody more current in the game: someone more like Buddy Bell and less like Tommy. But I felt like Lasorda could do the job well, and he brought a lot of intangibles to the table. This was not going to be a six-month season, this was only a four-week assignment."

So as the group was leaning more toward Lasorda, Alderson decided that he needed to make absolutely sure that, if given the chance, the 73-year-old retiree could handle the rigors of the brutal travel schedule halfway around the world, along with the daily grind of the Olympic media contingent following his every move. Bavasi distinctly remembers a turning point in the conference-call discussions.

"At first, we weren't all that worried about his ability to manage the team, the bigger concern was about his ability to physically handle the demands of the assignment at his age, considering this was a man that had had a heart attack five years prior," said Bavasi. "We didn't need someone who was going to end up in the hospital in Australia during the middle of the Olympics."

The Committee also wasn't sure that the trip was going to offer Lasorda the conveniences that he had become accustomed to in the major leagues, mostly a first-class travel ticket and hotel accommodations in Sydney that a Hall of Famer would come to expect. This was far from being a major-league road trip—the United States Olympic Committee would only be providing every athlete, coach, and staff person with a round-trip airline ticket to Australia in coach seating—no exceptions. On top of that, it was a 15-hour flight from Los Angeles to Sydney, and once there, Lasorda would be expected to stay with his team in the Athletes Village, just like all of the other Team USA coaches of other sports. The Athletes Village can best be described as more like a college dormitory, where they serve cafeteria-style food.

As the Committee continued the debate over who should manage Team USA, Bavasi eventually stepped in.

"I remember somehow interrupting the discussion, and I didn't make a speech or anything, I just mentioned that this team has a chance to be great, and I thought the industry wanted someone who would be likeable internationally. Maybe we'd better rethink Tommy and give him a little more consideration," said Bavasi. "All I was saying is that he couldn't really cause that much of a problem in a month. He has a way of motivating. The players will believe him when he tells them they're good, so maybe we've got to rethink that."

It was then that Alderson asked both Bavasi and Watson to sit down with Lasorda and explain the differences of this assignment, to make sure he was completely aware of every single aspect of the job and the requirements surrounding the opportunity.

"So Bob and I take Tommy to lunch, and I'll never forget this. We met him at a Mimi's Café in Fullerton, California, and Mimi's is like a glorified Denny's with shade. So we're sitting there, and I start to tell him that this was going to be a lot of work, and very difficult travel, and I ask him, 'Are you sure you're up for this?'" said Bavasi. "And I've known Tommy since I was a kid, so he's talking to me like I'm his little nephew, like he always has. He's real comfortable chewing me out. And so I said, 'Look, you know we're considering you for the job.' And he says, 'Considering? Who the fuck else do you have who's a Hall of Famer on your list?' And I said, 'Hey, we don't have another Hall of Famer, but we don't have anyone your age, either. And quite frankly, a lot of people may have interest in you doing this, but nobody has an interest in killing you.' And he just scoffed at that. He just said, 'That's ridiculous. I can't even believe you're thinking about that?'

"So I proceeded to tell him that he would need to stay in the Village with the rest of the team, and that they needed him to fly with the club in coach, and they're not getting three seats for every two guys like they do in the big leagues; it's one man per seat," said Bavasi. "And he said that he would do whatever everybody else was doing. That was enough for me, because by then everybody in the restaurant was staring at us."

On the next Committee conference call, it was reported that Lasorda was fully aware of the demands of the job and was still on board. At that point, the final decision rested with Alderson.

"I was aware that Tommy was Commissioner Selig's preferred candidate, but had I wanted to name another candidate, I would have made that case to Bud," said Alderson. "But in the end, Lasorda was the right choice for us based on all team- and non-team-related considerations."

7

WATCH LIST

In May of 2000, the Team USA Selection Committee began with a list of 603 names on the initial Olympic Team USA watch list, and this time USA Baseball was planning on only bringing a total of 29 players with them to the Gold Coast of Australia, approximately two weeks prior to the official start of the Olympic Games. There, Team USA would play a series of exhibition games against other Olympic baseball teams from Italy, Korea, the Netherlands, and South Africa. The goal was to invite those 29 players to the practice sessions as a final live "tryout," where three position players and two pitchers were going to be cut and sent back to the United States, while staff had a chance to finalize the 24-man roster for the Games.

"The idea was to be able to have a slight bit of flexibility with who we name to the final roster, to be able to go with the hot hand," said Watson. "We were going to be travelling so far away, we wanted to have additional players available in case a guy got injured during the exhibitions or just wasn't playing or pitching well. That way, if something did go wrong, we didn't have to try and find a minor leaguer back in the States and fly him all the way to Australia in an emergency."

But first things first, and that was to name a coaching staff to assist Lasorda. For the role of pitching coach, Marcel Lachemann, the '99 Pan Am team's pitching coach, had moved on to Colorado with Buddy Bell, so he was no longer available either. Some of the names given to the Committee on the initial ballot included Hall of Famer Sandy Koufax and former major leaguers Charlie Hough, Bruce Kison, and Al Nipper.

The Committee ended up selecting former major leaguer Phil Regan, with whom Lasorda was very familiar. The two had worked together in the Dodgers' farm system, when Regan was their special assignment and advance scout. Regan had just come off a season in 1999 as the pitching coach for the Cleveland Indians, so it was imperative that most clubs could trust Regan's judgment when it came to monitoring the pitch counts their prospects would be throwing. They knew that Regan would stick to the drill.

At first-base and hitting coach, Reggie Smith was available again and accepted the opportunity. He of course was very comfortable working with Lasorda, after having played for Tommy from 1976 to 1981 in Los Angeles. Other candidates who were mentioned for that role included former major leaguers Steve Henderson, George Hendrick, Mitchell Page, and Harry Spilman. But it was Smith who received the most support.

At third-base coach, an array of new candidates included such names as Collins and Lefebvre (now that they were not going to be managing the team), former longtime Lasorda sidekick in Los Angeles Joe Amalfitano, former major-league catchers Terry Kennedy and Joel Skinner, and a couple of well-respected minor-league managers in Tom Gamboa and John Gibbons. One name that was very unfamiliar to the group but that had been gaining a lot of support was Toronto Blue Jays triple-A manager Eddie Rodriguez.

Rodriguez was being thought of as the leading candidate because of his wide-ranging baseball knowledge and because he was originally from Cuba and could speak Spanish. Not only did the Committee and USA Baseball like that idea,

Lasorda did as well. With Rodriguez standing on the field during games in the third-base coaching box, he would be able to understand anything that the Cuban coaches might communicate to their players from the dugout using Spanish.

"Being nominated for the opportunity was a total surprise to me at first, because I was of Cuban descent and didn't really have a good grasp on what USA Baseball stood for," said Rodriguez. "But it was a tremendous honor to have the chance to wear the red, white, and blue uniform and to be able to work with Tommy, Reggie, and Phil, I knew we had a great chance to do well."

Finally, just as they had done in Winnipeg, USA Baseball brought with them two collegiate coaches to act as batting-practice pitchers and auxiliary coaches, to basically do whatever else the on-field staff needed help with. Some of the nominees for those two spots included Jerry Kindall of Arizona, Paul Maneiri of Notre Dame, Pat McMahon of Mississippi State, Mark Johnson of Texas A&M, and Joe Carbone of Ohio University. Although Carbone had been one of the two auxiliary coaches with Team USA in 1999, he was not selected this time around. Instead, the Committee went with the very well-respected Ray Tanner of South Carolina, and the second auxiliary coach from Winnipeg, Dick Cooke of Davidson. Both coaches were very familiar with how USA Baseball operated, and Tanner threw right-handed batting-practice pitches while Cooke threw left-handed BP pitches.

Once the staff was in place, it was on to the real business of determining the roster of players. Unlike many of the other Olympic sports, baseball players did not have the opportunity to qualify for the Games by earning points, racing fast enough, or holding world rankings. Essentially, the minor-league baseball season of 2000 was their Olympic trials. Play well for the first three months of the season, and you would surely end up on the USA Baseball radar. Play poorly, and you most likely were not going to be noticed. And following the success of the 1999 Pan Am Team, most American minor leaguers at the double-A level or higher were fully aware of the chance to become an Olympian that summer.

To start the dwindling process, USA Baseball and the Committee had to have a list of names to begin watching from the get-go. Then, as the season wore on and the Selection Committee would report back the action that they witnessed each week around the minor leagues, players would drop off the list, and perhaps others—if a strong case was made by a Committee member—could be added.

To get the watch list started, USA Baseball asked the Major League Baseball Scouting Bureau to compile a list of their top American minor-league eligible players going into the season, based on reports and grading potential from the previous year. Secondly, the Team USA Selection Committee, made up of 15 club scouting- and player-personnel directors, were allowed to submit names of players from either of the two clubs that they were each assigned to cover. For instance, Bavasi was assigned to monitor the Florida Marlins and Montreal Expos, while Don Welke was assigned to cover the Los Angeles Dodgers and Toronto Blue Jays. Each Committee member was assigned his own organization, along with a second in which he happened to be somewhat educated about the players in that system as well.

Once both the Bureau and the Committee had submitted their pre-season lists, it contained over 600 eligible players, all broken down by position.

<u>Starting Pitching</u>

The Committee had no preference whether they had right-handed or left-handed starters: They simply wanted the four best arms they could possibly get in the Team USA rotation. "That being said, we were hoping that one left-hander would really step up and make the team, so that we would have the opportunity to start a lefty if we wanted to, against a particularly strong left-handed hitting opponent," said Watson.

Preferably, they were looking for pitchers who had not had any time spent on the disabled list during the season by the time the final selections would be made in late August, and secondly, pitchers who were throwing the ball well after the All-Star break. The plan was to pool a list of potential starters down to approximately 15, monitor their starts very closely after July, and then go with four of them to make the team. But a total of six starting pitchers would be selected to make the trip to Australia, with two being given the devastating news that they would miss the final cut overseas, after the exhibition games were played.

Over 100 starting pitchers made the original watch list, including all four starters from the 1999 Pan Am Team, some very big-name prospects, and others who went on to have outstanding major-league careers. A sampling of the list included:

Kurt Ainsworth – San Francisco
Ryan Anderson – Seattle (1999 Pan Am Team member)
Bronson Arroyo – Pittsburgh
Josh Beckett – Florida
Alan Benes – St. Louis
Mark Buehrle – Chicago White Sox
A.J. Burnett – Florida
Jeff D'Amico – Milwaukee
Doug Davis – Texas
Jon Garland – Chicago White Sox
Jason Jennings – Colorado
Rick Krivda – Baltimore
Ted Lilly – New York Yankees
Jason Marquis – Atlanta
Mark Mulder – Oakland (1999 Pan Am Team member)
John Patterson – Arizona (1999 Pan Am Team member)
Brad Penny – Florida (1999 Pan Am Team member)
C.C. Sabathia – Cleveland
Ben Sheets – Milwaukee
Brett Tomko – Seattle
Todd Van Poppel – Chicago Cubs
Jarrod Washburn – Anaheim

Jeff Weaver – Detroit (1996 USA Olympic Team)
Jake Westbrook – New York Yankees
Matt White – Tampa Bay
Barry Zito – Oakland

Relief Pitching

Another pool of over 100 names was on a list of possible relievers, and Team USA had a total of seven roster spots in the bullpen. The names on the original watch list included Team USA's hero from Winnipeg, Dan Wheeler, along with some other interesting candidates:

Norm Charlton – Cincinnati
Kyle Farnsworth – Chicago Cubs
Chris George – Kansas City
Brad Lidge – Houston
Jim Morris – Tampa Bay
Joe Nathan – San Francisco
Steve Rain – Chicago Cubs (who had originally been chosen for the 1999 Pan Am Team)
J.C. Romero – Minnesota (1999 Pan Am Team member)
Bobby Seay – Tampa Bay (1999 Pan Am Team member)
Ed Vosberg – Colorado
Dan Wheeler – Tampa Bay (1999 Pan Am Team member)
Todd Williams – Seattle (1999 Pan Am Team member)
Brad Wohlers – Cincinnati
Tim Young – Boston

Catcher

A list of 60 names was originally identified, and USA Baseball was looking at naming two full-time catchers to the roster, with an additional third player who could catch but also play elsewhere in the field and perhaps be a designated hitter as well.

One player who was identified early in the process as a very solid choice was Pat Borders, who was a two-time World Series champion with the Toronto Blue Jays and the MVP of the 1992 Series, when the Jays defeated the Atlanta Braves. During the spring of 2000, Borders was with the Tampa Bay Devil Rays, and it was looking as if he would be playing most of the season at triple-A Durham, making him eligible for the Olympic team.

"Here was a player that had so much experience behind the plate, we thought that would be a tremendous asset to the young pitchers we would have on the squad," said Watson. "If Pat was going to be available, I think we all considered him highly, because of his veteran presence."

Because of his switch-hitting ability and excellent performance in Canada with the USA Pan Am qualifying team, Marcus Jensen was also in the mix again to go to Sydney, along with several other prospects and former major leaguers at the position:

- Danny Ardoin – Oakland
- Rod Barajas – Arizona
- Charlie Greene – Toronto (1999 Pan Am Team member)
- A.J. Hinch – Oakland (1996 USA Olympic Team)
- Brandon Inge – Detroit
- Mike Kinkade – New York Mets
- Jason LaRue – Cincinnati
- Paul LoDuca – Los Angeles
- Chad Moeller – Minnesota
- Matt Nokes – Cleveland
- Joe Oliver – Seattle
- Tom Pagnozzi – New York Yankees
- A.J. Pierzynski – Minnesota
- Brian Schneider – Montreal
- Jayson Werth – Baltimore
- Rick Wilkins – Los Angeles

First Base

"We were hoping for some offense out of the first-base slot, but also somebody that was really solid defensively as well," said Watson.

Although Jon Zuber appeared on the original watch list, there were no votes from the Committee next to his name, so it appeared the 1999 Pan Am Team member was going to have to have an outstanding minor-league season in order to be reconsidered strongly.

The highest number of original votes at the position went to Nick Johnson, a left-handed-hitting power bat in the farm system of the New York Yankees. Other players being considered included:

Lance Berkman – Houston
Pat Burrell – Philadelphia
Jack Cust – Arizona
Dave Hollins – Tampa Bay
Aubrey Huff – Houston
Mark Johnson – New York Mets
Doug Mientkiewicz – Minnesota
Eric Munson – Detroit
John Roskos – San Diego

Second Base

Like Zuber, Jason Hardtke was on the watch list, but there were several other players who ranked ahead of him in number of initial votes. One of those players was Brent Abernathy of the Devil Rays, who had played for the 1995 USA Baseball Junior National Team and won a gold medal.

Some of the other potential two-baggers included:

Marlon Anderson – Philadelphia
Willie Bloomquist – Seattle
Brent Butler – Colorado

Casey Candaele – St. Louis
Craig Counsell – Arizona
David Eckstein – Boston
Jerry Hairston – Baltimore
Keith Lockhart – Atlanta
John McDonald – Cleveland
Joe McEwing – New York Mets
David Newhan - San Diego

Third Base

The hot corner had some very strong offensive players in the mix as well as some defensive specialists who were coming off impressive seasons the year before. Five players were garnering a high level of attention from the Committee right away:

Russell Branyan - Cleveland
Sean Burroughs - San Diego
Michael Cuddyer - Minnesota
Mike Lamb – Texas
Adam Piatt - Oakland

Other names they were watching at third base included:
Casey Blake – Toronto
Joe Crede – Chicago White Sox
Wes Helms – Atlanta
Drew Henson – New York Yankees
Dave Hollins – Tampa Bay
Mike Kinkade – New York Mets
Scott McClain – Colorado
Kevin Orie – Kansas City
Chris Snopek – Chicago White Sox
Chris Truby – Houston

Shortstop

"This position was probably our smallest pool of candidates, because we wanted the best possible defender we could find," said Watson. "We needed a player there that when the game was on the line in the bottom of the ninth, he would be able to catch the ball and make a good throw with absolute certainty. Whatever he could do offensively would be a bonus."

Under those parameters, it was fairly easy for the Committee to dwindle down their list of options for the starting shortstop role.

Travis "Gookie" Dawkins was again in the mix and was being given plenty of consideration. In fact, he garnered the highest number of pre-season votes. The second highest number of votes went to a light-hitting defender in the Houston Astros' farm system named Adam Everett, who had played collegiately for Ray Tanner at the University of South Carolina.

Everett was known in scouting circles as being a premium "catch and throw" guy who would make all of the plays and could solidify a defense. He might not make all of the highlight reels, but would rarely make any mistakes that would hurt you, and he would gobble up the routine ground balls with ease.

Right behind Everett in the discussion was a switch-hitting shortstop in the Philadelphia Phillies system who was well known as an up-and-coming superstar in the making, named Jimmy Rollins.

Other players being talked about were:

Willie Bloomquist – Seattle (who had played on the USA National Team while at Arizona State)
Alex Cora – Los Angeles
Mark DeRosa – Atlanta
Felipe Lopez – Toronto

There was also room on the roster for a utility-type infielder who could play more than one position and possibly substitute late in games in the outfield or offer Lasorda a decent chance at getting a pinch hit off the bench.

Some names being tossed around for that role included Shawn Gilbert of the Dodgers, whom Lasorda knew and who had played for Team USA in Winnipeg. Others included:

Geoff Blum – Montreal
Mike Caruso – Chicago White Sox
Kelly Dransfeldt – Texas
Jason Hardtke – Colorado (who had been an instrumental part of Team USA successfully qualifying for the Olympics)
Bobby Smith – Tampa Bay

<u>Outfield</u>

All four of Team USA's outfielders from 1999 who had helped them advance to Sydney were back in the fold:

Peter Bergeron – Montreal
Milton Bradley – Montreal
Mike Neill – Seattle
Dave Roberts – Cleveland

In fact, Bradley and Roberts were among the top early vote-getters, along with:
Dee Brown – Kansas City
Pat Burrell – Philadelphia
George Lombard – Atlanta
Corey Patterson – Chicago Cubs
Vernon Wells – Toronto
Randy Winn – Tampa Bay
Further down the list were players such as:
Jack Cust – Arizona
David Dellucci – Arizona
Adam Dunn – Cincinnati
Josh Hamilton – Tampa Bay

Terrence Long – Oakland
Jay Payton – New York Mets
Aaron Rowand – Chicago White Sox
Anthony Sanders – Seattle
Jason Tyner – New York Mets

Designated Hitter

The designated hitter would be used in the Olympic baseball event, so Team USA organizers would be reserving one roster spot for that role. Ideally, they were looking for a power bat who could also perhaps play fairly solid defense in the outfield. They did not want simply a hitter who was a liability defensively.

The most votes in early discussions went to Boston Red Sox prospect Dernell Stenson, a left-handed-hitting first baseman/outfielder with pop in his bat. Also mentioned were:

Todd Greene – Toronto (who could also play catcher)
Nick Johnson – New York Mets (if they selected another player to start at first base)
Eric Munson – Detroit (who played for the USA National Team while in college at USC)
Mike Simms – Texas

Further down the original watch list at the DH position was a player who intrigued some of the Committee members, but who had not received any initial votes, named Ernie Young. Young was well known to the Committee members and Alderson, having been up-and-down with the Oakland A's for the past several seasons and collecting hundreds of home runs in the minor leagues. A right-handed hitter with power, Young had moved to the St. Louis Cardinals system and was playing at the triple-A level.

"Ernie was a good candidate to provide that leadership in the clubhouse presence, an older veteran-type player that would fit in well," said Watson. "But we needed to make sure his skills hadn't diminished any that season, as we were still five months away from playing games in Australia."

And incredibly there was one other name on the initial list that most likely provoked plenty of discussion on the conference calls: Daryl Strawberry. Throughout the 1980s and early 1990s, Strawberry was one of the most feared sluggers in the game, known for his prodigious home runs and his intimidating presence in the batter's box with his 6-foot-6 frame and his long, looping swing.

During his 17-year career, he helped lead the New York Mets to a World Series championship in 1986 and the New York Yankees to three World Series championships in 1996, 1998, and 1999. A popular player during his career, Strawberry was voted to the All-Star Game eight straight times from 1984–1991.

At the beginning of the 2000 season, Strawberry was very near the end of his career. In a short four-week event, though, he likely could have provided Team USA with an intimidating presence at the designated hitter's spot.

But with a long history of personal drug abuse, it was highly unlikely that the Committee would ultimately be able to take a chance on adding a player like Strawberry to their roster. Testing all athletes for performance-enhancing drugs and recreational substances was a huge part of the Olympic Games, and any athletes caught breaking those rules during competition would be immediately disqualified. In a team sport like baseball, if an athlete tested positive, it would have resulted in an immediate loss of the game which that player participated in and it would have made that player immediately ineligible for the rest of the Olympics.

Lastly, the Committee had a group of players listed as "recently retired MLB prospects." These would have been well-known longtime major leaguers who may have recently announced their retirement from playing the game. Perhaps, though—the Committee felt that maybe—if given enough time to train and get back into the needed physical shape, the player could provide a huge name presence to Team USA, much like Lasorda would be doing. On top of that, perhaps these players would consider putting the uniform back on for a chance to do something they had never done: represent their country.

Some of the bigger names on that list included:

Wade Boggs - infielder
Tom Candiotti - pitcher
Chili Davis – outfielder
Dennis Eckersley – pitcher
Gary Gaetti – infielder
Jimmy Key – pitcher
Willie McGee – outfielder
Paul Molitor – infielder/DH
Tim Raines – outfielder
Ruben Sierra – outfielder
Terry Steinbach - catcher

"We had several of them even contact us through their agents, asking what their chances might be to make the club," said Watson. "Raines was still playing in independent ball somewhere, and I know Steinbach had a strong interest as well."

So as Steve Cobb of Major League Baseball sent out the original watch list to the Committee on May 4, 2000, those 603 players had already begun their minor-league seasons. They could all assume, if they knew what was going on later that summer in Australia, that they possibly were in the midst of trying to make the United States Olympic Baseball Team. But none of them knew for sure whether they were on the official watch list or not. What they did know was that in order to have a shot, they had better be playing well, especially when a USA Baseball Committee member, Watson, or Bavasi happened to be sitting in the stands watching their game that night. At that moment, according to the numbers, they had a 4% chance of making Team USA's roster.

8

MAKING THE TEAM

Over three successive Tuesday mornings in May of 2000, the USA Baseball Olympic Team Selection Committee held conference calls that would help them begin to pare down the watch list, in order to focus on a smaller group of players that they were all in favor of keeping a closer eye on. Essentially, they needed to cut down to a manageable list of the players that they could more easily monitor, both statistically and in person over the next two months.

Each call focused on three to four positions on the diamond, as both the positive and negative attributes of these players were debated. The athletes whom the Committee voted to keep alive for a spot on the team stayed above the line, and the ones that they determined were not going to make the cut, for whatever reason, fell out of the mix and were removed. Unless something dramatically changed for them, over 400 players had their chances of becoming an Olympian erased without ever even knowing it.

That exercise left the Committee with a working list of approximately 200 active and healthy players whom they had an interest in pursuing. The next step was to find out from each major-league general manager whether or not his club would give USA Baseball permission to contact each of the particular minor leaguers whom they were interested in speaking with. There were two potential hurdles: The first was to make sure that the player's club was willing to let him go play for Team USA in Australia in September, which happens to be right in the middle of the postseason pennant races. If a GM thought that perhaps he might want to call his player up to the majors in September, because his club might need that player to help them get to the playoffs, that particular player's chances of making Team USA were over. So a player's fate lay completely in the hands of his general manager.

The second way in which players would begin to drop off the list of 200 was when USA Baseball would contact the player after receiving permission, and the player himself would reject the opportunity. This was a much more rare circumstance, but it did happen. For reasons unknown, whether it be health, a fear of flying for 15 hours across the world and back, or a family concern such as a baby due to be born, whatever the circumstances, life did cause a few players to have to say, "Thanks, but no thanks" to the chance to play for Team USA. In addition, there were a few players who chose to take the chance on being called up to the major leagues in September, because they thought there was that opportunity with their club. USA Baseball had to realize that for every single one of these prospects, making it to the major leagues had been that player's singular goal since the day they were drafted. This "Olympic" opportunity had only been put in front of them within the past several months. Maybe it just was not something that these players had ever focused on.

So in late May, Cobb sent a letter to all 30 major-league general managers, asking for permission to contact the players in their farm systems whom "the Committee has identified as a player that warrants further consideration to represent the United States at the 2000 Summer Olympics in Australia." It was made clear in the letter that each organization had the final say with regards to player eligibility, and that this exercise was for the Committee's planning purposes only: They were not asking for any solid commitments quite yet. The only question at this time was whether any of the players listed from their club were ones that they currently planned to make completely unavailable for the Olympic Team.

"It was both a request for permission, as well as a way for us to continue to pare down the list," said Cobb. "Because we did have some clubs indicate that certain guys we liked were not going to be available to us anyways. That simply ended the discussion for those kids, and we moved forward with the ones that would most likely be made available to us."

By mid-June, the list was now cut down to 157 players who would most likely—according to their clubs—be made eligible for selection, who had responded positively to USA Baseball's questionnaire that was inside of the general information packet that was sent directly to each player.

The Committee, staying with the list broken down by each position on the field, had created a "probable" category and a second "desirable" category for each position. Under probable right-handed starting pitchers, Milwaukee Brewers prospect Ben Sheets was the top name on the list.

Sheets had graduated from St. Amant High School in Louisiana and gone on to pitch at Northeast Louisiana University (now the University of Louisiana at Monroe) on a baseball scholarship. Once there, he set a school record by striking out 20 batters in a game against Louisiana Tech.

After his sophomore season, he was invited by USA Baseball to try out for the USA National Team, made up of the best freshman and sophomore collegiate players in the country. But even after pitching well at the trials, he realized that he was going to fall short of making the team.

"The thing I remember is that being from a small school like ULM, I didn't think that I was going to be even close to some of the other pitchers there. But after a few days, I looked up and I was one of the two or three hardest throwers there. My stuff matched up with any of them, but Louisiana Monroe isn't LSU, Baylor, Texas, or Cal State Fullerton. It really opened my eyes though, to think, 'Dang! You know what, I got a pretty good arm.' It just boiled down to the fact that we had some coaches there from big-time college programs, and they had some kids there that they gave the innings to. I'm not saying they played favorites or the other guys weren't better than me at the time, but if I'm a college coach and my kid is at that trials, I'm going to make sure he gets a fair shake, if not the benefit of the doubt, to make the team." Drafted by the Milwaukee Brewers in the first round (10th overall) of the 1999 draft, Sheets made his professional debut with the Ogden Raptors of the Pioneer League later that summer. In August, against the Idaho Falls Chukars, Sheets struck out eight batters while allowing just one hit through five innings. Later in the month, he was promoted to Class A Stockton of the California League, and in his seven minor-league starts that year, Sheets averaged a strikeout ratio of 10.09 batters per nine innings.

The following season of 2000, Sheets started the year at double-A Huntsville in the Southern League and made 12 starts there before being promoted to triple-A Indianapolis by June.

"I don't remember when I was first informed that I was a candidate to play for Team USA, but it was sometime mid-season that year," said Sheets. "I received an information package and they wanted me to take a preliminary drug-screening pee test, so at that point, I kind of knew I was up for it. I thought it'd be cool, thinking that if I wasn't going to be in the big leagues, the Olympics were next best thing. But looking back, it turned out to be way better than a September call-up."

Sheets was having a solid year on the mound. He had an ERA around 1.80 for Huntsville and was hovering around 2.80 for Indianapolis. "I was only a 21-year-old at the time, so I was pretty young for triple-A, and I was holding my own and pitching real well," said Sheets.

"Ben was on our radar from the beginning," said Watson. "We loved his makeup and his arm, but he was progressing so fast, we weren't sure he wasn't going to get called up to Milwaukee or not. We were really hoping they would allow us to have him on the team."

For Brewers general manager Dean Taylor, there was never a doubt. "From our standpoint, it was a very straightforward decision. We knew Ben wanted the opportunity, and we felt like it would be a great honor for the Brewers organization," said Taylor. "We thought he'd have a great chance to be one of the front-line pitchers on Team USA, because within our organization, we knew that Ben Sheets had the makeup to be a perfect fit for the Olympic Team. There was no doubt he was the number-one Brewers prospect at the time, and we were hoping that this Olympic experience would give him even more confidence than he already had, not that he ever lacked any in the first place."

The second name on the probable right-handed starting pitcher list was Dan Wheeler, who had moved into a starter's role at triple-A Durham with the Devil Rays. USA Baseball officials certainly had an interest in Wheeler returning to Team USA from his Pan Am experience, but had a feeling he would be called up to the majors by Tampa Bay, even though they gave an initial green light for him to be contacted.

The other righties being closely followed were Kurt Ainsworth of San Francisco, Jeff Austin of Kansas City, Josh Beckett of Florida, Jon Garland of the Chicago White Sox, Nelson Figueroa of Arizona, Jason Marquis of Atlanta, Brian Tollberg of San Diego, and Matt White of Tampa Bay.

One pitcher had managed to play his way onto the watch list, discovered by the Committee after not even being mentioned on the initial list of over 600 players. Another 1999 draftee like Sheets, Chicago White Sox prospect Jon Rauch had gone 11-1 with a 2.48 ERA in 15 starts for single-A Winston-Salem, with 103 strikeouts in 94 innings pitched. Standing at 6-foot-11 inches tall, Rauch was an intimidating presence that seemed like he could throw a baseball through a brick wall.

Both USA Pan Am Team right-handed starters had fallen off the list by this point. John Patterson had suffered an injury and would spend most of the 2000 season recovering, while Penny was already up in the major leagues with the Florida Marlins.

The left-handed starting pitcher probable list contained only Ryan Anderson from the USA Pan Am Team, because Mark Mulder had also made it to the big leagues with the Oakland A's. Besides Anderson, the probable lefty list was highlighted by a pair of big-name prospects – C.C. Sabathia of the Cleveland Indians and Barry Zito, another 1999 draftee by the Oakland A's.

Both Sabathia and Zito had been given clearance by their GMs to be contacted by USA Baseball, and both were having solid seasons, Sabathia at double-A Akron and Zito at triple-A Sacramento of the Pacific Coast League.

On the next tier of left-handed names was 1999 Pan Am Team member Bobby Seay of Tampa Bay, who had gotten some critical outs in relief for Team USA in Winnipeg. Also on that tier was Kansas City Royals prospect Chris George, who was pitching well for double-A Wichita; veteran lefty Rick Krivda at triple-A Rochester in the Baltimore system; and three single-A farmhands: Mike Bynum of San Diego, Chuck Crowder of Colorado, and Geoff Goetz of Florida.

For bullpen and relief-pitching roles, the Committee had narrowed the field down to 18 names. Todd Williams had made it known to USA Baseball officials following the qualifying event in Canada that he would do anything to be considered for a spot on the Olympic team, and he was very clear about it. "I was all-in, and had such a great experience with the team in 1999, that I couldn't wait to get back to that level of excitement playing games for my country again," said Williams. "It was just a whole other level of pressure and excitement compared to a regular old minor-league game. I couldn't even imagine what it was going to be like pitching in the Olympics."

Another pitcher who had come out of nowhere and surprised the Selection Committee was right-handed reliever Shane Heams of the Detroit Tigers. Pitching at double-A

Jacksonville, Hearns had gone 4-1 with a 1.58 ERA in 28 appearances, with four saves, 48 strikeouts, and only 19 hits allowed in 40.0 innings pitched.

Also still above the cut line were Chad Bradford of the Chicago White Sox, Tom Davey of Seattle, Kyle Farnsworth of the Chicago Cubs, Chad Harville of Oakland, Steve Rain of the Chicago Cubs (who had missed playing for the 1999 Pan Am Team because he was called up to the majors), 1999 Pan Am Team member J.C. Romero of Minnesota, Bert Snow of Oakland, and Williams, who was now with Seattle.

At the catching position, 15 players were being monitored, with the top name on the list being Ben Petrick of the Colorado Rockies, who was hitting .319 with seven homers and 41 RBIs for triple-A Colorado Springs. Next was A.J. Hinch of the Oakland A's, whom Alderson had drafted out of Stanford, and with whom Seiler was very familiar as well. Hinch was one of only two players remaining anywhere under consideration who had already been an Olympian, having played for Team USA in the 1996 Games in Atlanta. But he warranted the consideration, as he was batting .300 through 67 games at triple-A Sacramento.

The veteran Pat Borders was also still being looked at and was remaining consistent at triple-A Durham, batting .260 with six homers and 37 RBIs. But one of Team USA's heroes in Winnipeg, Marcus Jensen, had advanced to the major leagues coming out of spring training with the Minnesota Twins, ironically alongside his teammate in Canada, Matt LeCroy. Both players were sharing time behind the plate in Minnesota until July, when Jensen was sent back down to the minors. "So as one opportunity closed, and I was disappointed about that, getting sent down," said Jensen. "But at the same time, it presented another opportunity for me. I had such a positive experience playing the year before in the Pan Am Games, so actually I took the initiative to call Paul Seiler on the phone and tell him that I wanted to play in the Olympics. I knew it had to be pretty late in their selection process, so I had no idea whether I would be picked or was even being looked at as an option. Paul didn't answer, so I left a message with him, saying that I'd love an opportunity to be considered again, and I left it at that."

Seiler did not return Jensen's call. Instead, he immediately dropped an information packet and questionnaire to Jensen in the mail, and made Cobb and the rest of the Selection Committee aware of Jensen's phone message.

"That was a great break for us," said Seiler. "We knew Marcus, he knew our drill from the year before, and I think we all had no doubt about what he could contribute."

At the first-base position, almost every player on the wish list was a left-handed bat. Eric Munson of Detroit and Dernell Stenson of Boston were near the top and being closely monitored. They were followed directly by players such as Morgan Burkhart of Boston, Mark Johnson of the New York Mets, Jeff Liefer of the Chicago White Sox, and Kevin Witt of Toronto. Somewhere along the road, the highly touted Nick Johnson of the New York Yankees had fallen out of the running. It was well known among the members of the Selection Committee that the Yankees were going to be the stingiest team when it came to offering up their prospects.

At second base, the clear-cut favorite at this stage was Abernathy. He was batting over .300 at triple-A Durham, and he had the pedigree of international experience that USA Baseball coveted. Known as a true "gamer," Abernathy did all of the little things well and had the fire in his belly that Seiler knew Lasorda would love.

"We had known Brent for several years, dating back to his experience with us in 1995 as a high school player from Georgia," said Seiler. "I always tried to impress upon the Committee how important we felt that experience was in these types of events."

The other second basemen pushing Abernathy for the starting job were Brent Butler of Colorado, who had very similar numbers to Abernathy statistically, and Keith Ginter of Houston, who was hitting .348 with 16 home runs and 60 RBIs at the double-A level.

At third base, Russell Branyan of Cleveland, Sean Burroughs of San Diego, Joe Crede of the Chicago White Sox, Michael Cuddyer of Minnesota, Wes Helms of Atlanta, Aubrey Huff of Tampa Bay, Scott McClain of Colorado, Ryan Minor of Baltimore, and Adam Piatt of Oakland were all still being considered and monitored on a daily basis by the Committee. In June, still more than a month away from naming the team, there was no clear-cut favorite yet for the hot corner.

But at shortstop, there was. Both of the Committee's top choices had been cleared by their teams to participate; they were Adam Everett of Houston and Jimmy Rollins of Philadelphia. The Committee was looking at choosing one of those two players, and possibly utilizing Travis "Gookie" Dawkins as their backup shortstop and pinch-runner off the bench. Neither Everett nor Rollins was putting up offensive numbers that would make one stand out above the other: Everett was batting .216 with four homers and 20 RBIs, while Rollins was hitting just .231 with two homers and 22 RBIs. But it was Everett who was generally considered the better defensive player.

Shawn Gilbert of the Dodgers was having another nice season at triple-A Albuquerque and was in the running as a utility player to be invited as one of the 28 men who would travel to Australia.

The outfield positions had been boiled down fairly well by this point, with Corey Patterson of the Chicago Cubs leading the discussion to grab the center-field spot and hit leadoff in the batting order. Known as a speedster and solid defender, the Committee wanted that strong defense up the middle of the diamond with Everett or Rollins and Abernathy or Butler on the infield and Patterson in center.

Other center fielders still alive were Milton Bradley of Montreal and Dave Roberts of Cleveland (both of whom had helped Team USA qualify), David Dellucci of Arizona, Josh Hamilton of Tampa Bay (who was batting .345 that summer at single-A level), Terrence Long of Oakland, Vernon Wells of Toronto, and Randy Winn of Tampa Bay.

At the corner outfield spots, some names still being considered were Chad Allen of Minnesota (a 1996 Olympian for Team USA), Dee Brown of Kansas City, Jack Cust of Arizona, George Lombard of Atlanta, Aaron Rowand of the Chicago White Sox, and interestingly enough, Lance Berkman of Houston, who had started the season in the major leagues with the Astros but had recently been sent to triple-A New Orleans, making him eligible again to play for Team USA.

Finally, the leading candidates to fill the designated-hitter role were John Roskos of San Diego, who was batting .363 in June with nine home runs and 43 RBIs, and Ernie Young, who was having a terrific year at triple-A Memphis, batting .293 with 23 home runs and 63 RBIs.

So as the calendar slowly turned and the days continued to creep up on the Committee, they were looking at a mid-August deadline to name an Olympic Team roster. A live press conference featuring Alderson, Seiler, Watson, Bavasi, Lasorda, and a couple of chosen players who were going to be selected to the team was scheduled to be held in Los Angeles to announce the names of the 29 minor leaguers whom USA Baseball had selected to take with them to their training sessions in Australia. The Olympics were slated for mid-September that year—summertime in Sydney—so Team USA would be gathering up those 29 players over the last week of August and heading overseas for two weeks of training, prior to the Games beginning.

"We were really getting down to crunch time, and by then we had a very good idea about the 50 or 60 players that we were keeping under serious consideration," said Watson. "Then, we also had a second tier of another 30 or 40 guys that were still available to us, that we were monitoring."

Both Bavasi and Watson, as well as some Selection Committee members and scouts from the Major League Baseball Scouting Bureau, were all out and about attending minor-league games all over America in order to take a personal look at the potential Olympians whom they had identified. All of them had been cleared to participate by their clubs and had taken a preliminary drug-screening test administered by Major League Baseball.

"The Commissioner's Office was doing early drug screenings on not only the potential American players, but every single minor-league player that was being considered to take part in the Olympics," said Cobb. "There were minor leaguers playing with MLB organizations from Australia, Italy, Korea, South Africa, and the Netherlands involved in the Olympics as well." Every player who had been submitted to MLB as a potential Olympian was being tested across the board, so that the national governing bodies putting together their teams could get an early indication of whether they had anybody that might come up as a positive test, and then, regardless of what the banned substance was, they would have the opportunity to speak to the athlete about it or remove him from consideration. There are many things that could create a positive test in an athlete's bloodstream or urine sample, including an overuse of smokeless tobacco, an over-the-counter cold remedy, asthma medication, human-growth hormone, or steroids.

As we've learned since then, baseball was right in the middle of suffering through what is now known as the "Steroid Era" in 2000, when many players were utilizing human-growth hormone and steroids to bulk up physically and remain in better shape throughout the season. But at the time of the Sydney Olympics, USA Baseball was equally concerned about the possibility of a player coming up positive for a high level of nicotine, due to the fact that so many minor leaguers were addicted to using smokeless tobacco or "chew" for such a long time. It was a very real possibility that a player would not be able to quit using it for a month-long period during the Games. Tobacco was not a banned substance, but very high levels of it found in a test could trigger a positive and cause a major problem for Team USA.

Out on the scouting trail, Watson specifically remembers a trip he made that had a huge impact on the Committee discussions the following week.

"I was living and working out of my home in Houston, and I drove out to Round Rock, Texas one day to take a look at Astros double-A prospect Keith Ginter, who was a middle infielder, and he was playing a home game against the Diamondbacks' double-A team that night. It was nice because I could also watch Jack Cust of Arizona play, who was also still on our list of candidates to be our designated hitter or an outfielder," said Watson.

"But it was neither one of those two guys that impressed me that night. The Astros had recently moved a pitcher up from single-A by the name of Roy Oswalt, and he threw for Round Rock that night and was absolutely phenomenal. He was lights out, I think he struck out Cust four times and won the game. I went up and asked Nolan Ryan, who was the owner and GM of the Round Rock club at the time, what he knew about this kid, and Nolan really liked him a lot. So I went home and called Astros GM Gerry Hunsicker to see if he'd make Oswalt available to us. When he agreed, I went back to the Committee the following week on the conference call and told them that this kid could make our team right now."

Oswalt had come out of nowhere to suddenly thrust himself into consideration for a spot on Team USA, and he probably didn't even know it.

Selected in the 26th round of the 1996 draft by Houston out of tiny Weir, Mississippi High School, Oswalt had spent two seasons at rookie ball and short-A before going 13-4 with 143 strikeouts at single-A Michigan in 1999. In 2000, he started at single-A Kissimmee and went 4-3 with a 2.98 ERA and 47 strikeouts in 45 innings pitched, before being moved up to Round Rock, where Watson ran into him.

At Round Rock, Oswalt went 11-4 with a 1.94 ERA and 141 strikeouts and a pair of complete-game shutouts.

In early July, Watson, Bavasi, Seiler, Cobb, and Alderson had planned to meet in Atlanta at the 2000 Major League Baseball All-Star Game, where Lasorda would also be doing some pre-Olympic media interviews and publicity appearances surrounding his new status as the manager of Team USA (which had been "officially" announced by USA Baseball in a press conference at Dodger Stadium in Los Angeles, back in late May).

The group had also planned on holding a very critical meeting one night during the three days of festivities in Atlanta, in which they could really begin to focus on making the final decisions about which direction they wanted to go, player-wise, at each position.

"As I recall it, Sandy (Alderson) basically came in and blew the roster up at that point," said Cobb. "I mean, we had been talking about this main group of players for a couple months, and he just wasn't happy with what we had on paper. It was a real eye-opener for all of us."

Alderson recalled, "I think the main difference that I was looking for going into the exercise in 2000 was that I wanted a little more firepower offensively than we had in 1999. The Pan Am Team had struggled to score runs at times and was more of a prospect-laden team with younger players and more defensive oriented, in my opinion. I just wasn't seeing the type of players that I was looking for on the Olympic Team roster at that point, because I wanted the Committee to be using more of a performance-based decision-making process than a tools-based process. We didn't need prospects on this team that were going to project to be a great major-league player in two or three years. We needed guys that were solid players right now, who had actually performed at a higher level. There were too many guys on the list that were 'toolsy' players that hadn't performed well enough, being favored over other guys that had put up great numbers that season."

Given the new approach by Alderson, the Committee went back to work and needed to find reinforcements at a couple of positions for their roster, fairly quickly. And just like that, players who had not even been discussed were now again being looked at.

Based on their performance in the minors that summer, several names made their first appearance on the watch list in early August:

Right-handed pitchers Robbie Crabtree of San Francisco and Ryan Franklin of Seattle; left-handed pitcher Eddie Priest of Cincinnati; infielders Mike Coolbaugh of the New York Yankees and Jason Hart of Oakland; and outfielders John Cotton of Colorado and Brad Wilkerson of Montreal.

Franklin was among the Pacific Coast League leaders as a starter for triple-A Tacoma. Cotton was batting over .300 from the left side and was among the PCL leaders in home runs and doubles for triple-A Colorado Springs, while Wilkerson, who had been a teammate of Abernathy's on the 1995 USA Junior National Team that won gold, was tearing through the Expos' farm system that summer.

And one other player had played his way back into consideration, after being pushed aside off the original list at the beginning of the season: first baseman Doug Mientkiewicz. The Minnesota Twins had the former University of Miami star and 1995 USA National Team member playing first base at triple-A Salt Lake, where Mientkiewicz was having a career year by hitting .334 with 18 homers and 96 RBIs.

So, although he was not always present on every Committee conference call throughout the selection process, it was the final adjustment that Alderson made in Atlanta that ultimately would shape the look and feel of the 29 players that would be named to the official Team USA Olympic roster at the press conference in late August. And that adjustment would turn out to be a rather significant one.

9

SELECTING OLYMPIANS

The date was August 17, 2000. USA Baseball, and the men who had volunteered to spend the past two years examining American-born minor-league baseball players to possibly give them the opportunity to represent their country in the Olympic Games, had reached their decisions. Hundreds of hours of studying statistics, reading scouting reports, and watching players live in action had all but come to a close.

Taking Alderson's new advice, the Selection Committee had boiled it down to the final 39 players whom they wanted to consider for 24 roster spots on Team USA and the 29 players that would be taken to Australia to have the chance to solidify their position on the team with a final live performance during exhibition games. USA Baseball would be announcing those names in a live press conference by the end of the month.

The list actually consisted of 32 of the Committee's first choices and 7 players who were on a second tier. So the core 32 players were finally being given notice about where they stood, as Watson, Bavasi, Cobb, and Seiler began informing these chosen potential Olympians of the good news. Here are the 39 players who remained on the roster, as of August 17:

Right-Handed Starting Pitchers
Ryan Franklin
Matt Ginter
Roy Oswalt
Jon Rauch
Ben Sheets
Matt White

Left-Handed Starting Pitchers
Rick Krivda
C.C. Sabathia

Right-Handed Relief Pitchers
Chad Bradford
Robbie Crabtree
Shane Heams
Todd Williams

Left-Handed Relief Pitchers
Bobby Seay
Tim Young

Catchers
Pat Borders
Marcus Jensen
Mike Kinkade
First Basemen
Doug Mientkiewicz
Mark Johnson
John Roskos

Second Basemen
Brent Abernathy
Brent Butler

Shortstop
Adam Everett
Jimmy Rollins

Third Basemen
Russell Branyan
Mike Coolbaugh

Outfielders
Shawn Gilbert
Mike Neill
Corey Patterson
Anthony Sanders
Brad Wilkerson
Ernie Young

Second Tier Options
Travis Dawkins	Infielder
Jason Hart	Infielder
Brandon Inge	Catcher
Scott McClain	Infielder
Tim Raines	Outfielder
Chris George	Left-handed relief pitcher
Eddie Priest	Left-handed relief pitcher

"We were focused on winning the gold medal, from Day One. So we were trying to put together a club that we thought could win the tournament, not just a medal," said Watson. "I believed that international experience meant a whole lot. The games being played were going to be different than the pro game in the States. I really believed that playing for your country is a whole lot different than playing the pro game."

To that end, the architects of the Olympic team placed a premium on international experience and a second premium on players who were performing well that summer (if they did not have any international experience), per Alderson's instructions.

Seiler and the staff at USA Baseball knew that there was an urgency to most games at major international baseball tournaments. They had seen and witnessed it firsthand just the past year in the Pan Am Games. One round-robin loss too many can keep a team out of the medal round, where the format is then single-elimination and any misstep is fatal.

International play is different on the field as well. The pace of games is usually slower, as pitchers are more deliberate. Pitchers also use a wider variety of arm angles and rely on more breaking balls than in the U.S. Offensively, teams use little-ball techniques such as the bunt, and they tend to try and steal bases more frequently.

It was no coincidence that USA Baseball's most successful two-year runs came in 1987-88 and 1995-96, when a nucleus of players from one summer returned the next. To that end, six players—shortstop Travis "Gookie" Dawkins, utilityman Shawn Gilbert, catcher Marcus Jensen, outfielder Mike Neill, left-handed reliever Bobby Seay, and closer Todd Williams—all had an upper hand at making the team, after playing in the Pan Ams.

That number would have been higher had Winnipeg veterans Peter Bergeron, Milton Bradley, Adam Kennedy, Mark Mulder, Craig Paquette, Brad Penny, and J.C. Romero not been promoted to the major leagues.

The Committee sought international experience from other competitions as well, and it was conceivable at that point that almost half of the possible 24-man Olympic roster would include players who had represented the United States in the past.

Shortstop Adam Everett and first baseman Doug Mientkiewicz played for the USA Baseball Collegiate National Team as amateurs. Second baseman Brent Abernathy, left-hander Chris George, right-hander Matt White, and outfielder Brad Wilkerson were part of the USA Junior National Team (ages 16-18) as high schoolers.

Abernathy, White, and Wilkerson were the only remaining names on the roster to have won gold medals in international baseball competition, doing so at the 1995 World Junior Championship in Boston. Wilkerson was named MVP after hitting three homers and winning three games, including a three-hit shutout of Taiwan in the championship game. Abernathy was the only player to hit a ball over the Green Monster during medal play, while White no-hit Italy during pool play.

"We wanted a Brad Wilkerson and a Brent Abernathy from our junior team program, guys who had that international experience," said Seiler. "They'd played against Cuba before, and understood that kind of pressure."

The pressure at the Olympics, though, was bound to be something different altogether. But Team USA's Pan Am veterans hoped the experience could take them to America's first gold medal since 1988, when baseball was a demonstration sport.

"I felt like I had a good chance to make the team because I had played the year before," Williams said. "It was good to have some of the guys from last year's team back in the mix, because I was hoping that would help the camaraderie in the clubhouse, which would also help us on the field."

On August 23, Watson and Bavasi were finally out of time and their player personnel decisions had to be made. It was the day of the live press conference to announce the Team USA roster. The choices they had to make between one player or the other were extremely difficult, and often it just came down to their gut instincts. But in a few instances, fate intervened and the decision was made for them.

Just two days prior, Team USA's potential starting center fielder Corey Patterson and the Cubs management declined his final invitation for Patterson to join the Olympic team. The 21-year-old appeared to be a lock for a shot at making the team and traveling to Australia, but the Cubs were not happy about the idea that Patterson wouldn't be starting for sure and would have to earn his starting role during the exhibition games. Watson and Bavasi just could not guarantee Patterson and the Cubs that he would make the final 24-man roster that would actually be competing in the Olympics.

But both Patterson and Cubs brass agreed it would be best for him to play somewhere, and not potentially be sitting on the bench. So they made plans to call him up to the big leagues that September.

That opened the door wide open for Wilkerson and gave him an even better shot at making the final roster, as he was now being looked at as the team's best option in center field.

Then, just two hours prior to the official live roster announcement, in what could be described as one of Team USA's bigger twists of fate, their planned starting first baseman, Mark Johnson of the New York Mets, had to be removed from consideration.

USA Baseball had gotten the final preliminary drug screening results back that morning on the last few players they had needed to test, right before they could officially name those players to the roster. One of those late tests happened to be Johnson's, and his result had come back positive.

It was not known what Johnson had tested positive for, but USA Baseball had to remove him from consideration. The news was so late in the proceedings that the triple-A team that Johnson was playing for at the time—the Norfolk Tides—was ready to make a big announcement that afternoon during their game and celebrate the fact that one of their players had made the Olympic Team. USA Baseball had to immediately call the Tides and tell them to cancel the ceremony, with no explanation as to why.

In addition, the official roster and the press release that USA Baseball had prepared to distribute to the media that day at the press conference had to be quickly rewritten and reprinted. "It happened extremely late in the process, so unfortunately we didn't have much of a choice," said Seiler. "We simply could not take a chance keeping him."

With Johnson no longer in the mix, it clearly made Mientkiewicz the leading candidate for the starting first baseman's job. It also opened up one last new opportunity for a player to be added to the group of 29 who might have originally been told that he did not make the team.

That player ended up being John Cotton, who was not even on the list of 39 players that the Committee was using the week prior. A veteran in his 12th minor-league season, Cotton was having the best year of his career at triple-A Colorado Springs, hitting .328 with 16 homers and 62 RBIs. A left-handed bat, he had less power than Johnson but more versatility, and was being looked at as a designated hitter and backup outfielder. It remained to be seen whether he would make it to Sydney, but he was going to get the chance, as the Committee chose Cotton as their last player above the cut line.

For Mientkiewicz, this was the opportunity he had been waiting for. Having spent all of 1999 in Minnesota playing first base in the big leagues for the Twins, and then being demoted back down to triple-A in 2000, Mientkiewicz was looking for something to really get him fired up again.

"I had missed out on a shot at making the 1996 Olympic Team back while I was in college for the Games in Atlanta, and my mom was pretty upset about that," said Mientkiewicz, who grew up in Florida and played at the University of Miami. "My family has always been very patriotic, so having a chance to play in the Olympics was something I always wanted to do. Deep down, I knew that I was the type of player that was built to compete and play well in a small, two-week type of tournament, so it would be right up my alley."

With a chance at making the 2000 USA Baseball Olympic Team in the back of his mind all season, he was having a tremendous year at Salt Lake. But he still wasn't positive it was going to happen.

"We were playing on the road at Sacramento, and Marcus Jensen was a teammate of mine at the time that the USA roster was being announced, and players started finding out that they'd been selected," said Mientkiewicz. "Marcus had gotten a letter in the clubhouse and confirmation from USA Baseball that he had been invited to go with the team to Australia, and I did not. So consequently, I was extremely disappointed."

Without a reason as to why he hadn't been chosen, Mientkiewicz had to assume that possibly it was the Twins front office that had blocked his opportunity, because they wanted him back in Minnesota. All communication that he had received from Watson was that Team USA was very interested in his services. Doug had made it very clear to Watson and to Twins general manager Terry Ryan during the process that if given his first choice, it would be to have the chance to play for three weeks in Sydney, not Minneapolis. The Twins were not in the pennant race that September, so there was no need for him to come up and help the club.

Not knowing how to take the bad news, Doug's wife, Jodi, who of course was just as upset about the fact that her husband wouldn't be playing in the Olympics, decided to write a very unfriendly letter to Terry Ryan, accusing the Twins of ruining Doug's chance of becoming an Olympian, a dream he had had since he was a kid.

"It was not a very nice letter, and she sent it straight to his e-mail account," said Mientkiewicz. "But within 10 minutes, Terry called me on my phone right after he had read it, telling me that he had given USA Baseball permission to take me on the team, and that it was his understanding that they just hadn't decided on the first-base position quite yet. We had a pretty good laugh, and of course I apologized about the letter."

It couldn't have been a much longer wait for Mientkiewicz, because soon thereafter he also would receive the great news that he was one of 29 players selected, with the caveat that his spot on the final 24-man roster needed to be earned by performing well in the exhibitions.

And with Johnson falling out of contention, the path to Mientkiewicz starting at first base for Team USA in Sydney was quite clear. He was the only true first baseman remaining on the list, with John Roskos of San Diego still being available, as well as Mike Coolbaugh of the New York Yankees, who could also play third base.

Finally, the last major move made to the roster was the

addition of Sean Burroughs, who had been on and off the watch-list radar for several months. When Russell Branyan of the Cleveland Indians was called back up to the major leagues in mid-August, it opened the door for another left-handed-hitting third baseman to be added into the fold. Burroughs had been watched almost all summer long, and although he had been left off the list of 39, his availability was still there when they needed to fill Branyan's hole.

Burroughs was drafted by the San Diego Padres out of high school in Long Beach, California and declined a scholarship offer to the University of Southern California to accept the Padres' contract offer. The son of 1974 American League MVP Jeff Burroughs, Sean had also starred in the Little League World Series as a pitcher when he was growing up in Long Beach, winning back-to-back Little League World Championship titles in 1992 and 1993 on a team his father coached.

In only his second professional season and throughout the summer of 2000, he was having a quality campaign at double-A Mobile, hitting .291 with 29 doubles, and was playing a steady third base.

With all of those last-minute situations working themselves out, Watson, Bavasi, Lasorda, and the rest of the USA Baseball brass stepped to the podium in California and announced their selections. And with that, the 29 players named to Team USA that afternoon were:

<u>Pitchers</u>
Kurt Ainsworth	San Francisco	B. Rouge, LA
Ryan Franklin	Seattle	Spiro, OK
Roy Oswalt	Houston	Weir, MS
Jon Rauch	Chicago WS	Westport, KY
Ben Sheets	Milwaukee	St. Amant, LA
Matt White	Tampa Bay	Pasadena, FL
Rick Krivda	Baltimore	McKeesport, PA
C.C. Sabathia	Cleveland	Vallejo, CA
Shane Heams	Detroit	Lambertville, MI

Todd Williams	Seattle	Syracuse, NY
Chris George	Kansas City	Spring, TX
Bobby Seay	Tampa Bay	Sarasota, FL
Tim Young	Boston	Bristol, FL

Catchers

Pat Borders	Tampa Bay	Lake Wales, FL
Marcus Jensen	Minnesota	Scottsdale, AZ

Infielders

Brent Abernathy	Tampa Bay	Marietta, GA
Sean Burroughs	San Diego	Long Beach, CA
Brent Butler	Colorado	Laurinburg, NC
Mike Coolbaugh	NY Yankees	San Antonio, TX
Travis Dawkins	Cincinnati	Newberry, SC
Adam Everett	Houston	Kennesaw, GA
Mike Kinkade	Baltimore	Tigard, OR
Doug Mientkiewicz	Minnesota	Fort Myers, FL

Outfielders

John Cotton	Colorado	Houston, TX
Shawn Gilbert	Los Angeles	Glendale, AZ
Mike Neill	Seattle	Seaford, DE
Anthony Sanders	Seattle	Tucson, AZ
Brad Wilkerson	Montreal	Owensboro, KY
Ernie Young	St. Louis	Mesa, AZ

The most obvious player-selection question was, why did they choose Adam Everett at shortstop over the highly touted Rollins?

"We thought that, if we ever had a game where we were having trouble scoring runs, we'd better do our best to stop them as well," said Bavasi. "Everybody on the Committee felt very good about Everett because of his defensive ability. We thought this kid was so exceptional, it was purely a glove decision, not a bat decision. It also might have been that we had a lot of scouts that had seen Everett play, and that didn't see Rollins as much. But we weren't so concerned about offense from the shortstop spot.

"But I do remember that when we announced that Rollins wasn't on the team, Phillies Assistant GM Ruben Amaro was pissed. He wanted Rollins on the team. He had called me and highly recommended the kid, and really wanted him to have that experience on our club, and when we didn't take him, he called me back and said, 'You missed it. You know, this kid would be great for you. I'm really upset. I thought he would be on the team.' He was really, really angry, and it was interesting to hear how he was responding as compared to some of the other teams that didn't want their players to play."

Watson was able to add Burroughs to the team because Russell Branyan (also a left-handed-hitting third baseman) had moved back up to Cleveland just prior to the announcement, and the same scenario took place with White Sox right-hander Matt Ginter, who was replaced in favor of Ainsworth. Ainsworth was a rising star, a first-round draft pick in the San Francisco Giants' farm system. He had been having an exceptional year at double-A Shreveport.

In the bullpen, the Committee made a conscious decision to add left-hander Chris George to the team—who had been listed on the second tier of players the week prior—over righties Chad Bradford and Robbie Crabtree.

"We had Hearns and Williams down there from the right side, and we knew that either Franklin or Ainsworth could provide right-handed long relief, and Krivda could help in long relief or start from the left side," said Watson. "So when the reports came back that the Japanese and Korean rosters were loaded with left-handed hitters, we wanted that extra relief help from the left side down there in the pen. That's why we added George, to go along with Seay and Young."

Anthony Sanders of Seattle was the only late surprise in the outfield mix. He and Neill had been making up two-thirds of the starting outfield that season for the triple-A Tacoma Rainiers of the Pacific Coast League, and now both of them were wearing a USA jersey.

"Anthony moved up very quickly when we began discussing defense, because he was exceptional at covering ground out there," said Watson. "We knew he struggled at times to hit a curve ball, but he was an experienced player that had been having a good season."

The Selection Committee members had dedicated countless hours to this process, and each and every one of them were instrumental in some way in helping to create this roster.

"Not just their playing ability, but judging their personal character was also an extremely important element, it was a big part of everything we did and it was a big focus of ours from the scouting side," said Selection Committee member Don Welke. "It had to be, because we were not allowed to take America's best baseball players: they were all in the major leagues. We weren't going to Sydney with A-Rod and Jeter and those guys, we were going there to compete with the guys we were given. So those were the qualities that we looked for in selecting this Team USA group: good character and ability."

At the end of the exercise, Alderson, Seiler, Watson, and Bavasi all felt good about what they had, at least on paper. And that was all that they could have asked for.

"I figured they'd be a pretty good team, but I probably attribute more of that to my attitude, which was that they'll just figure it out," said Bavasi. "We're Americans, and we figure things out. That's kind of the United States trademark. People can have better things than us, they can be better than us, but we'll find a way to figure it out, and I thought with Tommy leading the way, and with our advance scouting team giving us information on the opponents, that we would find a way to win. We had the talent to win one game against anybody. That might have been the wrong attitude to have when you're doing something like this, but we thought that we couldn't have done much better putting the best team out there that we could. There might have been a quarrel or two regarding Everett or Rollins, we could have fought more over that, but I don't remember a whole lot of arguments. We were tireless in using the Selection Committee, using those good scouts, to discuss these guys, and to vet out every single decision."

It was still to be determined which pitcher would be the team's fourth starter. In a game where good pitching usually always beats good hitting, USA Baseball was thrilled to have a potential starting rotation of Sheets, Oswalt, Rauch, and either Sabathia, Krivda, Ainsworth, Franklin, or Matt White.

"They were every bit as good as what we had going for us in Winnipeg, with Patterson, Mulder, Penny, and Anderson, so that was extremely exciting to know," said Seiler. "To be trusted again with pitchers of that quality by their major-league clubs said a lot about what we were doing and how we were going about our business. And it certainly gave us a great feeling that we had a legitimate shot at winning the gold medal."

Just days after the roster announcement, Team USA immediately lost some infield depth when Rockies prospect Brent Butler broke a bone in his right hand while swinging a bat during a game. Since their 29 players had already been chosen and the process of getting those athletes together was already in motion, there was no time to replace Butler. That dropped their roster size to 28, meaning that four more players would still need to be cut, as all active rosters in the Olympics would consist of 24 players. Team USA's final cuts from 28 to 24 would be determined in Australia during pre-Olympic training, which would include a series of exhibition games on Australia's Gold Coast, in the northeastern corner of the continent.

Butler was hitting .292 at the time with eight home runs and 54 RBIs for the triple-A Colorado Springs Sky Sox, and figured to be a backup at both second base and shortstop for Team USA behind Everett and Abernathy, a role that would now likely be filled by either Travis "Gookie" Dawkins of the Reds or Shawn Gilbert of the Dodgers, both of whom could also play in the middle infield and both of whom played for Team USA in Winnipeg at the Pan Ams. So Butler's loss was one that was absorbed rather painlessly.

But Team USA wasn't the only country to lose a player.

The host country Australia lost a much more important player in its plans, for a less understandable reason. The Los Angeles Dodgers promoted right hander Luke Prokopec from double-A San Antonio just 24 hours before Prokopec was expected to return to his native country in preparation for the Olympic tournament.

The Australian team was also going to be without Prokopec's former Missions teammate Adrian Burnside, as the Australian left-hander would be missing the Olympics with an injury. Montreal Expos right hander Shayne Bennett figured to be the ace of Australia's staff, and Prokopec had a shot at being one of his country's top four starters, along with Bennett, former big leaguer Mark Hutton, and 41-year-old Adrian Meagher.

Team USA finally convened and came together for the first time on September 1 in San Diego, as the United States Olympic Committee had set up the entire USA Olympic Team delegation processing center at the U.S. Naval Base there on the San Diego coastline.

Once all of the USA staff members had arrived on-site, Seiler held a brief meeting, and then Lasorda took the entire group of approximately 20 people (all of his coaches and non-player personnel associated with Team USA) out to dinner at his favorite local Italian restaurant. Always a lover of pasta, Lasorda saw it as an opportunity to build some camaraderie among the people who had given him this opportunity and had worked so hard to bring this team together. "We got a great idea that night what traveling with Tommy Lasorda and living with him for a month was going to be like," said Team USA Administrator Steve Cohen, who would become one of Lasorda's closest confidants. "He held court, served up the grand meal, toasted with some red wine, and had a lot of laughs. And all I know is that there was no bill to be found at the end of the night. It was a great time: We were all filled with such anticipation and excitement about what we were about to take part in."

USA Baseball had planned to hold their team's only

stateside workout at Qualcomm Stadium the next morning, where the media could come and interview players and coaches and get their first look at the American baseball team wearing the red, white, and blue. That would be Lasorda's first chance to address his players and to also tell the world how excited he was about putting on the USA uniform. Lasorda had missed wearing any baseball uniform, for that matter, and being in a dugout as well, and now that he was back managing a ballclub for the first time in over five years, he was basking in the spotlight that went with it.

"If they have the same attitude about going there as I have," Lasorda said of his players, "then you're going to see a bunch of guys that really want to win."

The exposure Lasorda brought to their operation was also important to USA Baseball. What better way to ensure that their team and the sport of baseball wasn't going to be overshadowed by the track stars, gymnasts, and swimmers who usually dominate Olympic Games media coverage, than by hiring baseball's most recognizable and enthusiastic ambassador?

"We were very fortunate to have him," said Watson. "There's no question about it." While both sides needed each other, Lasorda wasn't ashamed to admit his need might have been greater. He lobbied for the job for several months and jumped at the chance when it was officially offered to him back in May.

"When they called and said they wanted me to be the coach, I was so elated, so proud," Lasorda said. "I was honored. People think I'm wacky when I say how important this is to me, to be able to do something for my country. But I think it's an honor and a privilege."

In fact, Lasorda went so far as to say his appointment as Olympic coach overshadowed all the other high points of his Hall of Fame career, including the Cooperstown induction itself.

"The Olympics are something special to me," he said that day in San Diego. "I've done everything in the game of baseball. I started from the bottom as a player and I reached the major leagues as a player. I started at the bottom as a manager and I reached the major leagues as a manager. And then I was fortunate enough to be inducted into baseball's Hall of Fame. This is even greater. This is the utmost right here. This is a tremendous chapter in my life. There ain't nobody that's going to take it any more serious than me."

Lasorda planned to immerse himself in the Olympic experience, to participate in the opening ceremonies and to live with the U.S. athletes in the Olympic Village. He planned to treat every moment as the last hurrah of his career he knew this could be, and to share his unique brand of motivational speak with anyone who would listen.

"I want to be with all of the athletes from the United States. I want to pull for them all. I want to be part of the team, no matter what sport they were competing in. I want to know them and be able to tell them how proud I am of them. I can't wait until we walk into that stadium, and knowing that out of all those countries, I'm representing the greatest. That's going to be the main thrill for me, to walk in that opening parade. I get chills watching it on TV. Just think what I'm going to feel like doing it."

Lasorda's Olympic fervor stemmed from a sense of patriotism instilled in his youth. His father Sabatino came to the United States from Italy shortly after World War I. He married and supported a family of five sons (Tommy being the second) by driving a truck for a rock quarry in Pennsylvania. It was a hard life, but one for which Lasorda says his father was forever thankful because of the opportunities his adopted country provided.

"My father used to sit at the head of the table," Lasorda said. "And he'd say to us five boys, 'You guys are very lucky to be born in the greatest country in the world. You do everything you can to keep it that way. If you have to fight for your country, you must do it. And, maybe, you might even have to give up your life for your country.' Now, that's a father, speaking in broken English, talking about patriotism.

He wasn't born in this country. But he came here, and he wanted his children to grow up in this country. I've served my country. I was in the United States Army and I felt proud to do that. I wore that uniform with pride, and now I want to wear this uniform with pride. Because to me, this is bigger than the World Series."

A renowned motivational speaker, Lasorda planed to instill a similar sense of duty and national pride in his Olympic players.

"I will tell our players, 'Hey, you don't represent your hometown or that high school you came from or that organization you're in,'" Lasorda said. "'You represent the United States of America. And by golly, you're going to be proud and you're going to play your hearts out for the good of this country.'"

Of course, that cheerleading might only carry Team USA so far against the incredible talent of the Cubans, the advanced skill and precise pitching of the Japanese, and the overall efficiency of the Koreans. Even the Italian team and the host Australians (headed by former Brewers All-Star catcher Dave Nilsson) could threaten Team USA's quest to reach the medal round of the eight-team tournament.

But Lasorda was well aware of the challenges ahead. He knew that the Cuban national team split an exhibition series against the Baltimore Orioles just the past year and that that same Cuban roster would be in Sydney. He knew Japan would have players from its major-league teams. He knew the Korean league was shutting down in order to send its best players to Sydney, and the Italian team would feature several American-trained players of Italian descent.

His response to all of that? "The only thing I can say is, we're not going 6,000 miles to lose."

As part of the Team USA baseball delegation, Major League Baseball sent public relations executive Pat Courtney from their Commissioner's Office to assist with the media attention and overall coverage of the American team. Pat and I would work side-by-side throughout the month-long journey, focused on maneuvering Lasorda in and out of the dozens of interview requests we were going to receive and managing his time away from the Games and his team. It was not going to be an easy task, as we knew that Lasorda was bound to draw heavy attention to himself in Sydney.

But Courtney was excited to be a part of this brand new venture between Major League Baseball and USA Baseball, and I was happy to have him alongside to give an assist. "I wasn't sure what to expect when I first arrived on the scene, because I had spent the last several years working in the major-league environment. But I was amazed at how quickly that team came together, they seemed to be very close right from the start. I was blown away at how fast Tommy had formed a team-first atmosphere, and everybody involved—including myself—got caught up in it right away."

As Team USA moved through the USOC Processing Center that afternoon, receiving all of their baggage, uniforms, gear, and other items that they would need in Australia (much like the Pan Am Team did in Fargo, ND prior to the Pan Am Games), Seiler was busy making sure his entire delegation had the proper credentials, in particular Dr. Mattalino, Dr. Dicke, and trainer John Fierro. All three of them returned to take part in the Olympic experience, but only after they had gone through USOC mandated training courses and spent time volunteering to work with the United States Olympic Committee's other athletes that were preparing for the Games, in order to earn the proper identification as an official USOC trainer or medical personnel. Team USA also brought with them Chris "Gorbie" Gebeck as an equipment manager.

Once processing was finished, Lasorda held an impromptu team meeting in a conference room at the Naval Base. "We weren't sure what he wanted to do or what the meeting was about at first," said Neill. "All we knew was that there was a speaker phone on a table in the center of the room."

Lasorda had arranged a call with the legendary Hall of Famer Ted Williams, who wanted to say some words to the Team, and give them as much inspiration as he could over a phone.

Williams played his entire 22-year major-league career as the left fielder for the Boston Red Sox (1939-1942 and 1946-1960), and was a two-time American League Most Valuable Player winner, led the league in batting six times, and won the Triple Crown twice. A nineteen-time All-Star, he had a career batting average of .344, with 521 home runs, and was inducted into the Baseball Hall of Fame in 1966.

Williams was the last player to bat over .400 in a single season (.406 in 1941) and still holds the highest career batting average of anyone with 500 or more home runs. Nicknamed "The Splendid Splinter," "Teddy Ballgame," and, because of his hitting prowess, "The Greatest Hitter Who Ever Lived," Williams' career was twice interrupted by service as a U.S. Marine Corps fighter-bomber pilot. So he had a tremendous sense of patriotism as well and could identify with representing his country.

"What a great person to hear speak to us, very inspirational" said Neill. "That was pretty cool, a moment that none of us will forget."

The group then hopped on a bus and headed over to Sea World, where they took part in an official Team USA "Good Luck Send Off" reception and autograph signing session for fans. And from there, the team bus headed north for the two-hour drive to Los Angeles International Airport.

After training on Australia's Gold Coast for a couple of weeks, Team USA would reach Sydney on September 14, participate in the opening ceremonies, then open the Olympic baseball pool-play round on September 17 against Japan. The eight teams in the event (Australia, Cuba, Italy, Japan, Korea, the Netherlands, the United States, and South Africa) would play each team one time in the round robin, with the top four finishers advancing to the medal round. The team with the best first-round record would face the fourth-ranked team, while the No. 2 seed played No. 3 in the other semifinal. The gold-medal game was scheduled for September 27.

Lasorda said the format would force him to manage

virtually every game like it's the World Series.

"I think every game is important. Under the conditions you're going to be playing under, you can't wait and say, 'Well, we'll do something tomorrow.' No, we've got to do it every game. We've got to play every game like it's the one you have to win. You've got to try to win them all and be prepared to withstand certain types of ballclubs. It's going to be very exciting." Following the workout at Qualcomm Stadium in San Diego, future Hall of Famer and then current Padres star Tony Gwynn stopped by the locker room, to give the young American players a pep talk and some words of encouragement. The squad and all of the Team USA officials were scheduled to take the long flight to Australia for pre-Olympic training later that night. USA Baseball would be making its final roster decision in just 12 days.

10

GOLD COAST

When the USA Baseball traveling party arrived at LAX to begin checking in for what was to be a grueling 15-hour flight from California to Sydney, Seiler was still particularly concerned about how Lasorda was going to manage being in a coach seat for such a long time.

But, as it turned out, Seiler learned very quickly what it means to be a sports icon in a city like Los Angeles. As Lasorda went to check in at the counter, the airline agent of course happened to be a Dodgers fan and immediately found the 72-year-old a more comfortable first-class seat, in exchange for an autographed baseball, of course. One possible problematic scenario averted.

Upon arrival in Sydney, the USA Baseball delegation unfortunately wasn't finished traveling. They then had to collect their luggage, get through Customs, and then turn around and board a short flight to the Gold Coast of Australia, where six of the eight Olympic baseball teams in the event would be training and playing exhibition games against one another over the next ten days (Japan and Cuba were the only two Olympic teams that would not be).

Cobb had done his research as to which hotel he wanted to book for Team USA during their training period during a pre-Olympic test event in Australia back in November, some eight months prior. The best option he could come up with along the Gold Coast that would have the look and feel of a major-league experience was the Conrad Jupiter Hotel, one of the only high-rise hotels along the Gold Coast that had quality service and a variety of restaurants and that could accommodate the USA Baseball traveling party of approximately 50 people.

But Cobb's biggest concern about the Conrad Jupiter was that it had a live-action gambling casino in the lobby, the perfect place for Team USA's players to get themselves into potential trouble during downtime.

"One of the concerns we had talked about with Sandy Alderson was making sure that we didn't have any public relations disasters with this ballclub being in a foreign country," said Courtney. "I think that's why he and the Committee also tried to find the best character guys to represent the United States. We had just come off the 1998 Winter Olympic fiasco with the professional USA hockey team, that had been accused of trashing their rooms at the Olympic Village, and we did not want any negative publicity like that to happen with our first professional baseball team, especially when they would be under the microscope of the Olympic spotlight."

The second aspect of training on the Gold Coast that Cobb realized would be an issue was the quality level of the original baseball fields where the Australian Olympic Committee had wanted the games to be played. These exhibition games were no more than scrimmages that were going to be open to the public and played at the Aussie's Palm Meadows practice facility, where the groundskeeping was nowhere near major-league level quality or expectations.

When Cobb reported that back to the MLB Commissioner's Office, they immediately dispatched their highest level field-maintenance and ground-crew guru: a former Baltimore Orioles field supervisor named Murray Cook.

"Cook was absolutely critical," said Cobb. "He was able to get those fields into playable shape for all of these professional-level prospects to compete on, to where they weren't worried about bad-hop grounders or stepping into holes in the outfield. He did wonders over there, not just on the Gold Coast, but in Sydney, to the main baseball stadium and secondary facility as well."

(All Pre-Olympic exhibition game summaries provided by John Manuel – *Baseball America*)

EXHIBITION GAME ONE vs. ITALY

Sept. 7, 2000 - John Cotton went 2-for-3 with a home run and four RBIs leading Team USA to an impressive 11-2 victory over Italy in the squad's exhibition opener.

Center fielder Anthony Sanders led Team USA's 15-hit attack with three hits, right fielder Brad Wilkerson had two doubles and two RBIs, and left fielder Ernie Young added a double and single. Shawn Gilbert and Sean Burroughs each added pinch-hit solo home runs.

Left-hander Rick Krivda pitched four innings, giving up two runs on four hits for the victory, while righty Ryan Franklin followed with three scoreless innings. Four USA pitchers combined to hold the Italian team to just five hits.

"We swung the bats very well today, and showed that we could put some runs up on the board," said Lasorda. "I liked the way our pitchers threw the ball. It was a small first step in the right direction for our ballclub."

Trailing 2-1, Team USA scored five runs in the third inning, as Wilkerson and John Cotton each collected two-run doubles. Italian starter Jason Simontacchi allowed six runs (five earned) on six hits, suffering the loss.

MIRACLE ON GRASS

```
Italy 2                         USA 11

                  AB R H RBI                       AB R  H  RBI
De Francesch cf   4  1 3  0   Dawkins ss           3  1  1   0
Liverziani rf     4  0 1  2   Everett ph-ss        2  0  0   0
Madonna c         3  0 0  0   Wilkerson rf         5  2  2   2
Baldacci ph       1  0 0  0   Sanders cf           5  2  3   1
Sheldon 3b        4  0 0  0   E. Young lf          3  2  2   0
Dipace lf         3  0 0  0   Neill ph-lf          2  0  1   1
Frignani ph       1  0 0  0   Cotton dh            3  1  2   4
Carrozza 1b       3  0 0  0   Burroughs ph         2  1  1   1
Casolari dh       3  0 0  0   Coolbaugh 3b         3  0  0   0
D'Auria 2b        2  0 0  0   Kinkade 3b           1  0  1   0
Dallospedale ph-2b 1 0 0  0   Mientkiewicz 1b      4  0  0   0
LaFera ss         1  1 1  0   Borders c            3  0  0   0
Evangelisti ph-ss 1  0 0  0   Jensen c             1  0  0   0
Simontacchi p     0  0 0  0   Abernathy 2b         2  1  1   0
Ginanneschi p     0  0 0  0   Gilbert ph-2b        2  1  1   1
Toriaco p         0  0 0  0   Krivda p             0  0  0   0
Cerbone p         0  0 0  0   Franklin p           0  0  0   0
                              Seay p               0  0  0   0
                              Williams p           0  0  0   0
Totals           31  2 5  2   Totals              41 11 15  10

Italy      101 000 000 -  2  5 4
USA        105 021 11x  - 11 15 0
```

E - De Francesch, Carrozza, LaFera, Simontacchi. LOB - Italy 3, USA 6. 2B - De Francesch 2, Wilkerson 2 (2), Sanders (1), E. Young (1), Cotton (1), Kinkade (1). HR - Cotton (1), Burroughs (1), Gilbert (1). SB - Sanders (1).

```
Italy               IP  H R ER BB SO
Simontacchi L 0-1  3.0  6 6  5  0  2
Ginanneschi        3.0  5 3  3  0  3
Toriaco            1.0  2 1  1  0  2
Cerbone            1.0  2 1  1  0  0

USA                 IP  H R ER BB SO
Krivda W 1-0       4.0  4 2  2  0  3
Franklin           3.0  1 0  0  1  2
Seay               1.0  0 0  0  0  1
Williams           1.0  0 0  0  0  0
```

WP - Simontacchi. Strikeouts - Liverziani, Dipace, Carrozza, Casolari 2, D'Auria, Sanders 2, Coolbaugh 2, Borders, Jensen, Gilbert. Walks - LaFera.
Start: 1:00 PM. Time: 2:22. Attendance: 250

EXHIBITION GAME TWO vs. AUSTRALIA

Sept. 8, 2000 - Team USA moved to 2-0 in its six-game exhibition series leading up to the Sydney Olympics, defeating host Australia 3-1.

Winning pitcher Roy Oswalt struck out seven and gave up five hits in four shutout innings, walking only one. Team USA's offense was led by a pair of solo home runs by Wilkerson and third baseman Mike Kinkade. Wilkerson's shot gave Team USA a 1-0 lead in the first inning, while Kinkade's homer came in the sixth. Kinkade also scored the team's other run. He was hit by a pitch and scored on a fourth-inning double by catcher Marcus Jensen.

Team USA received strong pitching for the second straight game. Following Oswalt, right hander Matt White, lefty Tim Young, and right hander Shane Heams limited Australia to one run in 4 1/3 innings. Closer Todd Williams recorded the final two outs for his first save.

"Our pitching was once again outstanding tonight," said Team USA manager Tommy Lasorda. "It was a solid victory over a very good Australian team."

Former major-league pitcher Mark Hutton was tagged with the loss for Australia, after allowing two runs on four hits in four innings of work.

L-R: Shane Heams, Ben Sheets, Jon Rauch, Tommy Lasorda, and Sean Burroughs hold up the Olympic Torch that passed through the Gold Coast on the way to Sydney.

MIRACLE ON GRASS

```
USA 3                              Australia 1

                 AB  R  H RBI                     AB  R  H RBI
Gilbert ss/2b    4   0  0  0    Burton lf         2   0  1  0
Wilkerson rf     4   1  1  1    Roneberg ph/rf    2   0  0  0
Sanders cf       4   0  1  0    McDonald cf       4   0  0  0
E. Young lf      3   0  1  0    Nilsson dh        2   0  0  0
Neill lf         1   0  0  0    Vogler ph         1   0  0  0
Cotton dh        4   0  0  0    Johnson 1b        3   0  1  0
Kinkade 3b/1b    3   2  1  1    Gonzalez 3b       4   0  0  0
Mientkiewicz 1b  3   0  0  0    Byrne dh          2   1  2  0
Burroughs 3b     1   0  1  0    Reeves rf/lf      3   0  2  0
Jensen c         3   0  1  1    Williams 2b       4   0  0  0
Borders c        1   0  0  0    White c           3   0  0  0
Abernathy 2b     1   0  0  0    Van Buizen ss     3   0  0  0
Everett ss       2   0  0  0    Hutton p          0   0  0  0
Coolbaugh dh     1   0  0  0    Bennett p         0   0  0  0
Oswalt p         0   0  0  0    Ettles p          0   0  0  0
White p          0   0  0  0    Balfour p         0   0  0  0
T. Young p       0   0  0  0
Heams p          0   0  0  0
Williams p       0   0  0  0

Totals......    35   3  6  3    Totals......     33   1  6  0

Score by innings:                    R  H  E
---------------------------------------------
USA                      100 101 000 - 3  6  1
Australia                000 000 100 - 1  6  2
---------------------------------------------
```

E - Burroughs, Williams, Hutton. DP - USA 1. LOB - USA 9,
Australia 10. 2B - Jensen(1), Byrne. HR - Wilkerson(1),
Kinkade(1). SB - Wilkerson(1), Sanders(1), Abernathy(1).

```
              IP   H  R ER BB SO  WP BK HP IBB  AB BF Fly Gnd
Oswalt W 1-0  4.0  5  0  0  1  7   0  0  1  0   17 19  2  3
White         1.0  0  0  0  2  0   0  0  0  0    3  3  1  0
T. Young      1.1  1  1  1  1  1   0  0  0  0    6  7  1  2
Heams         2.0  0  0  0  2  0   0  0  0  0    5  7  2  3
Williams S,1  0.2  0  0  0  0  0   0  0  0  0    2  2  0  2

Hutton L 0-   4.0  4  2  2  2  3   0  0  1  0   17 20  6  3
Bennett       2.0  1  1  1  0  2   0  0  0  0    8  8  4  0
Ettles        2.0  0  0  0  1  1   0  0  0  0    6  7  4  1
Balfour       1.0  1  0  0  0  2   0  0  0  0    4  4  1  0
```

HBP - by Oswalt (Reeves), by Hutton (Kinkade). PB - White.

Strikeouts - Gilbert 2, Neill, Cotton 2, Kinkade 2, Borders,
Burton, Roneberg, McDonald, Nilsson, Gonzalez 2, Williams 2,
Van Buizen 2. Walks - Abernathy, Coolbaugh 2, Nilsson, Johnson,
Byrne 2.

Start: 6:30 pm   Time: 2:55   Attendance: 5000

EXHIBITION GAME THREE vs. AUSTRALIA

Sept. 9, 2000 - Team USA got another indication of how good host Australia's pitching could be in the 2000 Olympic Games. It also got another victory in its pre-Olympic exhibition play.

Team USA had just three hits, two of them belonging to first baseman Doug Mientkiewicz. But one of them was a two-run homer in the top of the first, and Team USA scored three unearned runs without a hit in the sixth to take a 5-3 decision.

Left-hander Chris George pitched three hitless, scoreless innings in relief of left-hander C.C. Sabathia, to get the win for the Americans. Bobby Seay came on to pitch the ninth for the save.

"For the third straight game it was our pitching that was the difference," said Lasorda. "George and Seay pitched well in relief, and we were able to scratch together enough runs to get the win."

Team USA's game-winning rally in the sixth started when Aussie right hander Tom Becker walked American catcher Marcus Jensen to lead off the inning. Becker then hit Brent Abernathy with a pitch, and Adam Everett laid down a good sacrifice bunt, but Australian third baseman Rodney Van Buizen threw the ball away, scoring both Jensen and Abernathy and giving Team USA a 4-3 lead. Everett, who advanced to third on the bad throw, then scored on a wild pitch by Becker.

Sabathia gave up six hits and three runs in five innings, walking none while striking out five. Team USA used its third different lineup, though Lasorda has been consistent by starting the same three outfielders every game: Ernie Young in left, Anthony Sanders in center, and Brad Wilkerson in right.

MIRACLE ON GRASS

Australia 3	AB	R	H	RBI
Reeves rf	4	0	1	0
Buckley ss	4	1	2	1
McDonald cf	4	0	1	1
Johnson dh	3	0	0	0
Gonzalez dh	2	0	1	0
Byrne lf	3	0	0	0
Roneberg 1b	3	0	0	0
Williams 2b	3	1	1	0
White c	3	0	0	1
Van Buizen 3b	3	1	1	0
Meagher p	0	0	0	0
Becker p	0	0	0	0
Nakamura p	0	0	0	0
Bevis p	0	0	0	0
Totals	32	3	7	3

USA 5	AB	R	H	RBI
Dawkins ss	2	0	0	0
Everett ss	1	1	0	0
Wilkerson rf	3	1	0	0
Mientkiewicz 1b	3	1	2	2
E. Young lf	2	0	0	0
Neill lf	0	0	0	0
Sanders cf	2	0	0	0
Gilbert cf	1	0	0	0
Cotton dh	3	0	0	0
Kinkade dh	2	0	0	0
Coolbaugh 3b	2	0	0	0
Burroughs 3b	1	0	0	0
Borders c	1	0	0	0
Jensen c	1	1	1	0
Abernathy 2b	2	1	0	0
Sabathia p	0	0	0	0
George p	0	0	0	0
Seay p	0	0	0	0
Totals	26	5	3	2

Score by innings:

```
                            R  H  E
Australia     101 010 000 - 3  7  1
USA           200 003 00  - 5  3  0
```

E - Van Buizen. DP - Australia 1, USA 1. LOB - Australia 3, USA 3. 2B - Reeves, Buckley, Gonzalez, Van Buizen, Mientkiewicz(1). 3B - Williams. HR - Mientkiewicz(1). SH - Everett. SB - Buckley. CS - McDonald, Mientkiewicz.

	IP	H	R	ER	BB	SO	WP	BK	HP	IBB	AB	BF	Fly	Gnd
Meagher	4.1	1	2	2	1	5	0	0	0	0	15	16	4	5
Becker L 0-1	1.0	1	3	2	3	0	2	0	1	0	3	8	1	1
Nakamura	1.2	0	0	0	0	2	0	0	0	0	4	4	1	1
Bevis	1.0	1	0	0	0	0	0	0	0	0	4	4	2	1
Sabathia	5.0	6	3	3	0	5	0	0	0	0	20	20	3	6
George W 1-0	3.0	0	0	0	1	2	0	0	0	0	8	9	2	4
Seay S,1	1.0	1	0	0	0	0	1	0	0	0	4	4	1	2

WP - Becker 2, Seay. HBP - by Becker (Abernathy). PB - White. Strikeouts - McDonald, Johnson 2, Gonzalez, Roneberg, Williams, Van Buizen, Dawkins, E. Young, Sanders 2, Gilbert, Burroughs, Abernathy. Walks - Gonzalez, Wilkerson, Neill, Kinkade, Jensen. Start: 6:30 pm Time: 2:30 Attendance: 4185

A total of nine hits in two games against the Australians was a cause for concern for Alderson, who was traveling with the team and helping Watson decide who their final cuts would be; Bavasi was unable to make the trip overseas. With only three more exhibition games to be played, the situation was murky at best as to which two position players and which two pitchers they were going to send home. It certainly had the players on edge.

"The feeling was not a good one yet, because I don't think any of us felt completely comfortable that we had locked up a roster spot on the team," said Mientkiewicz. "We were all very aware that they had options at every position, and that any of us could be one of the guys that got cut. I wasn't hitting the ball at all; I think that home run was the only ball I hit well in the first three games. I remember Coach Reggie Smith came up to me and basically told me that I needed to start hitting or I could be going home. I told him not to worry, that I was swinging well, and that when the bell rang, I'd be ready. But that was basically to let him know that I was still confident and knew what I was doing. That was a bluff—I was pretty scared."

Alderson was getting a bit frustrated as well, even though Team USA had won all three practice games. To understand why Alderson would feel that way, you have to understand his background in the game.

As the former general manager of the Oakland A's in the late '80s and early '90s, Alderson worked under the ownership of Walter A. Haas, Jr. The Athletics appeared in three consecutive World Series from 1988 through 1990 and had the highest payroll in baseball in 1991. Haas died in 1995, and new owners Stephen Schott and Ken Hofmann ordered Alderson to slash payroll. To field a competitive roster on a limited budget, Alderson began focusing on sabermetric principles, in order to obtain relatively undervalued players. He began to value on-base percentage among hitters, focusing on batters who only swung at strikes to give his team good at-bats. He taught his assistant GM Billy Beane to find value in players that other teams did not see, by using sabermetrics.

And on the Gold Coast through three games, Team USA was not getting on base enough for Alderson's liking.

"I was walking through the mobile home clubhouse out in right field, and Sandy, who I have always admired and respected and thought highly of, walked by me and said 'No one is getting on base and nobody is taking any pitches,'" said outfielder Mike Neill. "And I didn't mean to be a smartass to him, but I said, 'Well, it's pretty hard to get on base if you never play.'" Neill had only seen three at-bats in the three games.

Sticking to the principles that had helped him generate three straight American League pennant winners in Oakland, Alderson was trying to work a little of his philosophy into Lasorda's way of managing. He couldn't control what Lasorda did during games, but he could give his manager an idea about which players he felt should get more playing time.

As a routine, Alderson would hold a staff meeting every single morning in his hotel suite, that included Lasorda, Watson, Seiler, Cohen, the six Team USA coaches, doctors, trainers, advance scouts, and press officers. During the meeting, they would go over the day's schedule, set up a plan, discuss the opponent, and review where every player on the Team USA roster stood in their thinking, as far as the role that player would have on the team. Of course, there were heavy discussions about which four players might not make the club.

"Even with the small roster of players we had, there were certain guys that had playing characteristics, and others that had different playing characteristics, and I had always been an on-base percentage guy," said Alderson. "Mike Neill was a disciplined hitter, and so I obviously had a bias toward him, because he had a certain approach to the game that I liked. He wasn't a high-profile guy and wasn't going to be the next major-league All-Star, but he was a very solid player and had the right approach."

Team USA's hero in the '99 Pan Am Games, Neill had yet to start any of the exhibition games in the outfield under

Lasorda's watch.

"And I just remember the next day before the game, Sandy pulled me off the bus, and I thought, 'Oh shit, I'm in trouble.' But he just wanted to tell me that I was starting in left field that night and to prove him right. I knew that was my chance. Sandy, I felt, was always in my corner because he was the one who drafted me way back when in 1991 with the A's, so we had some history. I think he knew that I would give him good at-bats. I'm not going to hit a lot of homers, I'm not going to steal bases, but in these games, it wasn't a full season of stats. It was one game at a time, and I think he knew that I could do something, if given the opportunity."

Neill made Alderson's word hold up, as he went 1-for-3 with a pair of walks and three runs scored that night.

EXHIBITION GAME FOUR vs. SOUTH AFRICA

Sept. 10, 2000 - Kurt Ainsworth struck out seven in five two-hit innings, and DH John Cotton hit a grand slam as part of a seven-run fourth inning, as Team USA cruised to a 17-1 victory.

Center fielder Anthony Sanders, whose wife, Claudia, gave birth to a baby boy back in Tucson, Arizona the day before, also homered in the frame. With Team USA leading 17-1, the game was called after seven innings due to the international 10-run mercy rule (if a team leads by 10 runs or more after seven innings, or 6 ½ innings if the home team, the game is declared over).

Catcher Marcus Jensen went 2-for-4 with a double and three RBIs, while Brent Abernathy added two hits with a double and two RBIs to pace Team USA's 15-hit attack. Ainsworth picked up the win while Young and Heams each pitched a perfect inning in relief.

"We swung the bats really well today and continued to get strong pitching," said Lasorda. "Eleven players had hits today, the type of balanced attack we would like to see in Sydney."

MIRACLE ON GRASS

```
USA 17                              South Africa 1

                 AB  R  H RBI                       AB  R  H RBI
Dawkins ss        3  2  1  0       Bell ss           3  0  1  0
Everett ph/ss     3  0  1  1       De la Ray 3b      2  0  1  0
Wilkerson rf      4  2  1  1       F. Alfino 3b      1  0  0  0
Mientkiewicz 1b   4  2  1  0       Holness rf        3  0  0  0
Kinkade 3b        3  2  2  1       Dempsey 1b        3  0  0  0
Burroughs 3b      1  1  0  0       Cook cf           3  0  0  0
Cotton dh         1  2  1  4       Kemp c            3  0  0  0
Coolbaugh dh      2  0  0  0       Adonis dh         2  0  0  0
Sanders cf        2  1  1  1       Alfino lf         2  1  0  0
Gilbert ph/cf     2  1  1  2       Johnson 2b        2  0  0  0
Jensen c          4  0  2  3       Smith p           0  0  0  0
Neill lf          3  3  1  0       Berriman p        0  0  0  0
Abernathy 2b      4  1  2  2       Harrell p         0  0  0  0
Ainsworth p       0  0  0  0
T. Young p        0  0  0  0
Heams p           0  0  0  0
Totals......    36 17 14 15        Totals......    24  1  2  0

Score by innings:                    R  H  E
-------------------------------------------
USA                   212 750 0   - 17 14  2
South Africa          001 000 0   -  1  2  3
-------------------------------------------
```

E - Dawkins, Wilkerson, De la Ray 2, Berriman. LOB - USA 8,
South Africa 2. 2B - Jensen, Abernathy. HR - Cotton(2),
Sanders(1). SB - Dawkins, Wilkerson. CS - Abernathy.

```
                 IP   H  R ER BB SO WP BK HP IBB  AB BF Fly Gnd

Ainsworth W 1-0  5.0  2  1  0  0  7  0  0  0  0   18 18  3  5
T. Young         1.0  0  0  0  0  2  0  0  0  0    3  3  1  0
Heams            1.0  0  0  0  0  0  0  0  0  0    3  3  0  3

Smith L 0-1      3.1  6 10  8  7  2  1  0  0  0   16 23  4  3
Berriman         1.0  5  6  6  2  2  3  0  0  0    9 11  1  0
Harrell          2.2  3  1  1  1  0  0  0  0  0   11 12  3  5
```

WP - Smith, Berriman 3. PB - Kemp 2.

Strikeouts - Dawkins, Wilkerson 2, Coolbaugh, Bell, De la Ray,
Holness 3, Dempsey, Cook 2, Johnson. Walks - Wilkerson,
Mientkiewicz, Kinkade, Cotton 2, Sanders, Jensen, Neill 2,
Abernathy.

Start: 2:00 pm   Time: 2:32   Attendance: 1000

After four games, on the pitching side Sheets and Rauch were the only ones who had yet to get on the mound in a game, as pitching coach Phil Regan began to line up his rotation. When the team had arrived on the Gold Coast, Sheets had been told that he would be starting Team USA's first official Olympic game in Sydney on September 17 vs. Japan. Counting backwards five days to when he would need to pitch in an exhibition, Sheets knew that would fall on the team's final scrimmage against Korea on the 12th. Meanwhile, Rauch was slated to start the fifth exhibition game that night against the Netherlands, and Ainsworth had just made his first start in the contest against South Africa. Oswalt had pitched earlier in the week.

For Sheets, that schedule worked perfectly, especially since he knew something that Team USA officials did not.

"I had missed a start later in the minor-league season in Indianapolis, right as the Olympic Team was about to be selected, because my right shoulder had been a little sore, not a lot," said Sheets. "And I thought, oh man, no way am I going to let on to Tommy and the Team USA people that I was still hurting a bit. When we got to San Diego, everybody else was throwing bullpens at the workout, and I didn't. I hadn't thrown since the last time I pitched in a game in Indy. So I decided to let it rest, and maybe go over to Australia and then try to line myself up for one of the later exhibitions. I just needed a little rest, it had been a long year, a lot more throwing than I had ever done. And the Brewers wouldn't have known that my shoulder was that sore either."

They obviously did not, because it would not have been very likely that Sheets would have been named to the team, had either the Brewers or Team USA suspected anything was physically wrong with him.

"If you want to do something bad enough, you're willing to take the chance. You think you're pretty invincible, you can get away with it, and I wanted to play," said Sheets. "I wanted the opportunity to go out there and compete, and to be a part of something like that was going to be pretty special. As a competitor, I've always wanted to be the guy that's given the ball with everything on the line, you know."

So after four games, Lasorda and company seemed to be rolling pretty well. Players and staff members had adjusted their body clocks to Australian time, and there didn't seem to be any major injury issues, other than an inflamed elbow on pitcher Matt White. The Tampa Bay prospect had only worked one inning of relief in the four games, and anybody who wasn't 100 percent health-wise was a leading candidate to be sent home early.

But, just as Cobb feared, the casino at the Conrad Jupiter came into play and caused an issue. That night after the game, several of the Team USA players unwound themselves by spending some time together gambling. It was not uncommon for minor leaguers to gamble among themselves, even when there was no casino around. One of the most popular things that baseball players do to pass the time in the clubhouse and on airplanes is to break out a deck of cards and pony up some of their meal money.

On this night, Abernathy, Borders, and Mientkiewicz happened to be sitting at one table together playing blackjack, and it was a little after midnight.

"There were three guys and a woman standing right behind us, and I guess in Australia, players can place bets behind somebody that is gambling. So there's a spot where you can bet if you are sitting at the table as we were, and then people behind you can place a bet on you. So for instance, if Pat won his hand, not only does the casino pay Pat, but they pay the guy who had placed money behind him as well," said Mientkiewicz. "Well, one of these guys started to bet behind Pat, and he didn't really appreciate that very much. So Pat said something to the guy calmly the first time and asked him to stop. A few minutes later, Pat got up and went to the bathroom, came back, and the guy threw his money behind Pat again. And this time when he did it, he kind of elbowed or pushed Pat, maybe by accident or not. So Pat stood up and said, 'Look, I don't want any trouble. Let's take it easy and let's all just have a good time.' And all of a sudden, Lasorda comes over after he saw the commotion, and starts barking at the guy, 'I'll paralyze you with this left hook' and screaming at him and cussing him out. So the guy pushes Pat, and the next thing I know, Borders literally picks this guy up and throws him from the table we were at, over the table behind us into the pit area."

As the security guards were being called over and a scene began to ensue, Abernathy and Mientkiewicz immediately jumped in to back up their teammate, even as their 73-year-old manager had helped escalate the argument into a fight.

"I got one of the other guys into a bear hug from behind, and as I'm trying to wrestle him, all I saw was some woman beating Doug over the back with her purse, because Doug was holding her boyfriend back from doing anything else," said Abernathy. "Then the guy I had tries to break away from me, and bites me in the chest above my right nipple! He literally broke the skin through my shirt. I don't think any punches were thrown, but it got out of control really quick. You just had a feeling when those guys walked up behind us, just from the way they looked, that there was trouble written all over them.

"After Pat threw this guy to the floor, he got up but Pat chased him out of the place, literally running after him the entire length of the casino floor."

Finally, after the security guards got things to calm down, Conrad Jupiter officials called Watson, Cobb, and Seiler in their rooms, to make them aware of what just happened.

"I was sleeping in my room when the phone rang at like one in the morning, and Steve Cobb asked me to come downstairs," said Team USA doctor Fred Dicke. "We had to take Brent to the hospital to get a tetanus shot. It was a pretty nasty bite that left teeth marks."

To get his players' side of the story, Watson called Mientkiewicz and Borders up to his room. Lasorda was there as well.

"I started explaining to Bob as calmly as possible what had

happened, and that yes, maybe we were in the wrong place that late at night," said Mientkiewicz. "And Lasorda is back there screaming, 'Yeah, I love this shit! They stick up for each other! I want to go to war with these guys!' and finally I looked at Tommy and said, 'Skip, can you be quiet for a second! You're not helping the situation. Will you please allow us to explain what happened?' But I guess in his own way, he wanted us to know that he had our backs, because he kept telling Bob that this is what being teammates is all about."

There was no hiding the incident from the USA Baseball brass, or Major League Baseball's public relations rep Pat Courtney, because Courtney happened to be near the casino when things went down, and witnessed what had occurred. But since it was so late at night and there were not many media members staying at the Conrad Jupiter (most of the media was at another property, and of the ones who may have been staying at the Jupiter, none of them were present at the time of the fight), USA Baseball had a good chance of keeping the incident from making the papers.

So in Alderson's staff meeting the next morning, the USA Baseball brass had a chance to discuss everything, and came up with a plan to try and squash the subject, if any of them were ever to be questioned about it. Right away, they asked hotel management to downplay things as well. And to make sure that there were no more issues, and that the Team USA players could enjoy themselves and gamble in peace for the rest of their stay, the Conrad Jupiter opened up a private casino room for the USA players and USA Baseball and MLB personnel only.

"I think we were pretty fortunate that the media didn't catch on to it at all," said Courtney. "We did a nice job keeping it quiet, and the hotel didn't want the publicity either. We simply went about our business as if nothing had happened, and asked the players to do the same."

Borders, Mientkiewicz, and Abernathy were certainly glad that nothing came of it as well.

"I remember Nagano had just happened a few years before

that with the USA hockey players, and USA Baseball was adamant with us about being careful not to make a big stink about anything, and to represent ourselves with class," said Mientkiewicz. "And then here we were, throwing some little Vietnamese guys around in a casino. I wasn't sure if that was going to give them more of a reason to send me home."

USA Baseball later found out that hotel security had been made aware of those particular troublemakers in the past and that the main instigator who had started the problem with Borders carried a parole sheet the size of a scroll.

"I actually believe that the incident really helped our team bond and come together even more," said Abernathy. "Doug, Pat, and myself didn't know each other very well yet, and we were hanging out just having a good time that night. And our reactions showed that we had each other's backs no matter what, because we all stuck up for one another right away. And when the rest of our teammates heard about it, they supported us as well."

But, perhaps a bit shaken by the chaotic night and the nervousness surrounding what had occurred, Team USA went out and was beaten by the Netherlands, their first exhibition loss.

EXHIBITION GAME FIVE vs. THE NETHERLANDS

Sept. 11, 2000 - Former major leaguer Rikkert Faneyte drove in three runs with a second-inning double, then pitched the ninth inning to earn the save as the Netherlands defeated Team USA, 4-3.

Faneyte spent parts of four seasons in the major leagues with the San Francisco Giants and Texas Rangers from 1993-96. But he cleared the bases with a double in the second off USA starter Jon Rauch, who suffered the loss, giving up five runs in four innings.

Team USA tried to answer the Dutch offense, scoring two runs in the bottom of the second. Third baseman Mike Kinkade doubled home Ernie Young and John Cotton, who had both singled off the Netherlands' starting pitcher, Jurriaan

Lobbezoo. Reliever Ken Brauckmiller got the win for the Dutch with 2 2/3 scoreless innings.

The U.S. scored again in the ninth off Faneyte when shortstop Adam Everett doubled and scored on Brad Wilkerson's single. Wilkerson, who has batted third in every game for Team USA, had three of the Americans' nine hits.

"You have to give credit to the Dutch team," said Lasorda, who saw his team strand nine runners on base. "We definitely had opportunities offensively tonight, but just couldn't capitalize on them."

Rick Krivda came on in the sixth and limited the Netherlands to one hit in three innings of shutout relief. Bobby Seay pitched a scoreless ninth.

Team USA playing an exhibition game at one of the Australian Baseball Federation's practice facilities on the Gold Coast.

DAVID FANUCCHI

The Netherlands 4   USA 3

	AB	R	H	RBI		AB	R	H	RBI
Faneyte cf/p	4	0	2	3	Dawkins ss	3	0	0	0
Cranston cf	0	0	0	0	Everett ss	2	1	2	0
Milliard 2b	4	0	1	0	Wilkerson rf	4	0	3	1
Adriana dh	4	0	0	0	Mientkiewicz 1b	5	0	0	0
Muelens lf	4	0	2	0	E. Young lf	2	1	1	0
Isenia, P. 1b	4	0	0	0	Neill lf	2	0	0	0
Balentina c	4	0	0	0	Cotton dh	2	1	1	0
Eenhoorn ss	3	1	0	0	Coolbaugh dh	0	0	0	0
van't Kloost rf	4	2	3	0	Kinkade 3b	2	0	1	2
Legito 3b	3	1	1	1	Burroughs 3b	2	0	0	0
Lobbezoo p	0	0	0	0	Jensen c	4	0	1	0
Brauckmiller p	0	0	0	0	Sanders cf	4	0	0	0
Jongejan p	0	0	0	0	Abernathy 2b	2	0	0	0
					Gilbert 2b	2	0	0	0
					Rauch p	0	0	0	0
					Krivda p	0	0	0	0
					Seay p	0	0	0	0
Totals......	34	4	9	4	Totals......	36	3	9	3

Score by innings: R H E

The Netherlands   030 100 000 - 4 9 2
USA   020 000 001 - 3 9 0

E - Muelens, Eenhoorn. LOB - Holland 7, USA 9. 2B - Faneyte,
van't Kloost, Legito, Everett(1), Kinkade(2). SB -
Wilkerson(3), Mientkiewicz(1). CS - Milliard, Muelens.

	IP	H	R	ER	BB	SO	WP	BK	HP	IBB	AB	BF	Fly	Gnd
Lobbezoo	4.0	5	2	2	0	5	2	0	0	0	17	17	4	2
Brauck. W 1-0	2.2	2	0	0	2	2	0	0	0	0	10	12	3	2
Jongejan	1.1	0	0	0	1	2	0	0	0	0	4	5	2	0
Faneyte S,1	1.0	2	1	1	0	0	0	0	0	0	5	5	1	2
Rauch L 0-1	5.0	6	4	4	3	4	0	0	0	0	19	22	5	4
Krivda	3.0	1	0	0	1	2	0	0	0	0	10	11	2	5
Seay	1.0	2	0	0	0	0	0	0	0	0	5	5	2	1

WP - Lobbezoo 2.

Strikeouts - Adriana 2, Isenia, P. 2, Balentina, Eenhoorn,
Dawkins, Mientkiewicz, E. Young, Neill, Cotton, Burroughs,
Jensen, Sanders, Gilbert. Walks - Faneyte, Milliard, Eenhoorn,
Legito, Wilkerson, Coolbaugh 2.

Start: 6:00 pm   Time: 2:46   Attendance: 945

Following the tough loss, the Americans decided to take out their frustrations at the casino again, knowing that they now had access to a private gaming room that was only for them.

"A bunch of us decided to go play some blackjack for a little while after our late dinner back at the hotel, knowing that we'd have our privacy in that room they set up for us," said Abernathy. "But our luck didn't change in there, it got even worse. Most of us were getting our asses handed to us."

Having had enough of the "private" dealers that were taking all of their money in the luxury suite, several of the Team USA players decided to try their luck back out in the main casino with the general public.

"We probably shouldn't have done that, but it was pretty late and there weren't many people around at all," said Abernathy. "I found Ben (Sheets) sitting at a Caribbean Stud poker table and wanted to hang out with him for a few minutes."

After Sheets had decided that he had enough, Abernathy grabbed his seat at the table and began playing. "The table was one of those progressive poker jackpots that kept accumulating over time, with the payout getting higher every night that passed when somebody didn't win."

Just three hands after Sheets had left the table and Abernathy took his seat, Brent was dealt a royal flush of spades—10, Jack, Queen, King, Ace—and became an instant winner of the jackpot. "I couldn't believe my eyes. The casino boss told me that those only happened once or twice a year, and that they sometimes went six to eight months before one of those ever hits at that table," said Abernathy. "It was unbelievable."

Abernathy had won 126,000 Australian dollars, or what was the equivalent of $74,000 American. "I always have been very thankful that it was Ben that was sitting there when I took his seat," said Abernathy. "He's such a class act and was so happy for me. He didn't think anything of it at all, had such a great attitude about it, that's just the kind of guy he is."

(Following the Olympics, Abernathy went home and paid cash for a brand new Mercedes-Benz.)

And so even on a night when they had lost an exhibition game to the Netherlands, this United States Baseball Team was still coming together, and showing signs that maybe there was something special about this group.

"You just had a sense that there was something in the air, that these kids were going to do great things," said Seiler. "There were no egos involved, and you could feel the sense of team they were trying to build."

And there was no question that Lasorda was working behind the scenes on the hearts and minds of his starting pitchers, in particular Ben Sheets.

"I felt like those kids were great, I mean really super. I can remember talking to the entire pitching staff while we were training, and I told them, 'You guys just don't know how good you are!'" said Lasorda. "I told them that if they had given me this pitching staff in the major leagues, that we would be in the World Series within two years. Because these guys were that good, they just didn't know it yet. I had to make them understand and believe how good they were. On the Gold Coast, Ben and I would take a walk around the path of the hotel every night, and we would just talk baseball. We'd talk pitching. I knew this kid had a great arm, and I knew that if he got into the right frame of mind, he could beat the Cubans. So, we specifically saved him and lined him up to pitch the gold-medal game, just for that reason."

The time Lasorda spent with Sheets taking walks after dinner was certainly appreciated by the young right hander.

"I enjoyed those long walks on the beach, and around the hotel," said Sheets. "Tommy would usually just grab me after dinner and say 'Come take a walk with me, Sheetsy' and we'd just walk around the hotel, get some fresh air, and talk about baseball, talk about different little tips and ideas. He's been around the game a long time and the dude knows a lot. All he was saying was pretty simple stuff that's logical, but sometimes it was stuff that you might not think about while pitching. We both liked to talk and our personalities meshed really well. We're both outgoing guys with a little bit of charisma, a little bit of personality. So it was good to have somebody like that to talk to."

The next night, Sheets got the ball for his first start, after giving himself the rest his shoulder needed. It had been over two weeks since Sheets had pitched a game for the triple-A Indianapolis Indians, but on this night, it looked like he hadn't missed a beat.

EXHIBITION GAME SIX vs. KOREA

Sept. 12, 2000 – Right hander Ben Sheets solidified his place as Team USA's likely No. 1 starter with five shutout innings, and Team USA hit three more home runs to pound Korea, 15-0. While Korea did not use its top pitchers or Korean Baseball Organization home run king Lee Seung-Yeop in the game, its team is a collection of KBO all-stars and is still considered a strong medal contender.

But it didn't look that way against the Americans, as Team USA pounded out 17 hits. Three were longballs, bringing Team USA's total to 11 in six exhibition games. The Americans finished their practice schedule with a 5-1 record and will open play in the Olympics in five days against Japan.

"I am extremely pleased with the progress our team has made during these exhibition games," said Lasorda. "Tonight we showed that we are picking up our level of play and getting ready for the Olympics to begin. Our team will surely be ready to play by Sunday."

Sheets should start against the Japanese, taking his turn on his normal four days of rest. He was brilliant against Korea, giving up just two hits without a walk while striking out six. Triple-A Tacoma Rainers right handers Ryan Franklin and Todd Williams finished with two hitless innings of relief, as the game ended after seven innings due to the international 10-run mercy rule.

Team USA scored seven runs in the second inning to break open the game, with three key extra-base hits. Shortstop Adam

Everett, who has outplayed Travis Dawkins and figures to be Team USA's starter at the position, hit a two-run double off the left-field wall to score the first two runs of the inning. After a walk to Brent Abernathy, center fielder Brad Wilkerson tripled to right, scoring two runs. Ernie Young then followed with a two-run homer to right.

Pat Borders added a solo home run as part of a three-run third inning that extended Team USA's lead to 10-0. Abernathy and Young each reached base in all five plate appearances in the game, as each player went 3-for-3 with a pair of walks. Everett also had three hits and Mike Kinkade added a two-run homer.

Scouts from the Major League Baseball Scouting Bureau worked with Team USA during the exhibition games, by sharing their knowledge of the opposing teams.
L-R: Bart Johnson, Jim Walton, Carl Moesche

MIRACLE ON GRASS

```
USA 15                                 Korea 0

                 AB  R  H RBI                          AB  R  H RBI
Abernathy 2b      3  2  3  1    Lee lf/cf               3  0  1  0
Dawkins 2b        0  0  0  0    Jung cf/rf              3  0  0  0
Wilkerson cf      5  1  2  2    Park, JH rf/c           3  0  0  0
Neill lf          4  1  2  1    Kim, KT 1b              3  0  0  0
E. Young rf       3  2  3  5    Kim, DJ dh              3  0  1  0
Cotton dh         4  0  0  0    Kim, HS 3b              2  0  0  0
Kinkade 3b/1b     5  1  1  2    Hong c                  1  0  0  0
Mientkiewicz 1b   3  2  1  0    Jang ph/lf              1  0  0  0
Burroughs pr/3b   0  0  0  0    Kim, TG 2b              2  0  0  0
Borders c         4  3  2  1    Park, JM ss             2  0  0  0
Everett ss        5  3  3  2    Koo p                   0  0  0  0
Sheets p          0  0  0  0    Kim, SK p               0  0  0  0
Franklin p        0  0  0  0    Park, SJ p              0  0  0  0
Williams p        0  0  0  0    Jin p                   0  0  0  0
                                Lim, CY p               0  0  0  0

Totals......     36 15 17 14    Totals......           23  0  2  0

Score by innings:                    R  H  E
-------------------------------------------
USA                     073 122 0 - 15 17  0
Korea                   000 000 0 -  0  2  0
-------------------------------------------
```

LOB - USA 9, Korea 2. 2B - Borders(1), Everett(2). 3B - Wilkerson(1), Mientkiewicz(1). HR - E. Young(1), Kinkade(2), Borders(1). SB - Lee. CS - Abernathy.

```
              IP   H  R ER BB SO WP BK HP IBB  AB BF Fly Gnd
Sheets W 1-0  5.0  2  0  0  0  6  0  0  0  0   17 17  3   6
Franklin      1.0  0  0  0  0  0  0  0  0  0    3  3  1   2
Williams      1.0  0  0  0  0  2  0  0  0  0    3  3  0   1

Koo L 0-1     1.1  5  5  5  4  1  2  0  0  0    7 11  1   0
Kim, SK       1.1  6  5  5  2  2  1  0  0  0   10 12  1   1
Park, SJ      1.1  2  1  1  0  4  0  0  0  0    6  6  0   0
Jin           1.0  2  2  2  0  3  0  0  0  0    5  5  0   0
Lim, CY       2.0  2  2  2  2  5  0  0  1  0    8 11  0   1
```

WP - Koo 2, Kim, SK. HBP - by Lim, CY (Mientkiewicz).

Strikeouts - Wilkerson 3, Neill 2, Cotton 2, Kinkade 3, Mientkiewicz, Borders 2, Everett 2, Lee, Jung, Park, JH, Kim, KT 2, Kim, DJ 2, Jang. Walks - Abernathy 2, Neill, E. Young 2, Cotton, Mientkiewicz, Borders.

Start: 6:30 pm   Time: 2:45   Attendance: 2200

With their six exhibition games behind them, it was time for Alderson, Watson, and company to make their final cuts and decide who the four players were going to be whom they would have to send home brokenhearted. Two of them needed to be pitchers, the other two position players.

The first pitching cut was fairly straightforward. Matt White of Tampa Bay had developed arm problems during the exhibition week and was not fully ready to compete, and the USA Baseball brass could not take a chance on putting a pitcher on the final roster who was not healthy. As a right-handed starter, White had been beaten out by Ryan Franklin and Kurt Ainsworth for the fourth starter and long relief roles, as both had been pitching well in practice and were ready to go.

The Cleveland Indians made USA Baseball's decision about their final cut and their Olympic rotation a little easier, when they pulled left-hander C.C. Sabathia off the Olympic Team. Published reports out of Ohio quoted Indians assistant general manager Mark Shapiro saying Sabathia was returning home because Team USA had planned to use him out of the bullpen. Because the Indians agreed to let Sabathia go to Australia on the condition that he was a starter and work only on strict pitch counts, they decided to have him return rather than be relegated to the Team USA bullpen.

"C.C. ended up being chosen as their fourth starter," Shapiro said. "That meant that he also would be used in the bullpen possibly." Shapiro went on to say that he was considering using Sabathia as a spot starter during their upcoming series against the Boston Red Sox, when the two teams would be playing five games in three days.

With Sabathia suddenly removed from the team, Lasorda's starting rotation was lining up to look as if Sheets, Oswalt, and Rauch would get the first three opportunities. Young left-hander Chris George and veteran lefty Rick Krivda now figured into the fourth starter/swing reliever role, along with Ainsworth and Franklin from the right-handed side.

Team USA's Olympic schedule was such that they really

only needed three top starters. They opened with Japan in four days and would have Sheets ready to go, in all likelihood. He could then go again against Cuba in pool play, and would have three days' rest for a possible medal game, if needed.

The "which two position players to cut" debate was much longer and more difficult for Alderson, Watson, Lasorda, and crew to figure out.

Although he had been a contributor to Team USA's success in Winnipeg and carried with him that international experience, the brass was having a hard time finding a role that made sense for utilityman Shawn Gilbert.

Having gone 2-for-11 with 3 RBIs in the six games, Gilbert did not fit into a starting position in the outfield, as those spots would be taken by Young, Wilkerson, and Neill, along with Anthony Sanders as their backup. The infield positions that Gilbert could play best—shortstop and second base—were covered well by Everett and Abernathy, with Dawkins behind them. Sanders and Dawkins could also provide speed as pinch-runners and right-handed bats off the bench. It all added up to Gilbert being one of the two odd men out.

Watson clearly recalls the incredibly difficult task it was to tell Gilbert that he wasn't going to be an Olympian. "Paul (Seiler), Sandy, myself, and Tommy were in our suite at the hotel, and we had made our decisions, so we then had to inform those last two players," said Watson. "Shawn took the news pretty hard, and it was a gut-wrenching thing for us to have to do, especially since Shawn had helped us get to the Olympics the year before. Not only that, Shawn was in the Dodgers organization, so Tommy felt even worse about it."

The final cut came down to the only position that hadn't been completely solidified yet in Lasorda's mind, or in his starting lineup: third base. The candidates came down to left-handed-hitting youngster Sean Burroughs, right-handed-hitting veteran Mike Coolbaugh, and right-handed bat Mike Kinkade, who could also serve as a third-string catcher if anything were to happen to Borders or Jensen.

During the exhibition games, Kinkade had clearly won the

positional battle if you were looking at it from an offensive standpoint, going 6-for-16 (.375) with five runs scored and six RBIs. Burroughs had gone 2-for-7 with an RBI and a run scored, while Coolbaugh had struggled at the plate, going 0-for-8. Of the three, Coolbaugh brought the most defensive experience at third base to the table, while Burroughs could also handle the glove very well. Kinkade had a little less range over there and was considered to be more of a utility-type player.

"But at the end of the day, Coolbaugh just did not perform on the Gold Coast," said Alderson. "Kinkade had shown that he belonged on the team, and Tommy liked the option of having Sean's left-handed bat off the bench."

That made Coolbaugh the last man out. "When we told him, it seemed as if he was in disbelief," said Watson. "I think we all just sat there in the room in silence for about five minutes, and Mike didn't say a word. None of us knew what to say next and Mike had this blank stare on his face. Tough situation for sure."

Being sent home when you were ever so close to becoming an Olympian had to make the already long flight back to the States even longer for Coolbaugh, Gilbert, Sabathia, and White. The four players would each go on to have various levels of success in baseball.

The most successful of the four by far has been Sabathia, who reached the major leagues in 2001 and has been there ever since (even though he never threw another pitch again in 2000 for the Indians at any level, after being pulled off the Team USA roster). Following eight seasons with the Indians as one of the premier lefties in the game, he signed a lucrative long-term contract with the New York Yankees in 2009 and helped the Bronx Bombers win the World Series that season.

White never reached the majors in three more seasons, only getting as far as the triple-A level. Gilbert played in 15 games for the Los Angeles Dodgers in 2001 but spent most of the season at triple-A Las Vegas. He kept the uniform on for two more years in the minors with the Pittsburgh Pirates before hanging up his cleats in 2003.

And finally, Mike Coolbaugh's career ended up being notable in more ways than one. The third baseman reached the majors when he played in 39 games for the Milwaukee Brewers in 2001, and five more as a September call-up for the St. Louis Cardinals in 2002. After hitting a career-best 30 home runs in 2004 at triple-A New Orleans in the Houston Astros system, Coolbaugh retired in 2006 after 16 seasons.

Following his professional playing career, Coolbaugh turned to coaching, and in 2007, he was hired as the first-base coach for the Tulsa Drillers, a double-A affiliate of the Colorado Rockies.

But less than a month after he began the job, Coolbaugh was killed during a game against the Arkansas Travelers in North Little Rock, Arkansas, when a line drive hit by Drillers catcher Tino Sanchez struck him in the neck while he was standing in the first-base coach's box. The impact pulverized Coolbaugh's left vertebral artery, which severed the brain from the spinal cord. The result was a severe brain hemorrhage that essentially killed Coolbaugh on impact.

Later, after clinching the National League Wild Card playoff berth during the 2007 major-league season, the Colorado Rockies announced that the players had voted to award Coolbaugh's widow, Amanda, a full share of their playoff winnings. And when the Rockies made it to the World Series that season, her share ended up being $233,505.

During the following offseason, MLB general managers decided that it would be required of all base coaches to wear helmets, starting in the 2008 season. Minor League Baseball then began presenting the annual Mike Coolbaugh Award to someone who has "shown an outstanding baseball work ethic, knowledge of the game, and skill in mentoring young players on the field."

11

SYDNEY

Now that the 2000 USA Baseball Olympic Team roster had become official, the next day the entire traveling party left the Gold Coast and flew back to Sydney, where the 24 players, four official coaches, Seiler, Cohen, and Fierro would all prepare to check into the Olympic Athletes Village later that night. The Village is the home for all athletes, coaches, and trainers who participate in the Olympics, unless they are chosen by a national governing body that houses their athletes outside the Village in a team hotel (such as USA Basketball).

The Village can best be described as a massive, brand-new apartment complex with one giant cafeteria to feed the thousands of athletes and coaches from all over the world. In Sydney, the Village featured two bunk-style beds in each room, with approximately seven or eight rooms in each condo, along with a small kitchen unit and a bathroom. USA Baseball was given two condos to divide up the 32 people who needed to stay together in the Village. The other USA Baseball staffers, including Alderson, Cobb, Cooke, Tanner, Watson, the team medical personnel, and press officers would need to stay outside the Village, off-site at a hotel.

Team USA's apartments at the Athletes Village in Sydney.

In this case, Cobb had booked rooms for the extra USA Baseball executives and staff at the same hotel that USA Basketball had reserved for their entire delegation and the American Men's NBA Basketball stars.

With the USA Basketball operation taking first priority, they had managed to take over a sizeable portion of the available sleeping rooms on the property, as well as the meeting rooms. This was the Olympics, and every major hotel in the entire city was booked solid, either by Olympic fans or family and friends of all the athletes participating. Cobb did not have a lot of options.

"Because the rooms were in such high demand, I had to pre-pay in full for every room that I wanted to reserve, so I counted up what I needed and didn't pad it very much," said Cobb. "I did add one extra room for Commissioner Selig, in case he decided to make the trip over, but that was it."

And as much as Lasorda had suggested that he wanted to remain with his team in the Village, Seiler, Watson, and Alderson all knew that was going to be a major challenge for him, especially as it was going to be for over two weeks' time.

"We got in there the first night, and I don't think it was

anything like what Tommy had envisioned," said Seiler. "It's almost a college-type feeling being in a dormitory, very basic, nothing modern. He lasted one night."

The next day, knowing how uncomfortable Lasorda had been overnight, Seiler and Cobb devised a plan to put the Hall of Fame skipper into the one extra room Cobb had luckily reserved at the hotel: Bud Selig's.

"I had nothing else left, that was it," said Cobb. "I was out of rooms and so was the hotel; it was at 100% capacity. So we had no idea what we were going to do if Bud decided he wanted to make the trip to Sydney later in the Games."

Lasorda was certainly appreciative of the nicer accommodations, but the move caused another unexpected glitch in the USA Baseball operation. Since the hotel was a short distance from the Village and the baseball stadium venue—maybe a 15-minute ride by car—somebody needed to be put in charge of escorting Lasorda back and forth between the Village and the hotel during those times when he would want to be with his team, eating meals with them and also visiting with other American and foreign athletes.

So Seiler then called upon the United States Olympic Committee's Athlete Services staff, who then reached out to the Australian Olympic Committee's transportation volunteer brigade. It takes thousands of volunteers to successfully operate an Olympic Games, and in this instance, the USA Baseball contingent was in need of a driver with a vehicle to move around a celebrity. And ironically, the volunteer chosen to be assigned to the American baseball team happened to be a young man named Kurt Johnson, who was born in Australia but had spent time growing up in the United States.

When Johnson met up with Seiler and Lasorda to learn that he would be the Hall of Fame manager's personal chauffeur for the next two weeks, he was all for it and thrilled with his new gig. He and Lasorda seemed to get along well. The Team USA players got to know Johnson and vice versa.

Johnson was in his late thirties, stood about 5-foot-5, had a golden brown goatee, and was for the most part bald-headed.

So because he resembled the movie actor John Malcovich, who had recently starred in the 1997 film *Con Air*, Johnson acquired the nickname "Cyrus the Virus," which was the character Malcovich played in the movie. It is not known which Team USA player or staff gave him that moniker, but it stuck.

One other aspect of Lasorda's move to the hotel turned out to be a positive. He was now able to sit in on Alderson's early-morning staff meetings that were still being held in Sandy's hotel suite. Had he stayed in the Village, he would have been absent from the meetings, just as Seiler, Cohen, Fierro, and the three coaches (Rodriguez, Regan, and Smith) now were.

Still present besides Alderson and Lasorda each morning for their powwows in what became known as the "war room" were the usual suspects in Watson, Cobb, Cooke, Tanner, Doctors Mattalino and Dicke, and a group of very important advance scouts from the MLB Scouting Bureau.

Alderson (left) held a Team USA staff meeting each morning in his hotel suite (right: Watson, Cobb, Dicke).

One advantage that USA Baseball would come to enjoy was that they were being assisted in Sydney simply by the Bureau's presence covering the entire Olympic Baseball event. The MLB Scouting Bureau is a centralized scouting resource that operates under the auspices of the Commissioner's Office. Headquartered in Ontario, California, and supervised by its director, Frank Marcos, the MLBSB's efforts supplement the independent, proprietary amateur and professional scouting operations of the 30 major-league baseball clubs.

The MLBSB employed many scouts in the United States, Canada, and Puerto Rico, and for this event, they had sent three of their top scouts—Mike Larson, Carl Moesche, and Jim Walton—to Australia. And since the MLBSB staff was also staying at the same hotel, Larson, Moesche, and Walton would sit in on the Team USA meetings in order to discuss what they knew about that day's opponent, as well as their strengths and weaknesses. They provided Lasorda and his coaching staff with the background knowledge about the pitchers and players on Team USA's upcoming opponent.

The Bureau had been with the USA Baseball party in the Gold Coast as well, when they sent three videographers—Mike Fiol, Don Jacoby, and Christie Stancil—to shoot footage of every pitcher and player on those six Olympic Teams that were playing exhibition games. As the three video techs recorded game footage, they would drop it off to video coordinator Jerry Kelley back at the Conrad Jupiter Hotel. Kelley was in the midst of putting together an updated player "video profile" tape for each of the Olympic Teams; Cuba and Japan were not present on the Gold Coast, but the Bureau had accumulated footage of those teams in previous international baseball events.

Once all of the games were finished on the Gold Coast, Kelley moved his work station to the hotel in Sydney and began working in his personal room, which the crew dubbed the "High Performance Center." There, Kelley would file the footage he would receive twice daily; each player on every team would have his own tape, and each team was color coded so that Larson, Moesche, and Walton could analyze the tendencies of pitchers or look for weaknesses in opposing hitters. This was the information that would be critical in helping Lasorda understand what he was up against, going into each game.

As Team USA was settling into the Village, and the staff was getting used to maneuvering around the overly congested Sydney streets and planning for the delays due to security checkpoints during travel, Lasorda would meet up with his players at the scheduled team practice once a day. Afterwards, he and Cyrus the Virus would usually follow Pat Courtney and me to the International Media Center, in order to handle any media interview requests that we had received.

Lasorda was a very popular interview request in Sydney, as USA Baseball knew he would be. And he was in demand not just for the American media, but for news sources all over the world. In order to prioritize the influx of requests for his time, we had to stick with the main news outlets that fed back to the United States and then work with all of the foreign requests after that.

Some of the interviews and feature stories that were produced about Lasorda, this Hall of Fame manager coaching in the Olympics, were done by NBC Sports, which was broadcasting the Games back to the States; the *NBC Nightly News* with Tom Brokaw; MSNBC; CNN; the *New York Times*, *Washington Post*, and the *Los Angeles Times*. These were among many of the daily television stations and newspapers that were featuring one of the most unique stories going into these Sydney Games.

On the day before the Opening Ceremonies, NBC's *The Today Show* had requested a live interview with Team USA outfielder Anthony Sanders. *Today*'s producers had gotten word that Sanders had missed the birth of his son the previous week because he was with the USA Baseball team training for the Games on the Gold Coast.

As the USA Baseball Team's official press officer, I escorted Sanders to the *Today Show* set after practice that day.

When we arrived, Sanders was shown into the green room, or waiting room, to be prepped with makeup for his live television interview. Also there waiting in the green room to be interviewed on the *Today Show* was USA swimming sensation Lenny Krayzelburg, who was then recognized as the top backstroke swimmer in the world and one of the best in the history of that swimming style.

Krayzelburg would go on to win three gold medals in Sydney, shattering the Olympic record and nearing his own 1999 world record with 53.72 in the 100 backstroke, while making another Olympic Record in the 200 backstroke with a 1:56.76. He also played an important role in helping the American team win a gold medal in the 4x100 medley relay with a new world record of 3:33.73.

As soon as Sanders was finished meeting Krayzelburg and they had shaken hands, he ran into an even bigger star who was waiting backstage. Much to Anthony's surprise, standing there was none other than "The Greatest" Muhammad Ali. A former Olympic gold medalist himself at the 1960 Games in Rome, Ali was in Sydney to support the American Team and make his presence felt among the International Olympic Committee. But on this afternoon, he was standing backstage at the NBC complex, taking pictures with fans and security guards and shaking hands with as many people as he could.

After I was able to introduce Sanders to Ali and take his picture with the Champ, it was time for Anthony to get to the set. NBC's Katie Couric was going to be conducting the interview with Sanders, as a large crowd of American fans and Australian supporters lined the fence behind the stage, waving flags and signs.

The next surprise for Sanders was that once the interview started, NBC had sent a camera crew to Anthony's hometown of Tucson, Arizona and had a live shot being fed all the way to the set in Sydney of his wife, Claudia, and their newborn baby sitting at their home. As Sanders looked down to the TV set in front of him, with Couric by his side, it was the first time he had been able to see his newborn son. The look on his face was priceless.

"That was an incredibly special moment. What a nice surprise for NBC to have done that," said Sanders. "I had just met Muhammad Ali, and then ten minutes later I saw my son for the first time on TV. It was an awesome day."

Team USA outfielder Anthony Sanders meets "The Champ" Muhammad Ali on the set of NBC's *The Today Show*

As the Opening Ceremonies approached, the 24 USA Baseball players who had earned the right to be called Olympians continued to soak up the atmosphere of where they were and what they were about to do. They were light-years away from the long bus rides, dreary clubhouses, and old hotel rooms of the minor leagues.

"We got dressed in that Team USA uniform that looks identical to all of the other American athletes and went and waited with the rest of Team USA for the Parade of Athletes," said Abernathy. "I remember thinking how cool it all was, and how blessed I felt to be there. The anticipation for that moment when we could walk into that gigantic stadium, see all of the lights and over 100,000 people cheering for us, it was something I'll never forget."

For Neill, who had been such a major factor in helping Team USA qualify, and then had battled again to make the Olympic Team, the Opening Ceremonies meant something even more. "Walking into that stadium representing my county, that was the most amazing thing I've ever been a part of," said Neill. "The crowd, the waterfall, the orchestra, the fireworks, and you're a part of that? I was just so happy that I'd made the final roster, I remember thinking to myself, 'Wow, at least I did that,' without knowing what was going to happen in the Games we were going to play."

For the veteran Ernie Young, it was a special time. "The most memorable times for me were actually when we were able to get together with all the guys, just bonding, sitting around our apartment in the Village, watching some of the other Olympic events on TV and talking about baseball, and just really getting to know each other," said Young. "That brought us together like you wouldn't believe. The bond that we felt off the field was just unbelievable. Anything that we did off the field, we were all together, whether it was going to eat a meal at the café or doing something else."

Unlike in 1999, when Cobb and Seiler had made the conscious decision to house the USA Baseball Team away from the Village in Winnipeg, this time around, they made sure that their team got the full Olympic treatment inside the Village, and it was looking like another good decision.

"I think if we had been off-site from the Village, it would have been difficult for us to bond together as a team like that," said Young. "To be able to see all those other athletes in different sports going about their daily routine, I think it was helpful to us as well. Just being around that atmosphere and hanging our American flag up outside our house, and naming our apartment 'Club 99,' we were having such a great time, and we hadn't even started playing yet."

MIRACLE ON GRASS

The United States Olympic Team is introduced to the crowd as they walk into Olympic Stadium in Sydney.

On the first day of official competition, two days prior to Team USA's first game against Japan, the United States Olympic Committee held a press conference in the Main Press Center specifically to shine light on the USA Baseball Team (they usually held a conference for each team they had competing, as well as one for every individual sport). Selected to represent the baseball team at the presser were manager Tommy Lasorda, outfielder Mike Neill, pitcher Ben Sheets, outfielder Brad Wilkerson, pitcher Todd Williams, and outfielder Ernie Young, all wearing their Team USA-issued gear. Pat Courtney was alongside to help conduct the press conference, while I introduced Lasorda and the athletes from the podium and moderated the questions from the media.

The biggest news to come out of the conference that day was a comment that Lasorda had made when asked what his thoughts would be if the USA had earned a chance to play Cuba for the gold medal. "We would be playing that game for all of the Cuban Americans that have come to our country and who live in little Havana, on the streets of Miami and all across South Florida," said Lasorda. "That's who we would dedicate the victory to."

Needless to say, that made headlines in newspapers all over the world, and especially in Miami and Cuba the next day. "Baseball got a ton of media coverage out of that one particular quote," said Courtney. "It certainly ramped up the tension between the two teams and escalated what was already a pretty big rivalry into a bigger one."

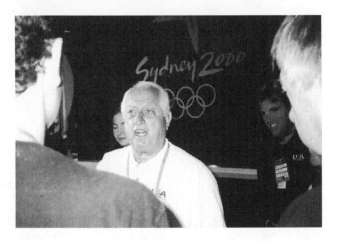

Lasorda speaking to the media at the official press conference for baseball, prior to the Games.

But for the most part, things went fairly smoothly during the session, as the worldwide media questioned the players and Lasorda about what they thought their chances were of winning. Many of the American baseball writers who had done Olympic preview articles prior to the Games did not have much faith in this band of fairly unknown minor leaguers, saying that they would have to play extremely well just to medal, let alone have a real shot at winning gold.

With the Cubans as everyone's favorite to win their third straight Olympic gold medal, and the highest level professional teams from Japan and Korea in the mix, most media members had the Americans pegged only for having a shot at the bronze medal. In fact, popular American ESPN baseball reporter Peter Gammons had mentioned on *SportsCenter* that he thought that the United States only had the *fifth* best team in the event, and that they wouldn't even medal at all.

Team USA players (L-R): Ernie Young, Mike Neill, Todd Williams, Ben Sheets, and Brad Wilkerson, spoke to the media at the Olympic Baseball press conference.

Here are the eight Olympic Team previews that were written by John Manuel and published in the September 2000 issue of *Baseball America* magazine:

AUSTRALIA
Head Coach: Jon Deeble
Key Players: Former Milwaukee Brewers All-Star Dave Nilsson played in Japan this year so that he would be available for the Olympics, though he was released in August after struggling with back pain and a .180 average with Chunichi. The team will have six players with major-league experience.
How Qualified: As host nation, Australia received an automatic bid representing Oceania.

Olympic History: Did not qualify in 1984 or 1992. Went 1-2 in the pool play in 1988. Went 2-5 in pool play in 1996.

Players with U.S. Ties: Most of the team plays in the United States, highlighted by Seattle Mariners outfielder Chris Snelling, Mariners LHP Craig Anderson, and Montreal Expos RHP Shayne Bennett. Just about every significant Australian player in the United States is on this team, except for a few such as Atlanta Braves LHP Damian Moss, LA Dodgers RHP Luke Prokopec, and Baltimore Orioles RHP John Stephens (injured).

Notes: Australia is excited about baseball after the home team upset a lower-level Cuban team (not the same roster that would be representing Cuba in the Olympics) to win the Intercontinental Cup in Sydney in November 1999. Bennett said it was the most important moment in Australian baseball history. Some of that momentum was later lost when head coach Mike Young resigned over a dispute about the distribution of bonus money after the tournament. Deeble, an assistant under Young, stepped in to take over the team.

Outlook: Australia will have the home fans on its side, and the roster looks more formidable than some might have expected. The Aussies will battle for the fourth spot in the medal round, and it could come down to their game against Team USA, the last contest of the round robin.

<u>Roster</u>

Pitchers: Craig Anderson (Mariners), Grant Balfour (Twins), Tom Becker (Tigers), Shayne Bennett (Expos), Mark Ettles, Mark Hutton (Astros), Adrian Meagher, Mike Nakamura (Twins), Brad Thomas (Twins), David White.

Catchers: Michael Moyle, Dave Nilsson (Yankees), Gary White.

Infielders: Mathew Buckley, Adam Burton, Clayton Byrne, Paul Gonzalez, Ronny Johnson, Rodney Van Buizen (Dodgers), Glenn Williams (Blue Jays).

Outfielders: Grant McDonald, Glenn Reeves, Brett Roneberg (Marlins), Chris Snelling (Mariners).

CUBA

Head Coach: None (team will be led by a "technical commission" headed by Servio Borges and Benito Camacho).

Key Players: 3B Omar Linares continues to serve as the bastion of Cuban baseball, both physically and symbolically. RHP Jose Contreras, who went 30, 0.98 in the Pan American Games last summer and was on the 1996 Olympic staff, leads an imposing pitching staff. He and RHP Norge Vera will be tough for anyone to beat.

How Qualified: Won the 1999 Pan Am Games in Winnipeg, Manitoba, beating the United States, 5-1.

Olympic History: Boycotted the 1984 and '88 Olympics. Beat Chinese Taipei 11-1 for the gold medal in 1992. Beat Japan 13-9 for the gold medal in 1996.

Players with U.S. Ties: None.

Notes: In spite of continued defections, the Cuban machine keeps on rolling. When they send their best players, the Cubans still rarely lose in international competition. Their exhibition games against the Orioles last year showed the A team can play with anyone in the world. Borges, 52, managed the national team to three Pan American Games titles during the 1970s and 1980s. He has not been the leader of the national team since 1990, but this year's squad will be familiar to him: Nine members of the 1990 team are going to Sydney. Camacho has no significant experience on the international stage.

Outlook: Four years ago, defections and an aging roster had Cuba looking vulnerable. Another gold medal and four years later—in spite of the addition of professional players to the mix—everyone still regards Cuba as the team to beat.

Roster

Pitchers: Omar Ajete, Yovany Aragon, Jose Contreras, Jose Ibar, Pedro Luis Lazo, Maels Rodriguez, Lazaro Valle, Norge Luis Vera.

Catchers: Juan Manrique, Rolando Merino, Ariel Pestano.

Infielders: Danel Castro, Orestes Kindelan, Omar Linares, Oscar Macias, German Mesa, Antonio Pacheco, Gabrielle

Pierre, Antonio Scull.

Outfielders: Miguel Caldes, Yobal Duenas, Yasser Gomez, Javier Mendez, Luis Ulacia.

ITALY

Head Coach: Silvano Ambrosioni (1992, '96 Olympic coach).

Key Players: RHP Jason Simontacchi is a California native who has played in the Royals and Pirates organizations and enjoyed his best season in the independent Frontier League in 1998, going 10-2, 2.95 ERA. Catcher Chris Madonna, a University of North Carolina product, hit better than .400 in Italy's top professional league this summer.

How Qualified: Finished second in the 1999 European championship last August.

Olympic History: Did not qualify in 1988. Went 1-2 in the round robin in 1984. Went 1-6 in the round robin in 1992. Went 2-5 in the round robin in 1996.

Players with U.S. Ties: Most of Italy's key players are Americans of Italian descent. In addition to Simontacchi and Madonna, outfielder Dan DiPace and infielder Seth LaFera were born in the United States. Italian native 1B Claudio Liverziani played in the Mariners system for a couple of years, batting .251-8-64 in 1997 and '98 at Class A Wisconsin.

Notes: Italy's top professional league wrapped up its playoffs early to allow the best possible team to compete in Sydney. The team held out hope of getting Florida Marlins RHP Jason Grilli, who easily would have been the ace of the staff, but that didn't work out.

Outlook: Italy won two games in 1996, and that's about the best it can hope for this time around. The team is realistic about its chances and hopes to avenge its loss to the Netherlands last year and establish itself as the best team in Europe.

Roster

Pitchers: Fabio Betto, Roberto Cabalisti, Marc Cerbone, Emiliano Ginanneschi, Christian Mura, Daniel Newman,

Battista Perri, Diego Ricci, Jason Simontacchi, Michele Toriaco.

Catchers: Matteo Baldacci, Stefano Landuzzi, Chris Madonna.

Infielders: Alberto D'auria, Davide Dallospedale, Andrea Evangelisti, Seth LaFera, David Sheldon.

Outfielders: Luigi Carrozza, Francesco Casolari, Roberto de Franceschi, Dan DiPace, Daniele Frignani, Claudio Liverziani.

JAPAN

Head Coach: Kozo Otagaki.

Key Players: RHP Daisuke Matsuzaka, a 19-year-old who leads the Pacific League in wins and strikeouts, will head the pitching staff. The league's top two home-run hitters, 3B Norihiro Nakamura and 1B Nobuhiko Matsunaka, will power the offense. Matsunaka is among the league leaders in all three triple-crown categories.

How Qualified: Finished second in the Asian qualifying tournament last September.

Olympic History: Japan is the only nation to win a medal in every Olympic baseball tournament. Defeated the United States 6-1 to win Gold in 1984. Lost to the U.S. 5-3 in 1988 to take Silver. Defeated the U.S. 8-3 to win Bronze in 1992. Lost to Cuba 13-9 in 1996 to take Silver.

Players with U.S. Ties: None.

Notes: Like the United States, Japan has struggled with how to put together its best team for the Olympics without disrupting its major-league season. Pacific League owners were willing to let players go (and even considered suspending their season), and each team contributed one of its better players. Central League owners wavered on the question all season and eventually contributed just two token reserves. As a result, the team will feature just eight professional players. Even the coach of the team is from Japan's industrial league and not its major leagues.

Outlook: A team that many had regarded as a threat to

Cuba in the spring hasn't come together as expected, though it will still be formidable. Japan's hopes will ride on how much of an impact its pros have and how good the amateur players are. It should be in the group behind Cuba competing for a spot in the medal round.

Roster

Pitchers: Yoseikazu Doi, Masanori Ishikawa, Masato Kawano, Tomohiro Kuroki, Daisuke Matsuzaka, Toshiya Sugiuchi, Masanori Sugiura, Shunsure Watanabe, Akichika Yamada, Yuji Yoshimi.

Catchers: Shinnosuke Abe, Kosuke Noda, Fumihiro Suzuki.

Infielders: Jun Heima, Nobuhiko Matsunaka, Norihiko Nakamura, Osamu Nogami, Yoshinori Okihara, Yukio Tanaka.

Outfielders: Nodihiro Akahosei, Jun Hirose, Tomohiro Iizuka, Yoshihiko Kajiyama, So Taguchi.

KOREA

Head Coach: Ung-Yong Kim.

Key Players: RHP Min-Tae Chung will be the team's ace and likely is headed to Japan or the United States after the Olympics. Side-arming RHP Chang-Yong Lim will remind people of Arizona's Byung-Hyun Kim as the likely closer. 1B Seung-Yuop Lee hit 54 home runs in 132 games last season.

How Qualified: Beat Japan to win the Asian qualifying tournament last September.

Olympic History: Lost the bronze-medal game 3-0 to Taiwan in 1984. Lost the bronze-medal game 7-0 to Puerto Rico in 1988. Did not qualify in 1992. Went 1-6 in the round robin in 1996.

Players with U.S. Ties: None.

Notes: By shutting down its professional league, Korea will send the closest thing to a dream team, lacking only a few players who are playing in the United States. The pitching will be particularly imposing, and at least a few of the players on this pitching staff will show up in major-league organizations down the road. The hitters are talented but not accustomed to seeing the power pitching that Cuba and the United States will present. This should be a cohesive team, as the players have been in international tournaments together before.

Outlook: Korea came into the 1996 Games as a medal contender and left with a dismal 1-6 showing. Hopes are even higher this time around, especially after Korea beat Japan in the Olympic qualifier last year and in the Asian Games in 1998. Anything less than a medal in Sydney will be a disappointment.

Roster

Pitchers: Tae-Hyon Chong, Min-Tae Chung, Pil-Jung Jin, Soo-Kyung Kim, Dae-Song Koo, Seung-Ho Lee, Chang-Yong Lim, Sun-Dong Lim, Seok-Jin Park, Min-Han Son, Jin-Woo Song.

Catchers: Sung-Heon Hong, Kyung-Oam Park.

Infielders: Dong-Joo Kim, Han-Soo Kim, Tae-Gyun Kim, Seung-Yuop Lee, Jin-Man Park, Jong-Ho Park.

Outfielders: Sung-Ho Jang, Soo-Keun Jung, Ki-Tae Kim, Byung-Kyu Lee, Jae-Hong Park.

THE NETHERLANDS

Head Coach: Pat Murphy (Arizona State).

Key Players: Murphy coached the Dutch to the European championship and an Olympic berth in 1988 behind SS Robert Eenhoorn and OF Rikkert Faneyte. The former big leaguers helped lure Murphy back and form the backbone of the team. LHP Jurrian Lobbezoo is an important part of the pitching staff.

How Qualified: Beat Italy to win the 1999 European championship last August.

Olympic History: Did not qualify in 1984 or '92. Went 1-2 in pool play in 1988. Went 2-5 in pool play in 1996.

Players with U.S. Ties: Along with Eenhoorn and Faneyte, 2B Ralph Milliard (Padres) and former Yankees OF Hensley Meulens have big-league experience. LHP Radhames Dykhoff (Mets), 3B E.J. t'Hoen (Angels), and ace RHP Rob Cordemans also have extensive pro experience in the United States.

Notes: The Netherlands' team strikes a balance between native Dutch players and natives of the Netherlands Antilles. Murphy was unable to land potentially his biggest bat, 1B Randall Simon (Yankees). The nation's two most famous baseball products—retired right hander Bert Blyleven and Braves outfielder Andruw Jones—obviously won't play.

Outlook: Murphy said his club and European rival Italy are closely matched in talent and experience. Give the Dutch the edge, though, because of coaching. The Netherlands won't reach the medal round, but don't be surprised if Murphy throws a scare into one of the tournament's favorites.

Roster

Pitchers: Patrick Beljaards, Ken Brauckmiller, Rob Cordemans, Patrick De Lange, Radhames Dykhoff (Mets), Eelco Jansen, Ferenc Joneejan, Jurriaan Lobbezoo, Erik Remmerswaal, Orlando Strewart.

Catchers: Johnny Balentina, Mike Crouwel (Pirates), Chairon Isenia (Devil Rays).

Infielders: Sharnol Adriana (Pirates), Robert Eenhoorn, E.J. t'Hoen (Angels), Percy Isenia, Reily Legito, Ralph Milliard (Padres).

Outfielders: Jeffrey Cranston, Rikkert Faneyte (Pirates), Remy Maduro (Pirates), Hensley Meulens, Dirk Van t'Klooster.

SOUTH AFRICA

Head Coach: Raymond Tew.

Key Players: RHP Tim Harrell, who plays in the Dodgers organization, is the team's ace and threw 8 2/3 innings with nine strikeouts in a key win against Guam. OF Ian Holness is the team's best hitter.

How Qualified: Beat Guam in three games to win the best-of-five Africa/Oceania Olympic qualifier in December.

Olympic History: None. Not only is this the first Olympic appearance for South Africa, but it's also the first appearance for any African nation.

Players with U.S. Ties: Harrell and his brothers Brian and Richard were born in South Africa to American missionary parents. They returned to the USA for high school and college, attending Liberty Univ. 3B Paul Bell plays in the Brewers system. Holness and 1B Nick Dempsey played in the Dodgers organization a couple of years ago. Team captain Bles Kemp was a bullpen catcher for the double-A Jackson Generals in the mid-1990s.

Notes: South Africa was able to qualify because of Australia's automatic bid. Africa and Oceania play each other for a single bid, and with the Aussies out of the picture, South Africa upset Guam. Their coaching staff includes Jim Murphy, a Canadian native who has worked for the Rangers and Royals.

Outlook: Like the unknown upstart that sneaks into the NCAA basketball tournament, South Africa is just glad to be here. A win would be a shock. Baseball is still in its early developmental stages in South Africa, and this is regarded as a great opportunity to build the sport there.

Roster

Pitchers: Vaughn Berriman, Ashley Dove, Brian Harrell, Richard Harrell, Tim Harrell (Dodgers), Liall Mauritz, Carl Michaels, Glen Morris, Alan Phillips, Darryn Smith, Russell Van Niekerk.

Catchers: Darryl Gonsalves, Bles Kemp.

Infielders: Neil Adonis, Francisco Alfino, Paul Bell, Simon de la Rey, Nick Dempsey, Kevin Johnson, Morne MacKay.

Outfielders: Clint Alfino, Jason Cook, Errol Davis, Ian Holness.

Reading between the lines of *Baseball America*'s previews, it was clear that they saw Cuba, Korea, and Japan as the clearest threats to the United States' success. And if you asked anyone who followed international baseball closely, they would say the same thing.

Australia, Italy, the Netherlands, and South Africa were going to be fighting an uphill battle just to win a berth in the medal round.

Just prior to the team's gathering on the Gold Coast for training, *Baseball America* also reported that Korea had lost two of its top reserves when the players refused to take the Olympic drug test. Pitcher Cho Young-joon of Yonsei University and outfielder Lee Hyun-kon were taken off the team and replaced by Dongkook University outfielder Park Han-I and Dankook University pitcher Lee Seung-hak. Both players were apparently upset at not being picked as starters and did not show up for the testing, saying they were busy with training. The Korea Baseball Association, the governing body for amateur baseball in Korea, already had submitted urine samples for all the other players on the team.

In the Olympic qualifying tournament in Seoul, Cho dominated by striking out 17 and allowing just two hits in 12.2 innings pitched, and was widely considered the best amateur pitcher in Korea.

But the Koreans had high hopes to atone for a shockingly dismal 1-6 performance at the 1996 Games in Atlanta, when it was expected to contend for a medal but instead finished eighth among eight teams. Embarrassed by its play four years earlier, Korea shut down its major leagues to send its top professional players to Sydney. Of course, the contingent would not include U.S. major leaguers such as Byung-Hyun Kim of the Diamondbacks or Chan Ho Park of the Dodgers, nor would it have any players from the U.S. minor leagues.

Even so, Korea's strength remained its pitching, led by Hanwha Eagles left hander Dae-Song Koo and Hyundai Unicorns right hander Min-Tae Chung. Koo threw in the mid-90s with pinpoint control, and at least five U.S. teams had been scouting him. Chung won 20 games in 1999 and was expected to seek free-agent millions from U.S. or Japanese major-league teams after the 2000 Korean season ended.

Though they didn't have the Diamondbacks' Kim, Korea did have a side-arming closer who could give opponents fits. Right hander Chang-Yong Lim led the KBO with a 2.14 ERA and 38 saves in '99 for the Samsung Lions and had major-league potential.

Other top pitchers included Hyundai right hander Soo-Kyung Kim—the 1998 KBO rookie of the year—and Hanwha left hander Jin-Woo Song, who threw a no-hitter in KBO play earlier that season.

Their offense was led by Samsung Lions first baseman Senug-Yeop Lee, who in 1999 came within one home run of the Asian record of 55, set by Japan's Sadaharu Oh. Lee hit 54 homers, obliterating the KBO mark by 12, and also set new Korean standards for RBIs and walks. Not surprisingly, he was named the league MVP.

Doosan Bears third baseman Dong-Joo Kim also offered power. That year, he hit the longest homer in the history of the KBO, an estimated 160-meter (520-foot) shot that landed on top of the subway station in front of Seoul's Olympic baseball stadium.

Two outfielders, Lotte's Byung-Kyu Lee and Hyundai's Jae-Hong Park, were regular 30-homer hitters in the KBO. Lee finished second in the 1999 batting race with a .349 average, while clubbing 30 homers and stealing 31 bases.

Lee is the only hitter who was on the 1996 Olympic team, and he was one of the few Koreans to stand out in Atlanta. He ranked second on the club with a .375 batting average while tying for the lead with six RBIs.

Recently, the Koreans had the upper hand against its archrival, Japan, winning the 1998 Asian Games and the 1999 Olympic qualifying tournament for Asian teams. But winning a medal would be a first for Korea, which lost bronze-medal games to Taiwan in 1984 and Puerto Rico in 1988.

Meanwhile in Japan, officials of the two major-league circuits couldn't reach an accord to alter their regular-season schedules and send professional players to Sydney. Organizers feared the indecision could well cost Japan a chance at medaling.

Pacific League people (who like the designated hitter) wanted to suspend the regular season and have Japan's 12 pro clubs send their best players to the Games. Central League bosses (who hate the DH) came down adamantly against any delay and refused to let any star players leave in the middle of a hot pennant race.

The result was that only eight Japanese major leaguers, one All-Star from each of the six Pacific League teams and two token reserves from Central League clubs, joined a group of industrial leaguers and amateurs in Sydney.

Japanese Olympic team manager Kozo Otagaki (from Toshiba Electric of Japan's Industrial League) would be counting on Seibu Lions phenom Daisuke Matsuzaka, Chiba Lotte, Marines right hander Tomohiro "Johnny" Kuroki to anchor his pitching staff. PL home-run-title contenders Norihiro Nakamura of the Kintetsu Buffaloes and Nobuhiko Matsunaka of the Fukuoka Daiei Hawks supplied power to the offense. Shortstop Yukio Tanaka of the Nippon Ham Fighters and outfielder So Taguchi of the Orix BlueWave also would play key roles, with Tanaka most likely the DH.

The team could not get Yakult Swallows star catcher Atsuya Furuta or Yomiuri Giants ace Koji Uehara, but it had backup backstop Fumihiro Suzuki of the Chunichi Dragons and second-line Hiroshima Carp pitcher Masato Kawano.

Matsuzaka, the Pacific League leader with 16 wins in '99, topped the PL again in 2000 with 12 victories through September. His 129 strikeouts in 149 innings also led the league, his 4.36 ERA ranked fifth, and his fastball was regularly clocking in at 95 mph.

Nakamura left for Sydney with the Pacific League lead in homers (37) and RBI (106), while Matsunaka ranked second in both categories (33 and 103, respectively). Matsunaka batted cleanup on Japan's 1996 Olympic team, homering in both medal-round games. Overall, he finished second in Atlanta among all players with 16 RBI and tied for third with five homers in nine games.

The most recognizable industrial leaguer on the Olympic team was Nihon Life Insurance right hander Masanori Sugiura. Sugiura pitched Japan to an 11-2 upset win over Kris Benson and Team USA in the semifinals of the 1996 Olympics, then started again the next day in the gold-medal game versus Cuba.

Sugiura gave up five runs in 1 2/3 innings, receiving a no-decision as Cuba won 13-9.

Since there was no time difference between Tokyo and Sydney, all Olympic baseball tournament games involving the Japanese team were going to be televised live throughout Japan by NHK, the government TV network. High viewer ratings were expected, despite the fact that the Japanese public knew their nation could have fielded a much better team with more professionals, had the Central League leaders been more flexible.

Finally, an in-depth look at the Cuban team that would be competing in Sydney showed that they were still the heavy favorites.

One advantage the Cubans had over Team USA was that this 2000 team will have trained together for almost three months, and nine members of the roster had been together on the national team for more than a decade.

The question was whether they would come to play. Cuban teams occasionally looked as if they were sleepwalking, only to burst out in crucial games to win gold medals. This was going to be the last hurrah for many of Cuba's all-time greats. Would they respond to this last chance in the international spotlight?

Two things were more certain: The players and coaching staff were under tremendous pressure from the government to bring back a gold medal, and Cuba's knowledgeable and passionate fans would be watching and discussing every pitch.

The two aces of the Cuban team were right handers Norge Luis Vera and Jose Ariel Contreras. Both pitched in the two-game exhibition series against the Baltimore Orioles in 1999. Contreras gave up no runs and struck out 10 batters in eight innings of relief in Havana, while Vera gave up three runs in seven innings of relief in Baltimore.

Vera was the Serie Nacional MVP in '99, going 17-2 with a league-leading eight shutouts and a 0.97 ERA. He also added three victories in the postseason. Contreras, who pitched on the 1996 Olympic team, went 13-2, with a 1.24 ERA in '99.

Reliever Maels Rodriguez's fastball had been clocked at more than 100 mph and he consistently threw in the high 90s. In December, he had pitched the first perfect game in the 39-year history of Serie Nacional. Rodriguez was likely to start against lesser teams such as Italy, the Netherlands, or South Africa, and become a short reliever in the medal round.

Veteran right handers included Jose Ibar, Pedro Luis Lazo, and Ormari Romero; all had extensive international experience. Another right-handed option was Ciro Licea, an impressive young arm.

Left-hander Omar Ajete, who had been on the national team since the late 1980s and already had two Olympic gold medals, was one of the possible closers. The other was right hander Lazaro Valle, 37, a national team starter for several years who had been moved to a relief role. Left-hander Yosvani Perez was cut from the roster in July before being added right before the Cubans left for training.

Cuba had three outstanding defensive catchers to choose from. Ariel Pestano had caught at the Pan Am Games, while Juan Manrique had played on the national team for a decade and was on the 1996 Olympic squad. Rolando Merino was the Serie Nacional All-Star catcher in 1999.

On the infield, first baseman Orestes Kindelan, third baseman Omar Linares, and second baseman Antonio Pacheco all had started on Cuba's Olympic gold-medal winners. Kindelan was Cuba's career home-run leader; Pacheco, who had become the all-time Cuban hits leader, could be paired with his former double-play partner, German Mesa (shortstop). Mesa had been banned from baseball by the government in 1996, before being reinstated in 1998. His skills had dropped off a bit, though he remained a superb fielder.

Other candidates included first baseman Antonio Scull, second baseman Oscar Macias, and third baseman Gabriel Pierre, all of whom were 31 or older and were Cuban league All-Stars. The youngest infielder was Michael Enriquez, who set a Cuban record with 152 hits in 1998-99.

One surprise omission from the team was 21-year-old Yorelvis Charles, who hit .354 to win the Serie Nacional batting title and was the shortstop on the postseason All-Star team. But his 27 errors probably accounted for his absence.

In the outfield, All-Stars Yobal Duenas and Yasser Gomez would start in center and right field, respectively. Duenas had evolved into one of the island's top hitters and won the 1998-99 batting title with a .418 average.

Gomez was one of the rising stars of Cuban baseball, hitting for average, though not much power, and was a solid defender with a strong arm. Two-time gold medalist Luis Ulacia offered speed and experience as a member of the national team since the late 1980s.

12

POOL PLAY

There were two fields being used for the baseball competition in Sydney. The larger, main stadium was Homebush Bay, which seated approximately 10,000 and was situated directly in the center of Sydney Olympic Park, where most of the other main Olympic venues were located. The massive structure being used for the track and field events, and where the Opening Ceremonies were held, was within walking distance, as were the basketball arena and the indoor bicycling venue.

The secondary field was located a few miles away in New South Wales and was called Blacktown Baseball Park. Much smaller, Blacktown was the equivalent of a typical Division I American collegiate baseball stadium: a little more intimate, with seating for up to 5,000.

Both fields had been finely manicured by MLB turf maintenance expert Murray Cook and his staff prior to the Games beginning. Having the two venues allowed for four games to be played on a daily basis: two during the day and two at night, as both facilities had lights.

Done randomly, the Americans ended up with a fairly favorable schedule for pool play, where all eight teams would face each other in one game. The top four teams with the best win-loss records after eight games would move on to the medal round, where the top seed would face the fourth seed, while seeds two and three would meet one another in the second semifinal. The two winners of those games would meet for the gold medal, while the other two teams would play for bronze.

Team USA was slated to open their Olympic gold-medal quest on September 17 at 1:00 p.m. against Japan at Homebush Bay, as organizers saw the game as a great matchup to kick off the overall baseball competition. They would also be facing games the following three consecutive days against South Africa, the Netherlands, and Korea, before a scheduled day off for all teams on September 21.

Lasorda and crew would pick back up and prepare for their three other scheduled pool-play games on September 22-24 against Italy, Cuba, and the host country, Australia. Another offday on the 25th would precede the semifinals on the 26th and the medal games on the 27th.

And so on a gloriously sunny and bright afternoon in Sydney, Lasorda sent his ace to the mound—Ben Sheets—to face the ace from Japan: Daisuke Matsuzaka. It was slated to be a tremendous pitching matchup, as the media had predicted for several days leading up to the game that these two strong right handers would end up dueling one another. Keep in mind that throughout the entire Olympic baseball event, none of the teams or their officials would ever be publicly announcing who their starting pitchers would be in advance of games. This information was held back on purpose, in fear of the competition being able to mentally prepare and practice specific hitting drills or skills in advance, based on knowing whether they would be facing a right-handed or left-handed pitcher, or a soft thrower or hard thrower.

Also, the Olympic teams did not want to tip their hands as

to who their starting pitcher would be, all the way up until the official lineup cards were exchanged at home plate. This meant that a team could not stack their lineup with righty or lefty hitters, based on the opposing pitcher. Japan, Cuba, and Korea took it so far as to actually warm up both a right-handed and left-handed pitcher in the bullpen prior to games, so that the opposition could not switch around their batting order or starting lineup, after visualizing only one particular opposing pitcher throwing in the bullpen prior to a game.

Lasorda and Team USA were less concerned about this type of information making much of a difference in the outcome of games, but since none of the other teams were required to give this information out, USA Baseball didn't either. Even though all of Team USA's internal plans for their starting pitchers were lined up well in advance, they chose not to tell anyone their pitching order outside of their inner circle. This approach was the exact opposite of what they normally did back home in the American minor leagues, where pitching rotations are common knowledge for the opposition, the media, and the public.

September 17, 2000 – Homebush Bay
GAME ONE: USA (0-0) vs. Japan (0-0)

Team USA was the home team on this day, so Sheets walked to the mound to take the ball and throw the first pitch of the game and of the Olympics, for the United States.

"Man, I was so amped up and excited for that moment, I went out there and early on, I was trying to strike everybody out," said Sheets. "But after the first or second inning, I reminded myself that my pitch count was limited to 90, and I wasn't going to be striking all these guys out: They were pretty good contact hitters. Once I settled in, and let that be the case, then everything started falling into place and I just started battling their hitters one by one."

Lasorda had gone with a starting lineup of: 2B Abernathy, CF Wilkerson, LF Neill, RF E. Young, DH Cotton, 3B

Kinkade, 1B Mientkiewicz, C Jensen, and SS Everett. But just as Sheets had brought his good stuff, so had Matsuzaka. The two aces were putting on a show, but for fans who had come to see home runs and a lot of offense, they weren't getting any.

The 13,404 fans who attended the game in the Homebush Bay stands were treated to a pitchers' duel, in the second Olympic baseball game ever played with wooden bats. (In a game that started an hour before Team USA's tilt with Japan, Cuba had pounded South Africa 16-0 over at Blacktown.) Matsuzaka and Sheets matched mid-90s fastballs and nasty breaking pitches, dominating the first seven innings of play.

But finally in the bottom of the seventh, the Americans were able to break through, when Cotton tripled to lead off the inning and scored on a single by Kinkade to give Team USA their first lead. They got a second run when Mientkiewicz executed a hit-and-run moving Kinkade to third, and then Kinkade scored when Jensen bounced into a fielder's choice, to put Team USA ahead 2-0 going to the eighth inning.

Now with the lead, Lasorda lifted Sheets after seven scoreless innings because like all the hurlers on the USA staff, he was on a strict pitch count. Pitch counts were given to pitching coach Phil Regan by each pitcher's MLB club. Sheets was brilliant, though, throwing 91 pitches and striking out three without a walk.

Matsuzaka remained in the game, though, and Japan battled back for him. Left fielder So Taguchi tripled with one out in the eighth off USA reliever Shane Heams and then scored on a groundout to make it 2-1. After the Americans failed to score in the bottom half, the ball was given to closer Todd Williams, to try and preserve the 2-1 win.

But in the ninth, Norihiro Nakamura, who had hit 37 home runs that season for the Kintetsu Buffaloes, singled to lead off the frame. After Williams got the next two hitters on a strikeout and a fly out to left, he was one out away from clinching the game for Team USA.

Amazingly, this was the exact same scenario he had found himself in, standing on the mound in Winnipeg one year earlier. And in that instance, Williams had failed to close the victory, as Team USA ended up on the wrong end of a heartbreaking 7-6 loss.

Battling Jun Hirose for the final out, the Japanese infielder—on what amounted to a swinging bunt down the third-base line—reached first base, as Kinkade had to eat Hirose's slow grounder.

Now with the tying run at second base, Jun Heima followed with an almost identical grounder very slow up the third-base line. This time, Kinkade fielded the ball, but his throw to first base was wide of the bag, and although it was caught by Mientkiewicz, it allowed the tying run to score all the way from second, because the runner never hesitated rounding third base and had been going on contact with two outs.

Although he stranded the go-ahead runs on base and got Team USA back into the dugout in a 2-2 tie, Williams had come oh-so-close once again to nailing down the win, but had failed, just like in the opening game of the Pan Ams.

"That certainly deflated us a little bit," said Cotton. "The way Matsuzaka was pitching, we knew it would be tough to come back again and score."

Matsuzaka stayed on the mound, as he was still hitting 93-94 mph on the stadium's radar gun in the ninth inning at the 120-pitch mark. Team USA failed to score, and the game went into extra innings, just as their opening game at the Pan Ams in Canada had.

At that point, Ryan Franklin took over on the mound for the Americans and was just as stellar as Sheets had been. In fact, he may have been a bit better. The Seattle Mariners' farmhand retired the Japanese side in order in the top of the 10th, and when Team USA failed to score in the bottom half, he did so again in the 11th, 12th, and 13th innings as well.

The game had already become the longest in Olympic baseball history, when the Americans came to bat in the bottom of the 13th. And as unlikely as it might sound, Mike Neill again seized an opportunity to build on his legend in international baseball.

Neill had been 1-for-3 in the game with a single. But the Mariners' farmhand—who had come off the bench to hit the game-winning single in the 10th inning of the Pan Am semifinals against Mexico, thus qualifying the United States to compete in Sydney—knew how to capitalize on an opportunity under this sort of pressure. He already had the most significant base hit in USA Baseball history.

And on this day one year later, Neill finally ended the longest Olympic game since baseball became a medal sport, when he launched a dramatic, game-winning home run, a towering two-run shot to right field that gave Team USA a 4-2 walk-off victory.

Neill stood in the batter's box and admired his homer for a second before rounding the bases and being mobbed by his teammates. He sounded almost embarrassed by his emotion over the homer, which gave Team USA a win in its first-ever Olympic extra-inning game and its third victory in seven Olympic matchups with Japan.

"I wouldn't say anything about it was normal," said Neill, who hit the homer on a 3-2 pitch. "I got caught up in the moment. It was an unbelievable feeling, because I knew it was gone when I hit it. It was an intense game, and I'm glad it's over with. Last year's hit in the Pan Ams, there was more pressure, because if not for that, we wouldn't be here. But today was just an unbelievable atmosphere."

Neill's homer came off Japan's 19-year-old reliever Toshiya Sugiuchi, who had walked Brad Wilkerson to lead off the inning. The long, grueling at-bat included a two-minute delay when Neill's foul tip caught Japanese catcher Fumihiro Suzuki, and a smaller delay when Neill fouled a ball off his foot.

"After the wild pitch moved Wilkerson to second (a 1-2 pitch), I was looking for something inside I could pull, to at least move him to third," Neill said. "and I was looking fastball. I got both."

Lasorda, Sheets, and company had beaten one of the heavy favorites to medal and were off to an incredible start. "What was so great about that moment was that for the first time in a long time, is wasn't about me getting the win, or Todd getting the save," said Sheets. "It didn't matter, and it had been a long time since we had played a game when our stats didn't matter. In pro ball, all of that matters. You need to win for your stats and it's a dog-eat-dog world. So, that was the first time in a very long time that we all just wanted to win the game, and none of us cared how. We were all out there just battling for our country. When Neilly hit that ball over the wall, we all just went crazy, like kids do when they play in Little League."

The legendary Hall of Fame Italian-American skipper had gotten his first dose of the intensity of Olympic baseball and was loving every minute of it. He celebrated like Lasorda always had with the Dodgers, leaping up after Neill's game-winning homer and hugging with his players.

Afterwards, he commanded the media room, both while he was asked questions and when he wasn't. When asked about the atmosphere that day in Homebush Bay Stadium, Lasorda reminisced straight back to his glory days in Los Angeles.

"It felt like the seventh game of the playoffs (in 1988) with Orel Hershiser on the mound. I can't describe the joy I felt with this young man (Neill) hitting that home run. I was jumping up and down like it was a World Series game. I jumped when (Kirk) Gibson hit his home run (in the 1988 World Series) and now, but this is bigger. This is bigger than the Dodgers, bigger than Major League Baseball. We're doing this for America."

Lasorda was also very well aware of how important it was for his team to post a victory in their first game. "We needed that game. These guys are tremendous. They could've gotten down on themselves after (Japan) tied the game in the ninth, but they didn't. If you took six months to build a team with character, you couldn't come up with a better bunch."

And finally, when discussing the quality level of pitching that was on display that day, he wasn't shy. "If you don't like Ben Sheets, you don't like Christmas. He was just outstanding. Matsuzaka looks like he's 14 years old, but I told him after it was over that he pitched a great game. He reminds me of Hershiser, and our winning pitcher Franklin has a lot of Bulldog in him as well."

Ben Sheets throws the first pitch for Team USA at the 2000 Olympic Games, in the Americans' first game vs. Japan.

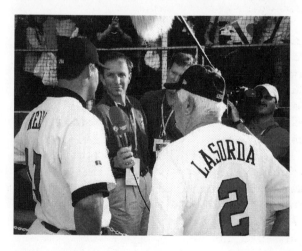

Mike Neill and Tommy Lasorda are interviewed by Ted Robinson of NBC Sports following Neill's game-winning two-run homer to beat Japan.

DAVID FANUCCHI

```
Japan 2 (0-1)                        USA 4 (1-0)
              AB  R  H RBI                        AB  R  H RBI
Taguchi lf     6  1  2  0      Abernathy 2b       6  0  2  0
Iizuka cf      2  0  0  0      Wilkerson cf/rf    5  1  0  0
Okihara ph/ss  3  0  0  1      Neill lf           4  1  2  2
Matsunaka 1b   4  0  2  0      E. Young rf        4  0  1  0
Akahoshi cf    2  0  0  0      Sanders cf         1  0  0  0
Nakamura 3b    4  0  2  0      Cotton dh          5  1  1  0
Nogami pr/2b   1  1  0  0      Kinkade 3b/1b      5  1  2  1
Tanaka ss/1b   4  0  0  0      Mientkiewicz 1b    4  0  2  0
Abe dh         4  0  0  0      Dawkins pr/ss      1  0  0  0
Kajiyama rf    3  0  0  0      Jensen c           5  0  0  1
Hirose ph/rf   2  0  1  0      Everett ss/3b      5  0  0  0
Heima 2b/3b    5  0  0  0      Sheets p           0  0  0  0
Suzuki c       5  0  0  0      Heams p            0  0  0  0
Matsuzaka p    0  0  0  0      Seay p             0  0  0  0
Sugiuchi p     0  0  0  0      Williams p         0  0  0  0
                               Franklin p         0  0  0  0

Totals......  45  2  7  1      Totals......     45  4 10  4

Score by innings:                    R  H  E
-----------------------------------------------------
Japan                000 000 011 000 0 - 2  7  1
USA                  000 000 200 000 2 - 4 10  3
-----------------------------------------------------
```

Note: None out, 0 runner(s) LOB when the game ended.

E - Suzuki, Kinkade, Mientkiewicz, Everett. DP - USA 1. LOB - Japan 7, USA 8. 3B - Taguchi, Cotton(1). HR - Neill(1). SH - Iizuka, Abe. SB - Neill(1), Dawkins(1). CS - Hirose. SO - Iizuka, Okihara, Akahoshi, Tanaka 2, Hirose, Heima, Suzuki, Cotton 2, Mientkiewicz, Dawkins, Jensen, Everett 2. BB - Tanaka, Wilkerson, Neill 2.

```
                IP   H  R ER BB SO WP BK HP IBB  AB BF Fly Gnd
Matsuzaka      10.0  8  2  2  2  5  0  0  0  0   37 39 15  9
Sugiuchi L 0-1  2.0  2  2  2  1  2  1  0  0  0    8  9  2  2

Sheets          7.0  4  0  0  0  3  0  0  0  0   24 26  3 14
Heams           0.1  1  1  1  0  0  0  0  0  0    2  2  1  0
Seay            0.2  0  0  0  0  0  0  0  0  0    2  2  0  2
Williams        1.0  2  1  0  0  1  0  0  0  0    5  5  1  0
Franklin W 1-0  4.0  0  0  0  1  4  0  0  0  0   12 13  4  4
```

WP - Sugiuchi.

Umpires - Home:Rosario 1st:Valdes 2nd:Leone 3rd:Castillo
Start: 12:30 pm   Time: 3:33   Attendance: 13,404

In other action on the first day of the baseball competition, the Cubans came out of the gates strong with a 16-0 win in seven innings against South Africa, falling a two-out error in the seventh inning short of a perfect game.

The Cubans, who used their top three starters and perhaps their top arm, settled for the Olympics' first no-hitter. Right hander Norge Luis Vera started and threw five innings, striking out six. Pan Am Games hero Jose Contreras threw an inning in relief, striking out one, while flame-throwing 20-year-old Maels Rodriguez and his 99-mph fastball struck out three in the seventh.

But the bid for a first-ever Olympic perfect game went by the boards when third baseman Gabrielle Pierre, who had entered the game in the seventh as a replacement for star Omar Linares, booted a grounder hit by Ian Holness, South Africa's best hitter.

Cuba rapped 18 hits against three South African pitchers, including three doubles and a triple by second baseman Oscar Macias. Right fielder Miguel Caldes had four hits, including a double, while second baseman Antonio Pacheco had three hits and a team-high three RBIs.

After what amounted to an incredible afternoon of baseball, Lasorda's squad headed back to their Village apartments to prepare for their second contest, which would take place the following night.

In the first of a pair of night games on Day One, The Netherlands stunned the host Australians in front of a vocal home crowd of more than 14,000 with a 6-4 win. The Dutch—who were led by Arizona State coach Pat Murphy—weren't considered a medal contender coming into the Games, but beat the favored Aussies with a combination of solid pitching by left-hander Jurriaan Lobbezzoo and power hitting.

Trailing 1-0 after a solo homer by Australian third baseman Paul Gonzalez, the Netherlands took the lead in the third inning with a power barrage against the Aussie ace, former big-league right hander Shayne Bennett. Dutch DH Sharnol Adriana, a former Blue Jays farmhand and Mexican Leaguer, drilled a three-run line-drive homer to left field, followed by a double by former big-leaguer Hensley "Bam Bam" Meulens that hit off the top of the wall in straightaway center field. Meulens scored on a line-drive double to left by Percy Insenia to give the Dutch a 4-1 lead.

They stretched their lead to 6-1 in the sixth and then held on for the victory. Lobbezoo pitched the first 7 1/3 innings, giving up four runs on seven hits. He was helped along by a pair of Dutch double plays and other nifty plays by the Netherlands' middle-infield combination of one-time major leaguers Robert Eenhoorn and Ralph Milliard.

Also, Korea got off to a nice start by downing Italy 10-2, outhitting the Italians 11-4. Seok-Jin Park picked up the win with 3 1/3 innings of hitless relief. Starter Sun-Dong Lim gave up both Italian runs, leaving when left fielder Dan DiPace homered to lead off the fourth. First baseman Ki-Tai Kim went 2-for-4 and drove in three runs to pace a balanced offensive attack for Korea. Catcher Kyong-Oan Park doubled twice and drove in a run as well. The Italians kept the game close for a while and were down 4-2 heading into the seventh before Korea broke the game open.

September 18, 2000 – Blacktown Park
<u>GAME TWO: USA (1-0) vs. South Africa (0-1)</u>

The Americans shifted to the smaller secondary ballpark in Blacktown and were scheduled to face South Africa next in a night game that would start at 7:00 p.m. Lasorda gave the ball to 6-foot-11 right hander Jon Rauch, who had pitched himself onto the American Olympic Team that summer with an outstanding minor-league season in the Chicago White Sox farm system.

Shaking off the expected Olympic jitters, Rauch gave up two hits and a run to the South Africans in the first inning, their first two hits and run scored in the competition. And so although he couldn't match Cuba, which had three pitchers combine to no-hit South Africa the previous day, after one half inning, Rauch and Team USA trailed the South Africans, who were playing only their second Olympic baseball game ever, 1-0.

But that lead was short-lived, as Team USA scored a pair of runs in the bottom half of the first. With one out, Brad Wilkerson tripled on a fly ball to right that should have been caught, the first of several South African fly-ball miscues. One out later, Ernie Young walked, and Cotton ripped a 3-2 pitch just inside the first-base line for a two-run double, giving Team USA a 2-1 lead.

In the second, *Baseball America*'s 2000 Minor League Player of the Year (Rauch) began to steady himself on the mound. After surrendering a leadoff single, he retired the next three batters and got the Americans back into the dugout.

South African starter Liall Mauritz was hurt by his own wildness and poor defense as Team USA then stretched its lead. The Americans turned four hits, a hit batsman, an error, and a wild pitch into five runs in the second. Cotton again had the inning's big hit, a two-run single that put Lasorda and company on top 7-1. It came after South African center fielder Jason Cook dropped Neill's routine fly ball, which should have been the third out of the inning.

From that point on, Rauch only made one other mistake, hitting a batter with a pitch. He finished with 13 strikeouts, fanning seven of eight batters in the fifth and sixth innings. Rauch fell one short of the Team USA Olympic record for strikeouts in a game, set in 1992 by left-hander B.J. Wallace. But after that first inning, Rauch wasn't thinking records. He was thinking win.

"I was still a little shaky in the second inning," said Rauch. "I was relying a little too much on my fastball, and I was a little excited. I had to settle down and focus and get back to what I do best, which is throw strikes. It took me a while to settle down and get in a rhythm with (Pat) Borders, but once I did that, I threw well."

Rauch didn't walk a batter and ended up giving up only three hits, and Team USA's offense produced the expected rout after all. Cotton tied a Team USA Olympic record with five RBIs, and left fielder Mike Neill hit his second home run in as many days. While not as dramatic, his solo shot in the bottom of the sixth gave Team USA the 10-run cushion it needed to end the game early, due to the international 10-run mercy rule.

Cotton got his fifth RBI of the game in the fourth with a bases-loaded groundout, pushing him to the Team USA RBIs-in-a-game record. His five was the most for Team USA since baseball became a medal sport. Outfielder Oddibe McDowell had five in a game in 1984, when baseball was still a demonstration sport.

And while most players weren't talking much about individual records just yet, for Cotton, his Olympic spot and accomplishments after two games (he tripled and scored Team USA's first run against Japan) were worth noting.

"The record really does mean everything," said Cotton, who had been jockeying back and forth with Devil Rays farmhand Jim Buccheri that summer as the minor-league player with the most appearances without ever having played in the major leagues. "Hopefully, the Olympics will fast-forward my career," said the current version of Crash Davis. "I'm getting a chance to show teams in the U.S. and overseas that I can play this game, and hopefully help us win a gold medal, too."

MIRACLE ON GRASS

```
South Africa 1 (0-2)                USA 11 (2-0)

                 AB  R  H RBI                        AB  R  H RBI
Bell ss           3  0  0  0      Abernathy 2b        2  1  1  1
Alfino, C. lf     3  0  0  0      Everett ph/ss       1  0  0  0
Holness rf        3  1  1  0      Wilkerson cf/rf     3  3  2  0
Dempsey 1b        3  0  1  1      Neill lf            3  3  1  1
Cook cf           3  0  0  0      E. Young rf         1  2  1  1
Kemp c            3  0  1  0      Sanders cf          1  0  0  0
Adonis dh         3  0  0  0      Cotton dh           4  0  2  5
Alfino, F. 3b     2  0  0  0      Kinkade 3b          2  0  0  0
Johnson 2b        2  0  0  0      Burroughs 3b        1  0  0  1
Mauritz p         0  0  0  0      Mientkiewicz 1b     3  1  1  0
Dove p            0  0  0  0      Borders c           3  0  1  0
                                  Dawkins ss/2b       2  1  0  0
                                  Rauch p             0  0  0  0

Totals......     25  1  3  1      Totals......      26 11  9  9

Score by innings:                       R  H  E
-------------------------------------------
South Africa             100 000 0  -   1  3  1
USA                      250 301    -  11  9  1
-------------------------------------------
```

E - Cook, Neill. LOB - South Africa 4, USA 4. 2B - Abernathy(1), Cotton(1), Borders(1). 3B - Wilkerson(1). HR - Neill(2). SH - Abernathy, Burroughs. SB - Abernathy(1), Wilkerson(1), Mientkiewicz(1). K - Bell 2, Alfino, C. 2, Holness 2, Dempsey, Cook 2, Adonis, Alfino, F. 2, Johnson, Neill, Sanders, Cotton, Kinkade, Dawkins. BB - Wilkerson, Neill, E. Young 2.

```
              IP   H  R ER BB SO  WP BK HP IBB  AB BF Fly Gnd
Mauritz L 0-1 3.0  7 10  7  3  3   2  0  1  0   16 21  2   4
Dove          3.0  2  1  1  1  2   0  0  0  0   10 12  5   2

Rauch W 1-0   7.0  3  1  0  0 13   1  0  1  0   25 26  3   6
```

WP - Mauritz 2, Rauch. HBP - by Mauritz (Dawkins), by Rauch (Alfino, F.). Mauritz faced 3 batters in the 4th.

Umpires - Home:Rouse 1st:Leone 2nd:Koyama 3rd:Hsieh
Start: 6:30 pm   Time: 2:01   Attendance: 3,474

Team USA improved to 2-0 with the victory and were slated to play their third game (and second consecutive at Blacktown) the next night, when they would face the Netherlands. The Dutch, who dropped to 1-1 with a 9-2 loss to Japan earlier in Day Two action, were the only team to beat the Americans during its exhibition schedule, defeating Rauch 4-3.

"It's important that we are off to a 2-0 start, but every night is important," Cotton said. "That's what's different about this tournament. The Netherlands beat us in the exhibition, so we know that's going to be a tough game. We have to win all of them here to accomplish what we set out to do: win a gold medal."

In the day game at Blacktown, Cuba was less than perfect, having to come from behind to beat Italy, 13-5. The underdog Italians (0-2) spotted Cuba (2-0) three runs in the first two innings before rallying with a five-run third against Cuban starter Yovany Aragon, who wasn't considered one of Cuba's top starters. Italy had six hits and took advantage of an error by Cuban center fielder Yobal Duenas to score its five runs.

Aragon gave way to Cuba's No. 4 starter, right hander Jose Ibar, who gave up one unearned run in 5 2/3 innings. Ibar struck out eight and gave up just two hits.

Cuba tied the game in the bottom of the third with a pair of runs as Duenas doubled to lead off and scored on a double by first baseman Orestes Kindelan, who had three hits and a game-high four RBIs. Kindelan scored the tying run on a single by DH Oscar Macias, who also had three hits. They then took the lead in the fourth on a two-run homer by Duenas, who had three hits and three RBIs, and put the game away with six runs in the fifth.

Over at Homebush Bay, the host Australians pulled off somewhat of an upset when they got by Korea, 5-3. Australia bounced back from their opening game loss to the Dutch, thanks to a pair of Mariners farmhands and a big hit by team captain Dave Nilsson, giving the home fans something to cheer about.

Nilsson, the former 1999 Milwaukee Brewers All-Star, tied the game with a run-scoring double in the seventh, and left fielder Glen Reeves had the game-winning hit, a two-run double in the eighth, giving the Aussies just their Olympic baseball game victory ever, and their second against Korea. Both teams were now 1-1 in the 2000 Games.

Outfielder Chris Snelling and left-hander Craig Anderson, both in the Seattle organization, played key roles for the Aussies. Snelling blunted Korea's momentum when he keyed a double play in the sixth inning, making a catch in right field and gunning down a runner at the plate to end a bases-loaded, one-out rally.

Anderson pitched 4 1/3 innings in relief of left-hander Brad Thomas of the Minnesota Twins organization, and got the win, holding Korea in check while his teammates rallied. He gave up only one hit and three walks while striking out two. Right hander Grant Balfour, also with the Twins, walked the leadoff man in the ninth but recovered for the save. Korea suffered a significant injury to star first baseman Lee Seung-Yuop, the nation's home-run champion, as he was hobbled by a sore back and ankle.

"I think it was a big hit, not just for me but for the team," said Nilsson, who had struck out looking with the bases loaded earlier in the game. "Obviously I had a chance to blow it open earlier and didn't come through. I got the same pitch that I struck out on before. This win gets us back on track, especially a win against one of the better teams here."

Team USA and Cuba emerged as the only undefeated teams left in the Olympic baseball tournament after the first two days, when Japan knocked off the Netherlands, 10-2. Both teams were now 1-1 and in a four-way tie for third place.

Japan jumped on the Netherlands quickly, scoring one in the first, three in the second, and three more in the fourth. The Japanese had 17 hits, including four by DH Nobuhiko Matsunaka, who had a homer and two RBIs. Third baseman Norihiro Nakamura had three hits, including a homer and three RBIs.

On the mound, left-hander Yuji Yoshimi went five solid innings, giving up three hits and one run while walking three and striking out nine. Dutch right fielder Dirk Van t'Klooster knocked in both Dutch runs, with a solo homer and a RBI single. The top five hitters in the Netherlands' order combined to go 0-for-13 with eight strikeouts.

September 19, 2000 – Blacktown Park
<u>GAME THREE: USA (2-0) vs. THE NETHERLANDS (1-1)</u>

Lasorda and Regan gave the ball to right hander Kurt Ainsworth, and the young Louisiana native admitted prior to the game that he would be starting what he called the most important game of his life.

In another evening start, Team USA would face Dutch starter Rob Cordemans, a former Indian River (Fla.) Junior College star and the owner of both Olympic victories in the Netherlands' history. Cordemans featured an 85-87 mph fastball, but he mostly attacked Team USA on this night with off-speed breaking balls and changeups.

Playing as the visiting team, the Americans jumped on Cordemans from the start as Brent Abernathy doubled to lead off the game. Brad Wilkerson followed by putting runners at the corners with a bunt single, and one out later both runners came home on a double to left field by Ernie Young, giving Team USA the early 2-0 advantage.

Ainsworth, who, like Rauch the night before, had to be fighting a little bit of nerves, gave up his only run in the bottom of the first, when the Dutch loaded the bases with no outs on two singles and a walk. But Ainsworth then got a pair of ground balls, one for a force play, the other a 4-6-3 double play, to escape further damage.

Young, who would have been playing for Memphis in the triple-A World Series if he weren't Team USA's cleanup hitter, added a solo homer in the third to give Ainsworth a 3-1 lead. From there, Ainsworth did alright with what he had. The Netherlands' hitters were sitting on his curveball, which was usually his strikeout pitch. So, starting in the third inning, Ainsworth went almost exclusively to his 92-93 mph fastball, moving it in and out of the strike zone. He estimated that he threw his fastball on more than 80 percent of his pitches and retired 18 of the last 22 batters he faced.

Ainsworth wasn't dominant, but he was plenty good. He gave up just one run on five hits in 6 2/3 innings, while walking two and striking out three, including the last batter he faced, before being lifted after having thrown 88 pitches.

"It wasn't a problem for me coming out of the game, because Tim (Young) needed some work, and it was good for him to come in and face a left-handed hitter, because that's what his role was going to be," said Ainsworth. "I was going to be the one hardest on myself anyway, because I thought I could have pitched better."

Team USA added to their lead with single runs in the sixth, seventh, and eighth innings, with Wilkerson adding a solo home run and Young keying another rally with a base hit.

"I hit a fastball away for the home run and didn't try to do too much with it, just hit it where it was pitched," said Young, whose blast went out to straightaway right field. "After a couple of innings, Cordemans was throwing his changeup a lot more. We had to stay back because he had a lot of guys off balance. We beat a good team: They beat us in the exhibition game. So it was important that we came back and won this one. We can't look past any team. We have to win every game, and it doesn't matter who we play."

With the win, Team USA moved to 3-0 to tie Cuba for the best record in the Olympic tournament. The Americans were slated to play Korea the next night at Homebush Bay, presumably with right hander Roy Oswalt ready to take the mound.

Oswalt would have a high standard to match after Ainsworth's start, the third dominating effort by Team USA's talented pitching staff. Sheets threw seven shutout innings against Japan; Rauch struck out 13 in a blowout win against South Africa, and Ainsworth had made it three in a row against the Dutch.

And in the game against the Netherlands, the offense finally began to click. It didn't matter who played well for Team USA; they were getting the proverbial different hero every night. While Mike Neill, who was announced at the plate in his first at-bat as the tournament's leading home run hitter (he had two), went 0-for-4, Young had his best game so far, and Wilkerson went 2-for-5 with a solo homer in the sixth. First baseman Doug Mientkiewicz also had his best game, driving in a pair of runs with a double and a sacrifice fly. Abernathy also added two hits and continued to form a formidable defensive combination with shortstop Adam Everett.

"This was the best game we've played as a team," Young said. "We put everything together today, with power, timely hits, and error-free baseball. That's important. Now we just have to keep doing it."

Team USA manager Tommy Lasorda discusses his team's chances in Sydney with *NBC Nightly News* anchor Tom Brokaw.

MIRACLE ON GRASS

```
USA 6 (3-0)                         The Netherlands 2 (1-2)
               AB  R  H  BI                         AB  R  H  BI
Abernathy 2b    4  1  2  0          Faneyte cf       4  1  1  0
Wilkerson cf    5  2  2  1          Milliard 2b      4  0  1  0
Neill lf        4  0  0  0          Adriana dh       3  1  1  1
E. Young rf     4  2  3  3          Muelens lf       4  0  2  1
Cotton dh       1  1  0  0          Isenia, P. 1b    4  0  0  0
Kinkade 3b      3  0  0  0          Eenhoorn ss      4  0  0  0
Dawkins ss      0  0  0  0          Balentina c      3  0  0  0
Mientkiewicz 1b 2  0  1  2          Brauckmiller ph  1  0  0  0
Jensen c        4  0  0  0          van t'Klooster rf 2 0  2  0
Everett ss/3b   3  0  0  0          t'Hoen 3b        3  0  1  0
Ainsworth p     0  0  0  0          Maduro ph        1  0  0  0
T. Young p      0  0  0  0          Cordemans p      0  0  0  0
Heams p         0  0  0  0          Jongejan p       0  0  0  0
Williams p      0  0  0  0          Jansen p         0  0  0  0

Totals......   30  6  8  6          Totals......    33  2  8  2

Score by innings:                     R  H  E
---------------------------------------------
USA                  201 001 110  -   6  8  0
The Netherlands      100 000 010  -   2  8  0
---------------------------------------------
```

DP - USA 2, Holland 1. LOB - USA 5, Holland 7. 2B - Abernathy(2), E. Young(1), Mientkiewicz(1). 3B - van t'Klooster. HR - Wilkerson(1), E. Young(1), Adriana. SH - Mientkiewicz. K - Wilkerson 2, Neill 2, Kinkade 2, Milliard, Balentina, t'Hoen 2. BB - Abernathy, Cotton 2, Kinkade, Mientkiewicz, Everett, Adriana, van t'Klooster.

```
              IP   H  R ER BB SO  WP BK HP IBB  AB BF Fly Gnd
Ainsworth W 1-0 6.2 5  1  1  2  3  0  0  0  0   23 25  3 12
T. Young      0.1  0  0  0  1  1  0  0  0  0    1  2  0  0
Heams         1.0  2  1  1  0  0  0  0  0  0    5  5  3  0
Williams      1.0  1  0  0  0  0  0  0  0  0    4  4  0  3

Cordemans L 0-1 6.1 6  4  4  4  5  1  0  0  0   24 28  9  4
Jongejan      0.2  2  2  2  0  0  0  0  1  0    3  4  0  1
Jansen        2.0  0  0  0  2  1  1  0  0  0    3  6  2  1
```

WP - Cordemans, Jansen. HBP - by Jongejan (Cotton). PB - Jensen.

Umpires - Home:Leone 1st:Koyama 2nd:Begg 3rd:McCabe
Start: 6:30 pm   Time: 2:42   Attendance: 3,352

The host country Australia saw their upset bid go by the boards, squandering a 3-1 lead in a 7-3 defeat to medal-favorite Japan, in front of 13,903 fans, the biggest crowd yet in the competition. Right hander Tomohiro Kuroki, who pitched for the Chiba Lotte Marines in Japan's major leagues, shut down the Aussies at Homebush Bay after giving up a three-run homer to 1999 major-league All-Star catcher David Nilsson.

Japan moved to 2-1, having rebounded nicely with wins against the Netherlands and Australia after losing to Team USA in the first game.

Australia entered the tournament touted as having one of the best pitching staffs, but none of its starters had performed well, and the Aussies clearly missed Dodgers right hander Luke Prokopec, who got his first major-league win just two days prior.

In this game, it was former major-league right hander Mark Hutton who labored through five innings for Australia, giving up three runs. But reliever Mark Ettles, another former major-league righty, couldn't hold the tie as Japan got four runs in the sixth. Catcher Fumihiro Suzuki had the go-ahead hit, an RBI single, which was followed by a three-run homer to left by leadoff-hitting shortstop Yoshinori Okihara.

Okihara led all hitters with four hits, including a double to go with his homer, and four RBIs. Left fielder So Taguchi, moved from the leadoff spot to the No. 3 hole, went 2-for-4 with two RBIs.

Nilsson continued his fine Olympic performance despite Australia's 1-2 start. His homer gave him five RBIs in the three games, and he was hitting .500 (6-for-12) overall for the tournament. But the rest of the lineup was powerless against Kuroki, who worked from the stretch the entire game. Kuroki gave up the three runs in eight innings, giving up just five hits while walking three and striking out nine.

Wrapping up play on Day Three were the two least likely medal contenders, who saved their best pitchers for their matchup. Italy (1-2) picked up their first win behind former

American independent league right hander Jason Simontacchi, getting the better of it in a seven-inning, 13-0 triumph over South Africa, which fell to 0-3.

Simontacchi pitched six strong innings, giving up one walk and six hits while striking out seven. The Italians got their first victory of the tournament by drawing eight walks and bashing 10 hits, including home runs by Franceso Casolari and Alberto D'auria. They did it against South Africa's top pitcher, right hander Tim Harrell of the Los Angeles Dodgers organization, who walked four and gave up six runs in 3 1/3 innings.

Former Mariners' farmhand Claudio Liverziani, playing right field, drew three walks, stole a base, and scored twice to help set the table for Italy, and former University of North Carolina and independent league catcher Chris Madonna drove in three runs with a single and sacrifice fly. Former American minor leaguer David Sheldon, the Italian third baseman, went 2-for-4 with a double and two RBIs.

September 20, 2000 – Homebush Bay
GAME FOUR: KOREA (1-2) vs. USA (3-0)

After three games, Lasorda was as happy as he could be. His squad had won a dramatic opening game over Japan and then took care of the business they should have in a pair of fairly routine wins over South Africa and the Netherlands. His starting pitching had lived up to the hype as being the strength of his roster, and the fourth member of that group was going to get his chance against Korea.

Just two months prior, USA Baseball Olympic Team General Manager Bob Watson had found the virtually unknown Roy Oswalt pitching in a double-A game in Round Rock, Texas. Now, the small-statured native of tiny Weir, Mississippi was about to be handed the ball for Team USA in the Olympic Games.

Oswalt was lined up for the start against Korea, because of the strength of the opponent. The Koreans were considered to be a medal contender, perhaps just a slight notch below

Japan in talent level.

Korea was coming off a heartbreaking loss to Cuba in which they had a very legitimate chance to beat the international powerhouse for the first time in Olympic history. But they let the game slip through their hands and lost 6-5.

In the exhibition game the two teams played on the Gold Coast, the Koreans had used most of their hardest throwers against the Americans, to see what they could do. And American minor leaguers know exactly what to do with fastballs: They hit them very hard. Team USA won that practice game 15-0, behind a lot of offense and the arm of Sheets.

So, when it counted, Korea decided to send soft-throwing submarine right hander Tae-Hyon Chong to the mound as their starting pitcher, to face Oswalt. And the strategy worked. Oswalt and Chong engaged in a classic pitchers' duel, Oswalt blowing away the Korean hitters with a mix of fastballs, sinkers, and changeups, while Chong kept the Team USA hitters off balance all night by slinging side-armed, slow curve balls and sliders that the Americans could never time very well.

The two righties matched zeroes through seven innings before each came out of the game, Chong allowing just six hits with five strikeouts, while Oswalt allowed seven hits with six strikeouts and a pair of walks, while throwing 100 pitches.

Oswalt was helped primarily by the left side of his defense. Shortstop Adam Everett handled five chances flawlessly, none of them routine plays. And in the seventh, he made a pair of splendid diving plays to his left to short-circuit a Korean rally.

But the play of the night belonged to third baseman Mike Kinkade, who had made a crucial error that prolonged the Japan game. Against Korea, he more than atoned. Oswalt loaded the bases in the sixth on two walks and a single by Kim Dong-Joo. With an 0-2 count, Korean shortstop Park Jin-Man lashed a one-hopper to Kinkade's right. He stepped, dived, and stopped the ball, tagged third base and threw to first, for the inning-ending double play.

Lefty Chris George then came on in relief of Oswalt to start the top of the eighth and retired the first two batters he faced, before hitting Korean designated hitter Byung-Kyu Lee with a pitch. Lasorda then turned to Ryan Franklin out of the bullpen and the move worked well, as Franklin struck out Han-Soo Kim to end the threat.

Korean reliever Jin-Woo Song was then brought on to replace Chong to start the bottom of the eighth, and it was a welcome sight for the Americans. They had struggled all night to get any sort of offense going off the soft-tossing Chong, and the change of pace turned out to be exactly what Team USA needed.

With one out, Mike Neill connected on a line-drive single to right field, and Ernie Young followed by coaxing a walk, putting runners at first and second base. Song then departed the game in favor of reliever Pil-Jung Jin, who was showing a 93-mph fastball. Jin managed to strike out pinch-hitter Anthony Sanders, but walked Mike Kinkade on a 3-2 pitch to load the bases. That set the stage for Doug Mientkiewicz.

And in a scoreless tie game in the bottom of the eighth inning, Mientkiewicz just needed one swing. No foul liners or off-balance misses. Just one short, quick, graceful swing, with the follow-through only a sweet left-handed stroke can produce.

With one swat at a 3-2 fastball, Mientkiewicz broke open a tense contest, crushing a Jin fastball deep into the Sydney night for a grand slam, giving the Americans a 4-0 lead.

"The pitch I hit was the first hittable pitch he threw me," Mientkiewicz said. "I'm not big on swinging early in the count in that situation. He was the one in trouble, not me. He couldn't walk in the winning run, so I was just telling myself to concentrate and don't chase a bad pitch. I played with it a little, moved up in the batter's box, then back, then up. On strike two I was questioning the call, and I was kind of in shock. I thought to myself, 'Well, if I'm a pitcher, I'm coming right back in there.'"

Jin did, and Mientkiewicz drilled the pitch into almost the

same place that Neill hit his game-winning homer in Team USA's 13-inning victory over Japan.

"I was at second base, so I had a perfect angle to see the pitch," Young said. "Doug was seeing the ball really clearly, because he laid off some tough pitches to hit. I knew the way he was seeing it, he was going to have a productive at-bat, and he didn't miss the fastball. The guy had to challenge him, with a full count."

Now ahead in the game by four runs, Lasorda turned to left-handed reliever Tim Young to try and secure the victory by getting the final three outs in the ninth. But Young walked the first batter he faced, so Lasorda wasted no time in going to his closer Todd Williams, who came in and secured the shutout.

As ecstatic as Mientkiewicz was, he knew that it was ultimately a team effort that had gotten the job done that night.

"If Kinkade doesn't make that double play, we lose," said Mientkiewicz, who had pumped his fist as he squeezed Kinkade's throw to first base. "I don't get my chance to shine. But I have a great still-frame memory of that moment, running up the line with my finger in the air, and (first-base coach) Reggie Smith high-fiving me. That was one of the longest home runs I've ever hit in my life."

Kinkade did make the play, Mientkiewicz hit the grand slam, and Team USA now stood at 4-0. One more victory would almost certainly clinch a spot in the four-team medal round.

MIRACLE ON GRASS

```
Korea 0 (1-3)                       USA 4 (4-0)
              AB  R  H  BI                        AB  R  H  BI
Lee, BK  lf    5  0  2  0     Abernathy   2b       4  0  1  0
Park, JH 2b    5  0  1  0     Wilkerson   cf       4  0  1  0
Park, Jae rf   3  0  0  0     Neill       lf       4  1  1  0
Kim, KT  1b    4  0  0  0     E. Young    rf       3  1  1  0
Lee      dh    2  0  0  0     Cotton      dh       3  0  0  0
Jang     pr    0  0  0  0     Sanders     ph       1  0  0  0
Kim, HS  3b    2  0  0  0     Kinkade     3b       3  1  0  0
Kim, DJ  3b    2  0  1  0     Mientkiewicz 1b      4  1  3  4
Park, JM ss    3  0  1  0     Borders     c        4  0  1  0
Hong     c     4  0  1  0     Everett     ss       3  0  0  0
Jung     cf    2  0  1  0     Oswalt      p        0  0  0  0
Chong    p     0  0  0  0     George      p        0  0  0  0
Song     p     0  0  0  0     Franklin    p        0  0  0  0
Jin      p     0  0  0  0     T. Young    p        0  0  0  0
                              Williams    p        0  0  0  0

Totals......  32  0  7  0     Totals......        33  4  8  4

Score by innings:                     R  H  E
-----------------------------------------------
Korea                   000 000 000 - 0  7  2
USA                     000 000 04  - 4  8  0
-----------------------------------------------
```

E - Kim, KT, Chong. DP - USA 1. LOB - Korea 11, USA 7. 2B -
Abernathy(3). HR - Mientkiewicz(1). SH - Jung. SB - Wilkerson,
E. Young. K - Lee, BK 2, Park, JH, Park, Jae 2, Kim, KT, Lee,
Kim, HS, Kim, DJ, Neill, E. Young, Sanders, Kinkade, Everett 2.
BB - Park, Jae, Lee, Park, JM, Jung, E. Young, Kinkade.

```
              IP   H  R ER BB SO  WP BK HP IBB  AB BF Fly Gnd
Chong        7.0   6  0  0  0  5   0  0  0  0   28 28  6   9
Song  L 0-1  0.1   1  2  2  1  0   0  0  0  0    2  3  0   1
Jin          0.2   1  2  2  1  1   0  0  0  0    3  4  0   1

Oswalt       7.0   7  0  0  2  6   0  0  0  1   26 29  4  10
George       0.2   0  0  0  0  1   0  0  1  0    2  3  1   0
Franklin W 2-0 0.1 0  0  0  0  1   0  0  0  0    1  1  0   0
T. Young     0.0   0  0  0  1  0   0  0  0  0    0  1  0   0
Williams     1.0   0  0  0  1  1   0  0  0  0    3  4  1   1
```

HBP - by George (Lee).

Umpires - Home:Koyama 1st:Hsieh 2nd:Bellrose 3rd:Poulton
Start: 7:30 pm   Attendance: 13818

Over at Homebush Bay, the Cubans pulled off their second straight come-from-behind win in even more dramatic fashion than their first. Pedro Luis Lazo struck out Korean hitting hero Park Jae-Hung on a full count in the bottom of the ninth, preserving Cuba's 6-5 win. The victory moved Cuba to 3-0 in the Olympic tournament, joining the United States as the only undefeated teams. Korea fell to 1-2.

After trailing 4-0, Cuba rallied for a 5-4 lead, then broke a 5-5 tie in the eighth on a solo home run by catcher Juan Manrique, off right hander Son Min-Han.

The Koreans took a 2-0 lead against Cuban ace right hander Jose Contreras in the first inning. Surprisingly, Contreras gave up three runs (two earned) on four hits in only 2.0 innings, walking one, striking out two, and hitting a batter. Korea stretched the lead to 4-0 through five innings as Park went 3-for-5 with a home run and three RBIs. Korean leadoff man Lee Byung-Kyu also had a big day, going 3-for-5 with one RBI and two runs.

Cuba's five-run sixth inning started when its veteran No. 3 and No. 4 hitters, third baseman Omar Linares and Orestes Kindelan, walked to lead off the inning. Second baseman Antonio Pacheco doubled to score both runners, then scored on Oscar Macias' double, making it 4-3. Kim was relieved by Seok-Jin Park, who gave up a single to right fielder Miguel Caldes to put runners on the corners. Then with two outs and runners at second and third, center fielder Yobal Duenas slapped a two-run single to give Cuba the lead.

After the Cubans had rallied, Korea tied the game on Park's solo homer off Lazo, who got the win by pitching the last 3 1/3 innings for Cuba. He struck out three while giving up one run and three hits. Korean starter Kim Soo-Kyung got off to a fast start before tiring. He pitched five innings, walking five and striking out five while giving up three runs.

Amazingly, the game played between the United States and Korea at Homebush Bay stadium wasn't even the most memorable of the day. That's because earlier that afternoon, the impossible, the unthinkable, happened.

In the biggest upset in Olympic baseball history, the Netherlands (2-2) defeated two-time defending gold-medal champion Cuba, 4-2, handing the Cubans (3-1) their first defeat ever in 22 Olympic baseball games.

Perhaps it shouldn't have come as such a surprise though, since the Cubans had shown some vulnerability in their first three games, trailing in a contest to Italy and barely escaping with a one-run victory over Korea.

"I can't begin to describe what this means to Dutch baseball," said Netherlands shortstop Robert Eenhoorn, the former major leaguer who played a key role in the win with his defense. "We didn't get a lot of respect from anybody coming into this tournament."

The Dutch won behind eight quality innings by Oregon native and former San Francisco Giants farmhand Ken Brauckmiller, a right hander who scattered seven hits and three walks while striking out just two. The Dutch got all the runs Brauckmiller needed in the third inning, against Cuban right hander Norge Vera, who was the MVP of Cuba's Serie Nacional in the winter while going 17-2, with a 0.97 ERA.

Dirk van t'Klooster walked to lead off the inning, and Johnny Balentina singled to follow. The Netherlands then loaded the bases when Cuba's star third baseman, Omar Linares, mishandled E.J. t'Hoen's sacrifice bunt. Rikkert Faneyte hit into a force play to keep the bases loaded before second baseman Ralph Milliard singled in a run, to tie the game 1-1.

Then, with former New York Yankee Hensley "Bam Bam" Meulens due up next, Cuba relieved Vera with flame-throwing 20-year-old Maels Rodriguez, whose fastball touched 99 mph on the stadium radar gun. Meulens turned around an 89-mph slider for a three-run double off the wall in left field, which turned out to be the difference in the game.

"That was the biggest hit of my career," said Meulens, who had spent part of the season in Korea before finishing the year in the Mexican League. "To have done that against Cuba, it was great satisfaction. Most of the teams had been throwing me a lot of breaking balls, and I'd seen so many, I adjusted to it. When somebody throws as hard as Rodriguez, though, you have to look fastball and adjust. His slider was hard enough, I didn't have to adjust too much."

Cuba never adjusted to Brauckmiller, who yielded a solo home run to Linares in the first, then pitched seven scoreless innings before leaving the game with two runners on and none out in the ninth inning.

Dutch coach Pat Murphy replaced his starter with Faneyte, who pitched in the Dutch domestic league. Faneyte then induced three straight groundballs from pinch-hitters Gabrielle Pierre and Javier Mendez, and center fielder Yobal Duenas, to notch the save and pull off the monumental upset.

"Rikkert's got ice water in his veins, he's just a strike thrower, so we knew he could do it," Murphy said. "This is really, really special. I'm really proud of this team and the way they believed. For Rikkert and Robert, I'm happy for them after all they've meant to Dutch baseball, to get a win like this late in their careers."

Cuba's invincibility had been pierced slightly in recent years, as the team lost to Japan and Australia, respectively, in the championship games of the 1997 and 1999 Intercontinental Cups, and also suffered round-robin defeats to the United States and Canada at the '99 Pan American Games. But nothing prepared the world for a Cuban upset, not even their close-call, come-from-behind 6-5 win against Korea the night before.

"We're not that worried," Cuban outfielder Luis Ulacia said through a translator after the upset. "We need to play better in our next few games so we won't repeat this loss. That goes to show that if the other team plays well, it can do the job better. We'll play hard and play better, but it's possible we could qualify for the medal round in fourth place. That's not embarrassing." Added second baseman Antonio Pacheco, a two-time Olympian: "We're not ashamed to lose to them. They're in the Olympics, aren't they?"

In the other two Day Four games, Japan (3-1) moved into

a tie with Cuba for second in the round-robin standings by handling Italy 6-1 at Blacktown.

Once again, Japan's big leaguers led the way offensively. First baseman Yukio Tanaka paced Japan's attack with a solo homer and three hits, scoring three runs. Catcher Fumihiro Suzuki had two hits and an RBI, while left fielder So Taguchi had a pair of doubles and scored a run. Third baseman Norihiro Nakamura, the team's cleanup hitter, had three walks, and also had a two-run double in the fifth inning to help Japan push out to a comfortable 4-1 lead.

The Italians (1-3) had their chances, leaving 13 men on base. Italy's lone run came when former Mariners' farmhand Claudio Liverziani doubled to open the bottom of the first, went to third on a single, and stole home on the front end of a double steal.

Also at Blacktown, in a game that was tied 1-1 going into the fifth, Australia (2-2) broke out with a four-run sixth, then put it away with four more in the eighth for a 10-4 win over South Africa (0-4).

Australia had 10 hits to back up five solid innings by 41-year-old Adrian Meagher. Mike Nakamura pitched three innings of relief to hold what was a 5-3 lead, until the Aussies could break it open.

South African center fielder Jason Cook had the team's first Olympic homer, a solo shot in the eighth, and three RBIs. First baseman Nick Dempsey had his second RBI of the tournament, and Cook, Dempsey, and right fielder Ian Holness had two hits apiece.

So, heading into the 2000 Olympic Baseball Tournament's first scheduled off day of competition, the United States remained as the only unbeaten team.

The Americans had a day off and Ernie Young had planned for the team to head out to the beach with an NBC television crew in tow, to catch some of the beach volleyball action and the overall Olympic crowd scene. They would be resuming play in two days against Italy. The loss by Cuba to the Netherlands was on the minds of fans and media, but not

Team USA.

"I'm worried to death about the Italians," said Lasorda, deadpanning after the game. Then he turned serious, adding, "The Cuba game showed that anything can happen in this tournament. I told our team, if you take anyone for granted, they can knock you on your rear end. We didn't come this far to lose. This is bigger than the World Series to me. Soon, all of America will know our players' names, because they're playing for what's on the front of their jersey, not the name on the back."

Homebush Bay Baseball Stadium in Sydney Olympic Park.

13

BUILDING MOMENTUM

For Paul Seiler and Steve Cohen, Sandy Alderson, and Bob Watson, all they could do now that the Olympic Games were under way was watch. They had done their jobs, and now it was up to Team USA's players and coaches to do theirs.

Seiler, USA Baseball's executive director, has served with Alderson and Watson on the Committee that had selected the players for Team USA. Watson co-chaired the Committee with Bill Bavasi, who couldn't make the trip due to prior commitments. Cohen, the director of National Team Operations for USA Baseball, was helping Seiler with administrative duties in Australia, but both acknowledged the hardest part of their jobs was over.

During Team USA's games, Cohen had a notebook out and was keeping score, but he wasn't doing it in any official capacity.

"It was more out of habit than anything else," Cohen said.

Team USA's cheering section behind home plate regularly included Cohen and Seiler, along with Major League Baseball Players Association representative Tony Bernazard, the former major-league infielder. Against South Africa, it also included former USA Baseball CEO and major-league general manager Dan O'Brien, who had helped guide USA Baseball during its transitional period from using amateurs to using professionals. Former Southern California coach Rod Dedeaux was also a constant, greeting visitors with his usual, "Hey, Tiger!" Dedeaux was a frequent companion of Lasorda's throughout the entire trip and during pregame batting practice.

Sitting behind Dedeaux at games were Team USA auxiliary coaches Dick Cooke and Ray Tanner. Tanner, *Baseball America*'s 2000 College Coach of the Year, was charting Team USA's batters, while Cooke tracked the pitchers. Cooke had experience doing that, serving in an identical capacity during the Pan Am Games in 1999. For Tanner, though, sitting in the stands during the game was something altogether new.

"It's one of the hardest things I've ever had to do," Tanner said. "During the exhibition games, we were in uniform during batting practice, but we can't be in uniform for the real Olympic games. It's just not what I'm used to."

Tanner did do a little coaching in the Team USA win against Japan, from the stands. His former player, Team USA shortstop Adam Everett, was asked to move to third base late in that contest, a position Tanner said Everett had never played, to his recollection. Tanner said Everett looked up at him in the stands between innings and asked, "Third base?" to which Tanner replied, "It's easy compared to shortstop."

Everett made it look easy, backhanding a ball headed down the line and making the throw to first right on target. In fact, in his short stint, he looked like Team USA's best option defensively at third, and he played at the hot corner again to close out the game against the Netherlands. So maybe Team USA's support staff had more to do than just cheer after all.

As significant as Cuba's first loss in Olympic baseball play was, another story was developing and beginning to overshadow that.

The number was 0.33. That was the earned run average for Team USA's four starting pitchers in its first four games. The Americans had won all four, two in dramatic fashion against

Asian qualifiers Japan and Korea and two with relative ease against the Netherlands and South Africa. The United States was the lone undefeated Olympic team.

The number—delivered by right handers Ben Sheets (Brewers), Jon Rauch (White Sox), Kurt Ainsworth (Giants), and Roy Oswalt (Astros)—stems from 27 2/3 innings pitched and only two runs allowed, one being earned. The quartet had given up just 20 hits and four walks while striking out 25 batters. If any other team was going to win the gold medal, it would have to go through Team USA's starting pitchers to earn it. And it wasn't going to be easy, because these pitchers weren't going to give anything away.

"These guys are unbelievable," said Team USA shortstop Adam Everett, whose defense had helped contribute to the low ERA. "It's obvious they have great arms, and we have some pitchers whose arms are better than others. But they all battle. They all have great heart, and they're battling like crazy."

Catcher Pat Borders, a 12-year major-league veteran, wasn't normally the type to gush. But since first catching the staff at Team USA's practice in San Diego, he hadn't been able to help himself. "You could put these guys in the big leagues right now," said Borders, "and they wouldn't embarrass themselves."

Considering that Ainsworth, Rauch, and Sheets were in college as recently as May 1999, Borders' comment shed light on what kind of stuff these pitchers had. Take Oswalt, who gave up eight hits against Korea. He walked two in his seven innings, but he had six key strikeouts—set up mostly by his 92-93 mph fastball—and kept the Koreans off the scoreboard.

"Ozzy made some mistakes, but he battled," said outfielder Ernie Young. "He never gave in. The best thing our guys do is they keep fighting and never give in."

The same could be said for the entire staff, which was off to about as impressive a start as could be. "There was no doubt that our pitching and defense have been superb, to this point," said Team USA general manager Bob Watson.

The bullpen hadn't been airtight, but right handers Ryan Franklin and Todd Williams had pitched very well, and left-handers Chris George and Bobby Seay had shown the ability to neutralize big left-handed bats late in close games.

Team USA officials, led by Alderson, had been adamant this time around that they were going to try to identify players that could provide offensive spark throughout the lineup. No one was expecting a team of minor leaguers to put up offensive numbers like the New York Yankees, but through four games, this version of Team USA had proven to be an improvement over its 1999 Pan Am Games predecessor. Only Everett, who was 0-for-14 at the plate, hadn't delivered. The rest of the team, with perhaps the exception of catchers Borders and Marcus Jensen, had come up with key hits when needed.

Lasorda had settled on a lineup, balancing left-handed and right-handed hitters. The Americans had not seen a left-handed pitcher yet, so continued production from the likes of lefties John Cotton, Mientkiewicz, Neill, and Wilkerson was going to be crucial. Lasorda and hitting coach Reggie Smith had displayed a knack for putting on the hit-and-run at the right time, and Team USA was 6-for-7 on stolen-base attempts.

"I really liked what we had seen through those first four games, and our pitching was as advertised," said Seiler. "We all certainly had reason to be optimistic about our medal chances, but there was still a long ways to go."

Of course, Cuba's 4-2 loss to the Dutch was keeping the baseball venue buzzing, and it would be talked about for the rest of the tournament. It was a shocking defeat, in that the Cubans were powerless at the plate against Ken Brauckmiller, who didn't have overpowering stuff but hit his spots with all his pitches. Scouts in attendance were shocked at the Cubans' approach at the plate, which saw even the smaller players on the roster swinging for the fences.

Cuba was also exhibiting its typical nonchalance during round-robin play. Omar Linares, the team's famed third baseman, made a crucial error that helped lead to the Dutch team's four-run inning. Veteran shortstop German Mesa, running at third base with one out, virtually gave up trying to score on a routine grounder to Dutch shortstop Robert Eenhoorn. Mesa offered no resistance after Eenhorn threw to catcher Johnny Balentina, who calmly applied the tag to the still-standing Mesa.

Observers wondered how much the Cubans could turn it on and off. On the heels of a 134-game winning streak at major international tournaments, Cuba had now lost games in four of the last five such competitions. At the '99 Pan Am qualifier for these Olympics, the Cubans had tanked their last round-robin game against Canada, so that they would not have to face Team USA in the Pan Am semifinal. It worked, as Cuba beat Canada 3-2 in the semis, then beat the United States with Jose Contreras to win the Pan Am gold.

Some were chalking Cuba's vulnerability up to the introduction of wood bats, others to the use of professionals, still others to age. All three were factors in making Cuba, while still a medal favorite, no longer the prohibitive gold-medal favorite. The Netherlands hadn't gotten its win against the back of the Cuban rotation, instead beating ace Norge Vera and wonder kid Maels Rodriguez.

To avoid any further trouble, the Cubans would have to avoid another upset in its last three pool play games, all of which could pose problems. Cuba plays Australia, which at 2-2 had struggled more than it had hoped, but still had a crucial win against Korea that kept them in medal contention. The Aussies were planning to start former major-league right-hander Shayne Bennett.

Cuba and Team USA would then square off the next night, and it was being discussed among Team USA circles to use veteran left-hander Rick Krivda as their starting pitcher. It was a bold choice by Lasorda and pitching coach Phil Regan, but they felt like Krivda's experience and the fact that he was a left-hander meant more than having a power-arm throw against Cuba. Last year's Pan Am experience supported their claim, as the Cubans pounded right hander Brad Penny in two appearances, and Penny's resume at the time closely resembled those of Team USA's current young righties.

In the final game of the round-robin, Cuba would face Japan. Unless the Cubans had lost to both the Aussies and the Americans, that game would likely be for positioning in the medal round and could end up as a preview of a semifinal rematch.

Japan (3-1) had an easier schedule from this point, playing South Africa, a grudge match with Korea, and then Cuba. The Japanese would have to decide when to use ace righty Daisuke Matsuzaka again, but pitching wasn't a problem for Japan. The team's offense, with five starters from the nation's major leagues, stalled against Team USA, but was consistent in wins against Australia, Italy, and the Netherlands. Japan had looked like the second-best team in the Olympics, ahead of Cuba.

Korea (1-3) and Australia (2-2) ranked as the biggest disappointments so far. The Koreans played well against Cuba and Team USA in defeat, but their loss to Australia meant they were facing an uphill battle to reach the medal round. Korea likely had to win out in its games against the Netherlands, Japan, and South Africa.

The host Aussies had a tough schedule ahead, with games remaining against Cuba and Team USA, as well as Italy. The Aussies likely would have to upset either Cuba or the United States to reach the medal round.

The tournament's surprise team of course was the Netherlands (2-2). The Dutch had the easiest remaining draw with games against Korea, South Africa, and European rival Italy. A very attainable 2-1 record in those games should have been good enough for a berth in the medal round.

But the Dutch were still looking at a No. 4 seed, in all probability. That would make Cuba, Japan, and Team USA all want the No. 1 seed even more. For all the Netherlands' moxie, its talent lagged behind those three powers, and it would be a significant advantage for the No. 1 seed to face the Netherlands in the semifinals, while the other two Gold-Medal contenders battled each other out.

Lasorda and Team USA were on their way to attaining their best-case scenario; they just had to continue doing what they were doing to make it a reality.

So, after a day of rest and relaxation and a chance to take in some of the sights and sounds of the Olympic fever in Sydney, Team USA geared up for their next contest: a night game on September 22, which just happened to be Tommy Lasorda's 73rd birthday. And, wouldn't you know it, Team USA would be playing against Italy, the country that Lasorda's father had migrated from to bring his family to America.

September 22, 2000 – Homebush Bay
<u>GAME FIVE: ITALY (1-3) vs. USA (4-0)</u>

Lasorda and Regan were back to the top of their pitching rotation, which meant that it was Ben Sheets' turn to take the ball. He would be facing Italian starter Battista Perri. And after Sheets got out of the top of the first inning, his teammates scored two runs quickly in the bottom half of the frame, unlike its first two games at Homebush. Against both Japan and Korea, the Americans waited until late in the game to score, getting their first runs against Japan in the seventh inning and all of their runs against Korea in the eighth. Against Perri, Team USA didn't wait.

Second baseman Brent Abernathy singled to lead off, and they put runners at the corners when Brad Wilkerson singled to right on a hit-and-run. Neill brought home the first run of the night with a fielder's choice and advanced to second on Perri's errant pickoff throw. He then scored on a single by Ernie Young, as Team USA grabbed an early 2-0 lead.

But Italy responded in the fourth against Sheets, scoring two runs without the benefit of a hard-hit ball. Catcher Chris Madonna, a former independent leaguer who played at the University of North Carolina, looped a double down the right-field line and came around to score on a similar bloop hit by former minor leaguer David Sheldon. Then Dan DiPace hit into a fielder's choice for the first out, went to second on a groundout, and moved to third on a wild pitch. With two out, Luigi Carrozza then beat out a slow ground ball up the middle, and the Italians had forged a 2-2 tie.

After the first inning, Team USA got very few good cuts against Perri, failing to wait on the right hander's assortment of off-speed pitches.

"Perri was just throwing strikes and spotting his pitches, sinking it a little, and it was just sitting up there," Neill said. "I don't remember facing somebody throwing so slow, and I feel like I'm a good off-speed hitter, but I would swing hard and hit it off the end of the bat. And as the game went along, we weren't scoring, and we started getting tighter and tighter."

Stuck in a tie game after six innings, Lasorda was forced to pull Sheets and bring on his most reliable reliever to that point, Ryan Franklin. The Mariners' farmhand had already picked up two victories in relief and had yet to allow a baserunner, let alone a hit in either of his two appearances.

Franklin set down the Italian lineup in order in both the seventh and eighth innings, but unfortunately Perri was keeping Team USA at bay. Finally, in the bottom of the eighth, Lasorda got the break he was looking for.

Perri, whose fastball was topping out at only 81 mph, got the first two outs of the eighth easily on grounders. Then Ernie Young, who had two of Team USA's six hits on the night, walked on five pitches. Perri then walked John Cotton as well, and the second base on balls brought out Italian manager Silvano Ambrosioni, who relieved Perri of his duties and brought in Jason Simontacchi.

Simontacchi, who beat South Africa and was being saved to start Italy's game against the rival Dutch, headed to the mound to face USA third baseman Mike Kinkade. On a 1-1 pitch, Kinkade hit a dribbler to the left of the mound that Simontacchi fielded cleanly, but his throw sailed over the head of first baseman Dan DiPace, and with the ample foul ground at Homebush Bay, both Team USA runners scored easily, giving the Americans a 4-2 lead. The error was a massive miscue that turned out to be a gift-wrapped birthday package for Lasorda.

When Todd Williams came on to record the final three outs of the game in the ninth, Lasorda's birthday had ended the right way. He finally got to unwind when Williams got pinch-hitter Dan Newman to ground out to end the game, triggering a Lasorda birthday celebration that included postgame cake in the clubhouse. Italy's close call made things tight, but couldn't spoil the party.

"Why don't you play like this all the time?" Lasorda asked Ambrosioni after the game. The night was supposed to be Lasorda's, and it was. Former Dodgers owner Peter O'Malley was one of many on hand to celebrate Lasorda's big day, but the Italians came ever so close to spoiling it.

"I lost my voice from yelling so much," Lasorda said, "because this was a tough, tough game. We were lucky to win tonight. But tomorrow when you look at the standings, it will say, 'United States of America, 5-0.'"

Franklin picked up the win with two shutout innings of relief, while Williams got his first save. It was Franklin's third win of the Olympics, tying the Team USA record set in 1996 by University of Virginia right hander Seth Greisinger. He had somehow been credited as the winning pitcher in all three of his relief appearances in Sydney, and was turning into Lasorda's good luck charm.

"Phil (Regan) and I joked about it a little," said Franklin. "It's just a matter of me getting in these games at the right time, but you also have to do your job and not let the other team score."

Sheets once again pitched well, but didn't get a decision, leaving with the score tied 2-2. Sheets went six innings, giving up four hits and one walk while striking out three, and after the game, he pronounced himself ready to pitch Team USA's final game, which would be in the medal round.

Many thought that perhaps Team USA's lack of solid play against Italy may have been because they were looking past the Italians, in preparation for Cuba the next night. Left fielder

Mike Neill, though, preferred to give Italy the credit.

"I don't think Cuba is as good as everybody says they are, but by the same token, some of these other teams aren't as bad as everybody thinks," Neill said. "There's a lot of parity in this tournament."

Lasorda shared his 73rd birthday in Australia with legendary USC head coach Rod Dedeaux (right), and former Los Angeles Dodgers owner Peter O'Malley.

MIRACLE ON GRASS

```
Italy 2 (1-4)                        USA 4 (5-0)
                 AB  R  H RBI                        AB  R  H RBI
Liverziani rf    3   0  1  0         Abernathy 2b    4   1  2  0
De Franceschi cf 4   0  0  0         Wilkerson cf    4   0  1  0
Madonna c        3   1  1  0         Neill lf        3   1  0  1
Sheldon 3b       4   0  1  1         E. Young rf     3   1  2  1
DiPace 1b        3   1  1  0         Cotton dh       3   1  0  0
D'Auria 2b       4   0  0  0         Kinkade 3b      4   0  0  0
Carrozza dh      4   0  1  1         Dawkins ss      0   0  0  0
Frignani lf      3   0  0  0         Mientkiewicz 1b 4   0  1  0
Newman ph        1   0  0  0         Jensen c        3   0  0  0
LaFera ss        2   0  0  0         Everett ss/3b   2   0  0  0
Perri p          0   0  0  0         Sheets p        0   0  0  0
Simontacchi p    0   0  0  0         Franklin p      0   0  0  0
                                     T. Young p      0   0  0  0
                                     Williams p      0   0  0  0

Totals......    31   2  5  2         Totals......   30   4  6  2

Score by innings:                             R  H  E
-----------------------------------------------------
Italy                     000 200 000    -    2  5  2
USA                       200 000 02     -    4  6  1
-----------------------------------------------------
```

E - Perri, Simontacchi, Everett. LOB - Italy 6, USA 6. 2B - Madonna. SH - Liverziani. SB - Abernathy. CS - DiPace. K - De Franceschi, Sheldon 2, D'Auria, Carrozza, LaFera, Wilkerson, Kinkade, Jensen 2. BB - Madonna, DiPace, LaFera, Neill, E. Young, Cotton, Everett.

```
              IP   H  R ER BB SO  WP BK HP IBB  AB BF Fly Gnd
Perri L 0-1   7.2  6  4  1  4  4   0  0  0  0   28 32  9   9
Simontacchi   0.1  0  0  0  0  0   0  0  0  0    2  2  0   1

Sheets        6.0  4  2  1  1  3   0  0  0  0   22 23  6   8
Franklin W 3-0 2.0 0  0  0  2  1   0  0  0  1    5  8  3   2
T. Young      0.0  1  0  0  0  0   0  0  0  0    1  1  0   0
Williams S,1  1.0  0  0  0  0  2   0  0  0  0    3  3  0   1
```

PB - Jensen.

T. Young faced 1 batter in the 9th.

Umpires - Home:Hsieh 1st:McCabe 2nd:Poulton 3rd:Koyama
Start: 7:30 pm   Time: 2:33   Attendance: 13,912

As a major-league All-Star, Australian catcher David Nilsson was one of the best non-Cuban players in the Olympic baseball tournament. But even he couldn't beat the tournament's best pitcher.

Nilsson had two hits and a walk in four trips to the plate earlier in the day at Homebush Bay. But the rest of his Australian team went 1-for-26 with 10 strikeouts against Cuban ace right hander Jose Contreras, in a 1-0 defeat.

The game was the quickest nine-inning game in Olympic history at two hours, four minutes. More significantly, it clinched a spot in the medal round for Cuba, which improved to 4-1.

Australia, which was now tied with Korea and the Netherlands at 2-3 for fourth place, had put themselves into a difficult position to try and grab the final medal-round berth. Team USA (5-0), Cuba (4-1), and Japan (4-1) were in position to advance, and Australia would need to beat Italy and upset the Americans, while also hoping that the Dutch lost to either South Africa or Italy.

"After the defeat to the Netherlands, I knew this was an important game for us to win," said Contreras, who threw the Olympics' first complete-game shutout since Nicaragua's Asdrudes Flores beat the Netherlands, 5-0, in 1996.

Contreras flashed the form that helped him dominate Team USA with 13 strikeouts in eight innings in the 1999 Pan Am Games gold-medal contest. His fastball was consistently in the low 90s, as he overmatched Nilsson's teammates.

"Contreras mixed it up well," Nilsson said. "He threw different fastballs, cutting and sinking. He had a good slider and a good splitter, and he threw hard. He pretty much dominated the game."

Over at Blacktown, Korea kept its slim medal hopes alive with a 2-0 win against the upstart Dutch, which created that three-way tie among itself, the Netherlands, and Australia for the fourth spot in the medal round, with two pool-play games remaining.

Korea was in position to grab that medal-round berth if

could beat archrival Japan and then South Africa, providing that Australia lost to either Italy or South Africa. The Netherlands had the easiest schedule remaining, with games against Italy and South Africa, though the Dutch needed Korea to lose a game.

If all three teams finished tied for the fourth spot, the tiebreaker would be the fewest runs allowed in the tournament. And through five games, Korea had given up 17, Australia 21, and the Netherlands 24.

Korean right hander Seok-Jin Park picked up the must-win with eight shutout innings against the Dutch, giving up just two hits and two walks while striking out seven. Righty Chang-Yong Lim finished up for the save.

The Netherlands lost some of the momentum it had gained with its shocking upset of Cuba, by giving up two first-inning runs, and the Dutch never recovered.

And in the third shutout of the day, Japan dominated South Africa 8-0 for their fourth straight win. Five Japanese pitchers gave up just three hits and struck out 10 against the overmatched South Africans (0-5). Two Japanese major leaguers, third baseman Norihiro Nakamura and first baseman Yukio Tanaka, hit home runs as their club pounded out 14 hits.

As Day Five concluded, all of the attention turned to what was easily the most anticipated pool-play matchup of the event: a Saturday night classic featuring the United States and Cuba.

The stage had been set. The United States, as the only undefeated team remaining, would be facing their archrival in Cuba. It would easily be Lasorda and company's toughest test, Japan's Daisuke Matsuzaka notwithstanding.

And making his first appearance in the Olympics for Team USA would be Rick Krivda, in a chance to step into the spotlight. The journeyman Orioles left hander, who had spent parts of six seasons going back and forth between triple-A Rochester and Baltimore, had a 5.57 career ERA in 258 major-league innings of work.

Lasorda and Regan were sticking with their strategy, so barring a last-second change of heart, Krivda was the guy. While Cuba hadn't announced a starter for the game, which was going to be broadcast in its entirety on MSNBC (though on a tape-delayed basis) by announcers Ted Robinson and Joe Magrane, it was certain that the Cuban hurler wouldn't have major-league experience, and Team USA officials figured that Krivda gave them the advantage.

"We wanted to go with a left-hander against Cuba, and Krivda was the most experienced and had good off-speed stuff," said Regan, who managed Krivda when he came up to the majors as a rookie with the Orioles in 1995. "We thought Rick would do a good job."

Regan's participation with Team USA was a strong reason why Krivda decided to sign up for service with the Olympic Team. The former Oriole, Red, Indian, and Royal knew he had drawn a choice assignment, and credited Regan for the opportunity.

"I don't know if they picked me because of my experience," Krivda said. "But maybe it was because we were in the middle of the tournament, it was an important game, and we started all of our young guys already. So to have them rested for the medal round, I can then be a swing guy or a setup man later on.

"But I know Phil stuck up for me to make this team, and I appreciated that. I wanted to pitch well for him. It had been a while since I played for him, but I wanted to show him he made a good choice."

Krivda, who went 11-9, with a 3.12 ERA at Rochester earlier that summer, didn't fit the mold of the rest of the USA staff of hard throwers, but that was a good thing. Cuba had knocked around Brad Penny twice in 1999 at the Pan Ams, and they were considered a good fastball-hitting team. However, in Team USA's 10-5 win over Cuba in Winnipeg, Dan Wheeler pitched 5 1/3 strong innings of relief, using mostly fastballs and sliders.

"They're a team that tried to intimidate you, and I had

major-league experience, so that was going to be harder for them to do to me, than maybe for a younger guy," Krivda said. "It was going to be a hostile environment to pitch in, so I think Tommy wanted my experience out there on the mound. Plus, our scouting reports said that Cuba was not a great breaking-ball-hitting team, so we hoped that would play to my strengths."

Cuban left fielder Luis Ulacia said it didn't matter whom Team USA used on the mound, and that it didn't even matter that the United States was his team's next opponent. "We play the same way no matter who the opponent is," Ulacia said. "Tomorrow is another game like any other. We will play hard and try to win, but it doesn't matter who pitches. A team has nine players, not one."

There was no advance word on who the Cuban starter would be, but Cuba had used three of its top arms in the previous two games. Norge Vera had started in the game they lost to the Dutch, and they had used righty Maels Rodriguez for 5.2 innings in that game as well. Jose Contreras had just beaten Australia, 1-0. That made right hander Jose Ibar, a former 20-game winner in Cuba's Serie Nacional, the most likely choice.

Cuba's pool of possible starters also included 35-year-old left-hander Omar Ajete, their only lefty, and righty Pedro Luis Lazo, who had mostly closed in international competition. Ajete beat Team USA in the 1992 Olympics, relieving then-current New York Yankees star Orlando "El Duque" Hernandez and pitching 8 2/3 innings, giving up one unearned run. Lazo had saved a 10-8 victory over the United States at the 1996 Atlanta Games.

Team USA and Cuba had split their two meetings in Winnipeg the previous summer. The United States won 10-5 in the round robin, roughing up Rodriguez with five runs in the ninth inning to break a tie. It was Team USA's first win against Cuba in a major international competition since 1987, when Ty Griffin's ninth-inning homer won a round-robin contest. In the gold-medal showdown in Winnipeg, Contreras took the mound on one day's rest and struck out 13 to beat Team USA, 5-1.

In Olympic competition, Team USA was 0-3 against Cuba. In 1992, Cuba beat then-current Texas Rangers ace Rick Helling twice, 9-6 in the round robin behind Ajete, and 6-1 in the semifinals behind Osvaldo Fernandez, who was now with the Cincinnati Reds.

In Atlanta, Cuba took a 10-8 decision in the round robin, getting two homers from third baseman Omar Linares and one each from Miguel Caldes and Ulacia. Then-current Toronto Blue Jays closer Billy Koch started and lost the contest for the Americans, despite being backed by five homers, two from Pittsburgh Pirates infielder Warren Morris.

September 23, 2000 – Homebush Bay
<u>GAME SIX: USA (5-0) vs. CUBA (4-1)</u>

On Lasorda's request, Team USA arrived at the ballpark a little earlier than normal, in order to soak up the atmosphere of what was going to be a special night. Very few of the American players had ever laced up their cleats wearing the red, white, and blue to play in a game against the Cuban powerhouse.

As the lineup cards were exchanged at home plate, the stadium was buzzing with anticipation—a full house was on hand to witness the first ever Olympic baseball game played between the USA and Cuba with professional players.

Taking the Team USA card to the meeting at home plate with the umpires was third-base coach Eddie Rodriguez. Lasorda had been having Rodriguez handle this assignment from the beginning of the event, and a big reason why Watson, Alderson, and Team USA officials had chosen Rodriguez to be a part of their coaching staff was because the native Cuban spoke fluent Spanish. Now an American citizen, he was coaching in the Toronto Blue Jays' farm system.

"I was so happy to be a part of that team, and to have that opportunity," said Rodriguez. "But I also knew that Tommy was relying on me to pick up anything that was being said by the Cubans in Spanish, while I was standing in the third-base coaches' box. Up until then, that hadn't been something for us to worry about, because none of the other teams we had played spoke any Spanish. But for this game, that was a big part of what I was expected to do over there."

It was certainly a great strategic idea, but it didn't get Team USA very far.

"As soon as I walked up to home plate with the lineup card, Cuban manager Servio Borges said to me 'We know who you are, so don't think you're going to get away with anything out of us tonight,'" said Rodriguez. "They had done their homework on me, so I knew right away that they wouldn't be talking too loudly over there in their dugout."

It was indeed Ibar that the Cubans would be starting on the mound, and he retired the American side in order in the top of the first. Then it was the veteran Krivda's turn, to try and go out and see if Lasorda and Regan's strategy would work.

It did not, as Cuba jumped on Krivda for four runs in the first inning. Left fielder Luis Ulacia reached on a bunt hit and Omar Linares walked. Then, with two outs, Krivda had a 1-2 count on designated hitter Antonio Pacheco, but the veteran singled to center to score Ulacia. Second baseman Oscar Macias followed with a run-scoring single to left, and Miguel Caldes followed with the game's biggest hit, a ripped double to the left-center-field gap that suddenly made it 4-0, before Lasorda could even warm up another pitcher in the bullpen.

The thought process of starting a left-hander with good off-speed stuff, had backfired. Krivda didn't get the job done, as he left pitches up in the strike zone and was punished for it.

"I ran into trouble when I walked Linares," Krivda said. "They hit some high changeups, and even when I made a better pitch, Caldes was able to hit it into the gap. If I could have that first inning back, maybe it would have been a different game."

Ibar was spotting his low-90s fastball and was able to reach back for something extra when he needed to. After three innings, Cuba still led 4-0, and Krivda had lasted only two frames. He was relieved by Jon Rauch—the pitcher whose regular turn it would have been to start, if Lasorda and Regan had stuck with their rotation.

In the top of the fourth, things got a little more tense between the two sides, as Cuba began to pull off some of their well-known intimidation tactics to try to thwart any potential Team USA comeback in the game. With Ernie Young at the plate, Ibar unleashed a fastball that drilled Young square in the middle of his back.

"Throughout the tournament and prior to, we had heard about some of the antics that the Cuban team would try to do against their opponents, somewhat of intimidating them. So when that happened, we probably should have just played our game and not let those antics take us away from what we had an opportunity to do that night," said Young. "I got caught up in it, though. They knew I was hitting the ball well and they were trying to send a message that they were the best. Ibar was having a good game and had great control that night, but he hit me in the middle of my back with a 95-mph fastball. I didn't like it at all, and I kind of lost my control for a second."

As Young threw down his bat and stared back at Ibar, both teams began to circulate out onto the field. But umpires quickly stepped in and made sure an all-out brawl didn't take place in what was supposed to be a competition filled with the Olympic spirit.

From there, Ibar escaped the inning with his 4-0 lead, and Rauch went back to the mound, with a warning from the home-plate umpire that if he retaliated in any way, he would be removed from the game. So Rauch got back at the Cubans the best way he could, by tossing four more shutout innings.

Ibar never let Team USA in the game thereafter, only allowing one American runner into scoring position, in the seventh inning.

"My fastball was fine, but what was most important was

my control," Ibar said. Regarding Young being hit by the pitch, he said, "It was not intentional. It got away from me and was badly interpreted."

Without being able to retaliate in any way, Team USA's frustration about the situation showed. Ibar was dominating them at the plate, and the Americans had lost focus about trying to score runs and create a comeback. On three different occasions, the USA players were on the top step of the dugout raring for a fight.

First baseman Doug Mientkiewicz didn't like the feeling one bit, and took it upon himself later in the game to send a message back to the Cubans, even if Rauch wasn't going to be allowed to. On a ground ball hit by Miguel Caldes, Mientkiewicz was covering first base, and after catching the throw to record the out, Mientkiewicz dropped down to his knees and blocked the path of Caldes to the base, forcing the runner to trip over him and go flying into the air, tumbling to the ground.

"That was me losing my cool a bit, because I was really frustrated. We all were frustrated and we weren't playing well. We were getting it shoved up our ass pretty good, and for me, I'd played against Cuba a couple of other times. So I was like, 'You know what? Here you go, take this.' I wanted them to know that we could play dirty like that as well, if that's what they wanted to do."

"I look back at it now and I think, 'What the heck was I doing?' But at the time, it was one of those things that I just needed to get out of my system, because I wanted to fight. I was so mad at that point, I wanted to punch somebody."

But obviously, starting a fistfight in the Olympics was not going to be a good publicity move for USA Baseball, Lasorda, or his team. So Mientkiewicz did the next best thing he could think of.

"Mike Neill accused me of trying to start World War III, but that was about as far as we could take it," said Mientkiewicz. "I think I got my point across."

But the incidents didn't end there. With Cuba leading 5-0

in the bottom of the eighth, they had pinch-runner Yobal Duenas at second base. When he rounded third and headed for home on a base hit, he came in sliding spikes-high on Team USA catcher Pat Borders as he awaited the throw. Borders went down writhing in pain, as the nasty slide had been one last message from the Cubans that this wasn't over.

Borders had to be helped off the field by Team USA medical personnel after the collision, and although X-rays taken after the game were negative, Borders' left ankle had swollen up to the size of a grapefruit.

"When I saw the collision happen, I thought Pat had broken his ankle," said Dr. Dicke. "So when the X-rays said there wasn't a fracture, I knew it had to be a bad strain, which it was. And I was very doubtful that he was going to be able to come back and play at the level that was needed for the medal round."

Ibar fanned 10 in seven three-hit shutout innings, and nine of his strikeouts came against Team USA's five left-handed hitters in its lineup. By the time Ibar left, the Cubans had a 5-0 lead.

Team USA was able to avoid the shutout by scoring a run in the top of the ninth off reliever Pedro Luis Lazo, but it was too little too late. Cuba had improved to 25-3 overall against Team USA in major international competition, with a decisive 6-1 triumph.

Afterwards, Cuban manager Servio Borges didn't understand what all the fuss was about. "There was no antagonism on our part. It's just baseball," Borges said. "Team USA is a good team. We tried to do things properly. Both teams are strong and both played hard. We proved to be better tonight."

And both Borges and Lasorda said they thought the Borders/Duenas incident was a clean play. Borges did, though, take the opportunity, when it was presented, to respond to Lasorda's statement prior to the Olympics, that he would dedicate a win against Cuba to the Cuban exiles in Miami.

"We dedicate this win to the 11 million people of Cuba who support us, watch us train, and were awaiting this victory tonight," said Borges.

Lasorda wasn't backing away from his comment, but made it known that his team had no antagonism for the Cubans, and that, if given another opportunity, his team would still want to win for the Cuban exiles in Miami.

Lasorda shows off his lucky USA Teddy Bear to NBC Olympic Sports anchor Bob Costas in the dugout

DAVID FANUCCHI

```
USA 1 (5-1)                         Cuba 6 (5-1)
                 AB  R  H RBI                       AB  R  H RBI
Abernathy 2b      5  0  1  0      Ulacia lf          4  1  1  0
Wilkerson cf      4  0  0  0      Gomez cf           3  0  0  0
Mientkiewicz 1b   4  0  1  0      Linares 3b         3  1  0  0
E. Young rf       2  0  0  0      Kindelan 1b        4  0  1  0
Cotton dh         4  0  0  0      Duenas pr/dh       0  1  0  0
Neill lf          3  0  0  0      Pacheco dh         2  1  2  1
Burroughs 3b      4  1  2  0      Scull ph/dh        2  0  0  0
Borders c         4  0  2  1      Macias 2b          4  1  1  1
Dawkins pr        0  0  0  0      Caldes rf          4  1  2  2
Everett ss        3  0  0  0      Pestano c          4  0  1  1
Kinkade ph        1  0  1  0      Mesa ss            2  0  2  1
Krivda p          0  0  0  0      Ibar p             0  0  0  0
Rauch p           0  0  0  0      Lazo p             0  0  0  0
George p          0  0  0  0
Heams p           0  0  0  0

Totals......     34  1  7  1      Totals......      32  6 10  6

Score by innings:                       R  H  E
-----------------------------------------------
USA                       000 000 001 - 1  7  2
Cuba                      400 100 01  - 6 10  0
-----------------------------------------------

E - E. Young, Burroughs. DP - USA 1. LOB - USA 9, Cuba 7.
2B - Burroughs(1), Caldes. 3B - Mesa. SH - Ulacia, Gomez.
K - Abernathy 2, Wilkerson 4, Cotton 3, Neill 3, Burroughs 2,
Ulacia, Gomez, Linares 2, Kindelan 2, Macias 2, Caldes, Pestano
2. BB - E. Young, Neill, Linares, Mesa 2.


             IP   H  R ER BB SO  WP BK HP IBB   AB BF Fly Gnd
Krivda L 0-1 2.0  5  4  4  1  1   0  0  0  0     9 11  0  4
Rauch        4.0  3  1  1  0  8   2  0  0  0    15 15  0  4
George       1.0  0  0  0  1  1   0  0  0  0     2  4  0  2
Heams        1.0  2  1  0  1  1   0  0  0  0     6  7  2  0

Ibar W 1-0   7.0  3  0  0  2 10   0  0  1  0    24 27  4  7
Lazo         2.0  4  1  1  0  4   0  0  0  0    10 10  1  1

WP - Rauch 2. HBP - by Ibar (E. Young).

Umpires - Home:Rey  1st:Leone  2nd:Yoon  3rd:Contreras
Attendance: 14,010
```

The United States and Cuba were now tied atop the standings with identical 5-1 records, because Korea (3-3) had managed to secure a critical victory in their hopes to medal, with a 7-6 triumph over their rival Japan (4-2).

In what would be the most important day of the Olympic baseball event in terms of movement in the standings, Day Six turned out to be quite a shocker.

Korea's victory over Japan at Homebush Bay prior to the USA-Cuba game couldn't have been much sweeter. They won their second straight game, 7-6 in 10 innings, in one of the best contests of the tournament. Meanwhile, Australia and the Netherlands, the other contenders for the fourth and final berth in the medal round, lost to the two weakest teams in the eight-team field.

At the midway point of the competition, Korea was battling injuries to its starting catcher and first baseman and had lost nine of its last 11 Olympic baseball games dating back to the 1996 Atlanta Games. Now, despite an injury to ace pitcher Min-Tae Chung that forced him to leave the Japan game after one inning, they were back in strong contention for a medal.

If the Koreans beat South Africa in their last pool-play game, they would qualify for medal play. And it got in this position by beating its archrival. "From a very young age, our mentality is that we have to win against the Japanese," Korean manager Euong-Yong Kim said. "We used this mentality today. We'll have to see how the other teams do to get to the medal round."

Added first baseman Lee Seung-Yuop, who had a two-run homer off Japanese ace right hander Daisuke Matsuzaka, "Disregarding all losses to other teams, this game meant the most to us as a country."

Matsuzaka gave up just one run in his final eight innings, but dug himself into a huge hole by giving up four runs in the top of the first. "That was very costly," Matsuzaka said. "Their swings were very sharp. I was sure we weren't going to win, because I gave up four runs. My fastball was not so good today."

Matsuzaka, who gave up seven hits and five walks while striking out 10, probably would be getting the ball in Japan's final game, be it for the Gold or the Bronze.

Japan (4-2) almost did come back to steal the victory. Korea had the bases loaded in the ninth with one out against Matsuzaka, when right fielder Byung-Kyu Lee grounded to second. Japan second baseman Jun Heima threw home, and Korean runner Sung-Heon Hong appeared to be safe, eluding the tag of catcher Fumihiro Suzuki. But the plate umpire called Hong out, and Matsuzaka escaped the inning. Japan then had runners at first and second with two out in the bottom of the ninth, when left fielder So Taguchi singled to right, but Lee threw out Heima at the plate to force extra innings.

Korea scored the winning runs in the 10th off Japanese reliever Yoshikazu Doi, both unearned. Left fielder Sung-Ho Jang reached on an error and moved to second on Ki-Tai Kim's single, and first baseman Seung-Yuop Lee's single loaded the bases. Jang and Kim scored when Japan third baseman Norihiro Nakamura booted a grounder, which bounded far into foul territory.

Japan rallied again in the bottom of the 10th, with Yukio Tanaka singling in first baseman Nobuhiko Matsunaka, who had doubled. But winning pitcher Jin Pil-Jung (who a few days earlier had been victimized by Doug Mientikewicz's game-winning grand slam) got pinch-hitter Shinnosuke Abe to hit into a game-ending 6-4-3 double play.

Just like when The Netherlands shook up the tournament by dealing Cuba its first-ever Olympic defeat, this time the Dutch found themselves on the other end of a shocking upset.

With their medal-round destiny firmly in their own control, the Dutch (2-4) let it slip away with a stunning 3-2 loss in 10 innings to South Africa (1-5) at Blacktown, handing the Africans their first ever victory in Olympic baseball competition. South Africa had lost its first five games by a combined score of 58-5, but got a pair of solo home runs from right fielder Ian Holness, including a game-winning shot in the 10th off Dutch closer Rikkert Faneyte.

"I'm extremely disappointed," Netherlands coach Pat Murphy said. "I think our players underestimated South Africa and were overconfident going into the game. We have moved from the penthouse to the outhouse. We'd beaten Cuba, who was ranked No. 1 in the world, yet we couldn't beat a team that had yet to win a game."

The Netherlands never led against right hander Tim Harrell of the Dodgers organization, as the South African ace went all 10 innings, after getting shelled by Italy in his prior start. Harrell gave up two unearned runs on five walks and six hits, striking out four.

Holness, who was now hitting .381 in the tournament, knocked in all three South Africa runs. He hit a solo homer in the sixth off Netherlands starter Patrick de Lange, but the Dutch tied the score in the bottom of the seventh on a pinch-hit single by Ken Brauckmiller, the pitcher who had beaten Cuba.

Holness put the South Africans back on top in the eighth against Dutch lefty Radhames Dykhoff. After Eelco Jansen walked left fielder Clint Alfino, Dykhoff came in to face Holness, who promptly delivered a run-scoring double.

The Netherlands tied it up in the bottom of the eighth when left fielder Hensley Meulens doubled home Faneyte, who had reached on an error. The Dutch had a runner on second with one out in the bottom of the ninth but couldn't score, as second baseman Ralph Milliard and shortstop Robert Eenhoorn failed to come through. And in the 10th, Harrell retired the side in order, getting Meulens on a grounder to shortstop Paul Bell to end the game.

To make the medal round, the Netherlands would need to beat Italy and hope for the improbable combination of an Australian upset of Team USA and a South African upset of Korea. Then the Dutch would have to win a three-way tiebreaker, the first of which is fewest runs allowed.

"This is destroying for us," Murphy said. "I don't know

how I am going to get the guys up for the game versus Italy."

To wrap up the night in Blacktown, the host country Australia squandered its medal chances by blowing leads of 5-1 and 6-4, losing to Italy 8-7 in 12 innings.

The Aussies (2-4) could still make the medal round, but they would need to beat Team USA and have Korea lose to South Africa, both of which looked unlikely. If both of those upsets occurred, it was also possible that the Netherlands could force a three-way tie for the final spot.

"I was disappointed, but we will come out and play a respectable game against the USA," said team captain David Nilsson, who went 3-for-3 with three walks and raised his batting average to a tournament-leading .571. "We had our chances to win it, and it was a game we should have won. We have given a good effort here, but we have underachieved."

Trailing 5-1, the Italians rallied against relievers Tom Becker and Mike Nakamura to get within 6-4 before facing closer Grant Balfour in the ninth. Chris Madonna then tied the game with a two-run homer off Balfour to send the game into extra innings, and Italian closer Marc Cerbone kept it tied with 3 1/3 scoreless innings through the 11th.

In the 12th, Italy got to left-hander Craig Anderson, who had been Australia's most reliable reliever to date. Alberto D'Auria reached on an error by second baseman Glenn Williams and DH Luigi Carrozza followed with a two-run homer to make it 8-6.

Australia rallied in the bottom half against Fabio Betto, who gave up a run when center fielder Grant McDonald doubled, advanced on a wild pitch and scored on third baseman Paul Gonzalez' groundout. But Betto got pinch-hitter Gary White on a groundout to end the game. Italy (2-4) still had a slim chance of advancing to the medal round, but that scenario was extremely complicated and improbable.

September 24, 2000 – Homebush Bay
GAME SEVEN: USA (5-1) vs. AUSTRALIA (2-4)

With a berth in the medal round already locked up, Team USA was facing their final game of pool play against the host country. The Aussies had underachieved so far in the event, and some speculated that perhaps the extra pressure of having to perform so well in front of their home fans, and the high expectations, had overwhelmed them a bit.

On the last day of the round robin, the only thing left to determine was the seeding of the four teams that would advance to the medal round, where the top seed #1 would face the #4 seed, while numbers 2 and 3 would meet in the other semifinal. After six games, the standings looked like this:

Cuba	5-1
United States	5-1
Japan	4-2
Korea	3-3
The Netherlands	2-4
Australia	2-4
Italy	2-4
South Africa	1-5

With Korea playing against South Africa in the afternoon on Day Seven, it was safe to assume that the Koreans would win and finish with a 4-3 record, in order to clinch their spot in the medal round. The Koreans took care of business in impressive fashion, scoring six runs in the fourth inning and cruising to a 13-3 win in a game ended in the bottom of the eighth by the international mercy rule.

Korean home-run champion Seung-Yuop Lee went 2-for-5 with two RBIs, and catcher Sung-Heon Hong, a backup who had replaced injured starter Kyung-Oan Park, went 3-for-4 with three RBIs to lead their offense, which had 15 hits and five walks against six pitchers.

In the other midday game at Blacktown, the Netherlands

earned a best-ever fifth-place finish in the Olympics, after edging European rival Italy, 3-2. The Dutch finished with a 3-4 record, while Italy ended up at 2-5.

"We certainly shocked the world with our win against Cuba, and we beat Australia, so we really progressed in the game," said manager Pat Murphy.

Netherlands right hander Rob Cordemans pitched eight strong innings for the win, giving up five hits and no walks while striking out four. "It's kind of a consolation prize," Cordemans said. "The loss to South Africa was disappointing, and we always expect a good game against Italy. We beat the best, but lost to the bottom team."

In the night game at Blacktown that was scheduled to start one hour before the USA vs. Australia tilt at Homebush, Japan and Cuba were facing one another. So the outcome of that game was going to have a severe effect on the 1-4 seedings, as was whether or not Team USA could beat what was likely to be an inspired Australian team playing in their last game, in front of a sold-out stadium of fans.

Both Cuba and Japan had clinched berths in the medal round, so they were playing only for positioning. It was clear that neither team wanted to face the starting pitching of Team USA in the semifinals, which was a must-win game in order to have a chance at winning the Gold.

So if Cuba could beat the Japanese, they would clinch the top seed with a 6-1 record, because even if the Americans beat Australia and secured the same 6-1 record, Cuba owned the tiebreaker by virtue of their head-to-head victory over the USA.

In the same vein, if Japan lost, they would end up being the fourth seed, with the same 4-3 record as Korea. And Korea owned the tiebreaker in that head-to-head matchup, by virtue of their win over Japan.

The heart of Cuba's lineup turned on their engine when they needed to, and helped the two-time defending Olympic champions wrap up the top seed for the medal round by pounding Japanese pitching in a 6-2 win.

This created the rematch that Cuba wanted with fourth-seeded Japan, as the two teams would tee it up again, likely with much more intensity, in the semifinals. But because this game was being played just an hour before the Americans took the field against the Aussies, the outcome was not known to Lasorda or any of the USA Baseball brass.

Cuban third baseman Omar Linares, who entered the game hitting just .227 for the tournament, went 3-for-4 with a pair of doubles. Orestes Kindelan hit his second homer of the Olympics, a three-run shot, and went 2-for-4 with four RBIs. First baseman Antonio Scull also went 2-for-4 as Cuba pounded 13 hits off four Japanese pitchers.

Veteran reliever Lazaro Valle went 3 1/3 innings for the win. Maels Rodriguez worked two innings in a tune-up outing, striking out five, to finish up.

So as Team USA took the field at Homebush Bay in the last scheduled pool-play game of the competition, depending on the outcome of their game and the Cuba-Japan game, the Americans knew they would either be facing Japan or Korea in the semifinals, and not the mighty Cubans. And Cuba knew the same thing: Team USA and Cuba would be the 1 & 2 seeds, while Japan and Korea would be the 3 & 4 seeds. It was just a matter of what order they would finish.

"That was a great feeling, knowing that we had already put ourselves into the best position to advance, and wouldn't have to face Cuba in a knockout game," said Seiler. "That was the last place you wanted to be, because it was just so difficult to beat them. If you don't, then the best you could do was a bronze medal, and that would have been disappointing to everybody involved. It was not going to be easy to beat one of the Far East teams, but it was the best chance we had."

For an Australian team that started with such high hopes, the finale of the Olympic baseball tournament was too fitting. An enthusiastic flag-waving crowd of 14,018 was on hand at Homebush Stadium, just waiting for the opportunity to be won over. A prime enemy, Team USA, was the opponent, and former major leaguer Mark Hutton was on the mound for the home team.

But as with the rest of the Olympic tournament, everything went wrong for Australia. Team USA jumped out to a big early lead, knocking out Hutton. A rain delay of 34 minutes helped drown the crowd's early enthusiasm and the Americans broke open a 5-0 game with five more runs in the fourth inning, and they sealed a 12-1 victory in a mercy-rule game that ended after seven innings.

Team USA, rebounding from a smarting loss to Cuba the previous night, did everything right against the Aussies. Right hander Kurt Ainsworth, spotted to an early lead, pitched five solid innings, giving up just one run and needing fewer than 70 pitches to do it. He was followed in relief by lefty Chris George, who throughout the Olympics had been given the nickname of "Sandy" by Lasorda, due to his thin build and blazing, left-handed fastball. Instead of calling him by his name, Tommy would refer to George as "Sandy," because Chris reminded him of Sandy Koufax. George finished off the Australians by throwing two shutout innings of relief.

And after getting just 13 hits in the last two games, Team USA's offense busted out with 14 hits against four Australian right handers.

Three of the hits came in a four-run second, and five more came in the fourth. Catcher Marcus Jensen (filling in for the injured Pat Borders), went 3-for-4 with three RBIs, and made it a mercy-rule game with a solo homer in the sixth, the Americans' sixth home run of the tournament.

"We needed this game," said Doug Mientkiewicz, who had a single and an RBI in three plate appearances. "Our emotions had dropped a little after last night, and tonight we got our intensity back. We focused right in and got Kurt some runs and got off to a good start, which we haven't been doing enough. We had a more businesslike attitude tonight, and that's what we need for the final two games."

Every Team USA player either had a hit or scored a run. Second baseman Brent Abernathy had two doubles, tying a Team USA record shared by five others and giving him five in the tournament, breaking the U.S. Olympic record set by major leaguers Mark Kotsay and Travis Lee in 1996. Abernathy went 4-for-5 with three RBIs on the night, the four hits tying a U.S. Olympic record shared by Lee, Jacque Jones (1996), and Will Clark (1984).

Center fielder Anthony Sanders scored three runs and had an RBI in his first start of the tournament, and helped Abernathy provide flawless defense up the middle. And third baseman Mike Kinkade had his best game, going 2-for-5 with a double and two RBIs.

Lasorda tinkered with the lineup elsewhere, sitting DH John Cotton for the first time and starting Gookie Dawkins at shortstop ahead of Adam Everett. Dawkins' 0-for-3 effort meant that Team USA shortstops, while playing excellent defense, were now 0-for-23 at the plate in the tournament, with three walks and seven strikeouts.

Still, hitting coach Reggie Smith said he was encouraged with the way his charges had come back from an offensive slump against soft tossers from Korea and Italy and Cuba's hard-throwing Jose Ibar, who dominated them in a 6-1 defeat.

"We were more relaxed tonight, and we went out and hit like we did in the exhibitions," Smith said. "The last few games, we've had some struggles, but the team made some adjustments."

Team USA starting pitcher Kurt Ainsworth and catcher Pat Borders talk strategy in the dugout, prior to the game vs. Australia.

DAVID FANUCCHI

```
USA 12 (6-1)                        Australia 1 (2-5)
                 AB  R  H RBI                        AB  R  H RBI
Abernathy 2b     5   0  4  3        Reeves rf        3   0  0  0
Wilkerson rf     5   0  1  0        Snelling cf      3   0  0  0
Neill lf         3   2  1  0        Nilsson dh       2   1  1  0
E. Young dh      2   1  0  1        Johnson ph/dh    1   0  1  0
Mientkiewicz 1b  2   2  1  1        Byrne lf         3   0  1  0
Burroughs 3b     2   0  1  0        Gonzalez 3b      2   0  0  1
Kinkade 3b/1b    5   1  2  2        Van Buizen ph/3b 1   0  1  0
Sanders cf       3   3  1  1        Moyle c          3   0  0  0
Jensen c         4   2  3  3        Roneberg 1b      3   0  1  0
Dawkins ss       3   1  0  0        Williams 2b      3   0  0  0
Ainsworth p      0   0  0  0        Buckley ss       3   0  2  0
George p         0   0  0  0        Hutton p         0   0  0  0
                                    White p/c        0   0  0  0
                                    Ettles p         0   0  0  0
                                    Meagher p        0   0  0  0

Totals......    34  12 14 11        Totals......    27   1  7  1

Score by innings:                   R  H  E
-------------------------------------------
USA                      041 501 1 - 12 14  0
Australia                000 100 0 -  1  7  2
-------------------------------------------
```

E - Reeves, Ettles. DP - USA 1, Australia 2. LOB - USA 10, Australia 5. 2B - Abernathy 2(5), Kinkade(1), Nilsson, Johnson. HR - Jensen(1). SB - Mientkiewicz, Sanders. Strikeouts - Wilkerson 2, E. Young, Kinkade, Sanders 2, Dawkins, Reeves, Byrne 2, Moyle. Walks - Neill 2, E. Young 2, Mientkiewicz, Sanders, Dawkins.

```
              IP  H  R ER BB SO  WP BK HP IBB  AB BF Fly Gnd
Ainsworth W 2-0 5.0 5 1 1  0  3   0  0  0  0   19 19  7   4
George         2.0 2  0 0  0  1   0  0  0  0    8  8  4   1

Hutton L 0-1   2.0 5  4 4  4  0   0  0  0  0   10 14  3   2
White          1.0 5  5 5  1  1   1  0  1  0    8 10  2   0
Ettles         3.0 2  2 2  1  3   1  0  1  0   11 13  3   2
Meagher        1.0 2  1 1  1  3   0  0  0  0    5  6  0   0
```

WP - White, Ettles. HBP - by White (Sanders), by Ettles (E. Young).

Umpires - Home:Bellerose 1st:Contreras 2nd:Leone 3rd:Rey
Attendance: 14,018

Team USA finished the preliminary round at 6-1, tied with Cuba, and earned the second seed in the medal round. After Cuba beat Japan, Lasorda and company learned that they would be playing third-seeded Korea Tuesday night at Homebush. Cuba, the top seed, would play fourth-seeded Japan Tuesday afternoon. The winners were slated to play Wednesday night for the gold medal, while the losers would meet that afternoon for the bronze.

"I was hopeful we would be 7-0, but I did expect us to be able to be 6-1 after seeing this team in the exhibitions," Lasorda said. "I felt good about our ballclub, and I liked our chances. If we played like we were capable of, we should have good results."

There would be no medal round for the host nation. The mercy-rule defeat summed up the whole tournament for Australia, which had lofty goals after winning the 1999 Intercontinental Cup there the previous November. But the Australians finished seventh with a 2-5 record, thanks to crushing losses to the Netherlands (6-2 in the Aussies' Olympic opener) and Italy (8-7 in 12 innings).

"It's pretty disappointing," Australian left fielder Clayton Byrne said. "The club just never got it going. We had legitimate hopes of going further in the tournament, but that didn't happen. We didn't hit, we didn't pitch, and we didn't field. It was pretty simple."

Lasorda and Smith said they had plenty of information on Korea (thanks to the MLB Scouting Bureau), which indicated it would start submariner Tae-Hyon Chong in Tuesday's semifinal. Team USA was expected to counter with right hander Roy Oswalt against Korea in a rematch of their 4-0 victory, with right hander Ben Sheets on tap to start the medal game. Lasorda indicated the rest of the staff would be available for relief duty in both games.

Korea had lost an outfielder during its exhibition schedule and Park during the round robin, and ace right hander Chung Min-Tae left his start against Japan after just one-third of an inning after getting struck on his shin by a line drive. Though

X-rays were negative, his prognosis for the medal round was unknown.

"Apart from the injured players, the rest of us will be trying our best," outfielder Soo-Keun Jung said. "If Chong is pitching well, we will have a chance to go to the final."

The Americans were confident as well, and liked their position. "I think when we play the way we're capable of, there's no team in this tournament that can beat us," Abernathy said. "It's up to us to play up to our capability."

Abernathy had shined both offensively and defensively for the red, white, and blue. Yet given his outstanding play on the field, Lasorda still couldn't seem to get his name right, calling the young second baseman "Trent" instead of "Brent" the entire time the team was together. "Maybe he wanted to keep calling me Trent, because he liked the way I was playing," said Abernathy. "I didn't mind, as long as we were winning."

Team USA knew they would have to save their best two games for last, if they were to win a gold medal. As Lasorda was fond of reminding everyone who would listen, he didn't come 10,000 miles to lose.

14

CAPTURING THE GOLD

On the off day before the medal round, the question on everyone's mind was: Would Team USA's starting pitching hold up enough to beat the strongest field in Olympic history, and would they be able to score enough runs? The first Olympic baseball games with professional players had produced upsets nearly every day and some of the most exciting baseball ever played outside of the major leagues.

The 1999 Pan American Games, which had marked the first time USA Baseball used pros, was considered to this point to have been the best international baseball tournament ever held. Pros also comprised teams from Canada, the Dominican Republic, and Mexico, among others. As deep as that tournament was, observers said that this tournament was better.

"The pitching here in Sydney is much better than the Pan Ams," said Tony Bernazard, the former major leaguer who was working for the MLB Players Association. "The Far East teams, Japan and Korea, have much better pitching than teams like Canada did. These teams have major leaguer talent on their rosters. Maybe the bottom teams weren't as good as in the Pan Ams, but the top teams here are all very strong."

The top four teams separated themselves from the pack late in the tournament. Korea won its last three games after losing to Team USA. Included in that three-game winning streak was an impressive 7-6 win against Japan, its biggest rival and the biggest victory of the tournament.

Hard to believe, but that was more significant than the Netherlands handing the Cubans their first-ever Olympic loss. When the Dutch then suffered their own shocking upset, a 3-2 loss that gave South Africa its first-ever Olympic win, the Koreans had their shot at the medal round, and they took full advantage.

But it was extremely difficult to call how the two semifinal games were going to play out. Any of the four remaining teams had a legitimate shot at winning the Gold, and they also each had a chance of not even medaling at all. One of the four would end up without a medal—but which one was it going to be?

The strength of the Cubans was their pitching, and Cuba's top arms had delivered, for the most part. Jose Contreras tossed a crucial shutout against Australia, and Jose Ibar dominated the USA. Their offense had been good enough in the preliminary round, but their whole lineup looked mortal against hard-throwing Team USA righty Jon Rauch after he relieved Krivda. And they had been held to only two runs by an unknown pitcher from the Netherlands. Cuba got through a slump when in games against Korea, the Netherlands, and Australia, it scored a total of nine runs, while also giving up nine. But Team USA woke up the sleeping giant, and Kindelan and Linares look primed to once again provide big hits when they really counted.

Keeping in mind that Cuba was an aging team, they had lost their veneer of invincibility with three losses in the last two international competitions, and the switch to wood bats in that span had sapped some of the strength from their lineup. Perhaps this was the opportunity—if there ever was one—to knock out the defending champs.

Team USA's strength was supposed to be its starting

pitching, and they absolutely had fulfilled that prediction. Excluding the Rick Krivda experiment against Cuba, Team USA's rotation had posted a 0.81 ERA. No team had rivaled Team USA's defense up the middle in the infield, given by Brent Abernathy, Adam Everett, and Gookie Dawkins.

The USA lineup had found three consistent hitters in leadoff man Abernathy, first baseman Doug Mientkiewicz, and outfielder/DH Ernie Young. But their left-handed hitters (aside from Mientkiewicz) were slowing down after a strong start. To beat Korean submariner Tae-Hyon Chong and whomever they might face in a medal game, John Cotton, Mike Neill, and Brad Wilkerson would need to snap out of their funks and produce.

Their offense did get back on track against solid pitching from Australia, and with a second look against Chong, they should have a good knowledge of what to expect. If they could get by Korea, the Americans' gold-medal hopes would rest on the arm of right hander Ben Sheets, Lasorda's pick to face Cuba or Japan with the gold medal on the line.

But with a loss to Korea, it would be hard to imagine this team getting up for the bronze-medal game and beating either Japan or Cuba in that situation, no matter how well Sheets pitched.

After a 1-3 start and a string of injuries, Korea gained confidence and momentum by beating Japan. But their top starting pitcher was hit in the shin with a shattered bat in the game against Japan, and although he didn't break a bone, his availability for the medal round was questionable.

Their hopes rested with Tae-Hyon Chong, hoping he could handle Team USA with the ease with which he did in his first start against them, allowing just five hits and no walks in seven shutout innings.

But the Koreans seemed determined to find a way to bring home a medal, and would be much more excited about playing in a bronze-medal game than any of the other three teams.

Finally, Japan had played like a professional team, led by Japanese major leaguers such as first baseman Nobuhiko

Matsunaka, third baseman Norihiro Nakamura, catcher Fumihiro Suzuki, outfielder So Taguchi, and DH Yukio Tanaka. Top pitchers Matsuzaka and Tomohiro Kuroki had pitched well, with Kuroki expected to start against Cuba in the semifinals.

But Japan was 0-3 against the three teams remaining: Cuba, Korea, and the United States, and had lost both of Matsuzaka's starts, which was unexpected. Japan's industrial-league players had not produced offensively, leaving the big leaguers to pick up too much of the slack.

If Kuroki could dominate Cuba in much the same manner that Brauckmiller did, and if their big-league hitters could score some runs, they had an outside shot at beating the Cubans. That would give the ball in the gold-medal game to Matsuzaka, who perhaps was the tournament's best player. It was unfathomable that the Japanese would go 0-for-3 in his starts.

But Cuba was Cuba, and Japan's confidence wasn't high after losing its last two games.

September 26, 2000 – Homebush Bay
SEMIFINAL # 1: CUBA (6-1) vs. JAPAN (4-3)

Jose Contreras and Orestes Kindelan both had big-game reputations for Cuba in international play, and they did nothing to tarnish those well-earned reputations in the semifinals. In a surprise move by Cuban manager Servio Borges, he chose to have his best right hander start the semifinal game against Japan, instead of saving him for a possible gold-medal game.

Contreras rewarded Borges by throwing his second straight Olympic shutout and Kindelan drove in all of the game's runs in Cuba's 3-0 victory.

The game was a rematch of the 1996 gold-medal matchup, which Cuba had won 13-9. This time, Japan had five members of its major leagues in the lineup and one on the mound, yet Contreras still dominated. He gave up six hits, walked none, and struck out nine, four days after shutting out Australia in a 1-0 win. Most observers had expected Cuba to save Contreras for the medal game, but Borges reasoned, "You must win the semifinal first," so he went with his ace.

Contreras had complete command of his fastball, changeup, split-finger fastball, and breaking pitches. Whenever he got into trouble, he picked his game up a notch, including a 97-mph fastball (on his 108th pitch) to get a ninth-inning groundout from Japan's powerful third baseman, Norihiro Nakamura.

Japan had runners in scoring position three times, and each time Contreras rose to the occasion. In the fourth, an error and a single by Nakamura had runners at first and second with one out. On a 2-1 pitch, Contreras jammed first baseman Nobuhiko Matsunaka, and the big leaguer hit into a 1-6-3 double play to end the inning.

In the sixth, with runners at first and third and one out after hits by Matsunaka and So Taguchi, Contreras faced veteran Yukio Tanaka. He struck out Tanaka with a split-fingered fastball for the second out, then retired pinch-hitter Shinnosuke Abe on a routine grounder to second to end that threat.

And in the eighth, Japan right fielder Jun Hirose led off with his team's hardest-hit ball, a lined double to left-center field. But Contreras easily handled the next three hitters as Hirose remained anchored at second.

"We had opportunities, but their pitcher was too good," Japanese manager Kozo Ohtagaki said. "They were better in terms of their concentration, taking advantage of their opportunities when we did not."

Cuba had Kindelan, who pushed his Olympic-leading RBI total to 11 by knocking in the game's first run in the fourth, as Cuba responded after Japan's missed opportunity. Yasser Gomez singled to lead off and Omar Linares hit a soft liner to second baseman Jun Heima, who made the catch but threw wildly to first in an attempt to double-up Gomez, so Gomez took second. Kindelan then punished a high fastball from

Japanese starter Tomohiro Kuroki, drilling a single to left that scored Gomez for the 1-0 lead.

Cuba got its other runs in the sixth. Luis Ulacia ignited the rally with an infield hit and went to second on Gomez' single to right. After Kuroki retired Linares on a routine fly out, both runners moved up on what turned out to be a crucial wild pitch. With first base open, the Japanese pitched to Kindelan, who again teed off on a high pitch, this time for a two-run single to left.

"We knew we were going to face good pitching, because Japan traditionally has good pitchers," Ulacia said. "We have put forth more effort lately, because we knew we were going to face very good pitching."

Kuroki was good, scattering eight hits and not allowing a walk in seven-plus innings. But Contreras and Kindelan were better. Kindelan upped his batting average to a robust .387 with two home runs and 11 RBIs over 31 at-bats in Sydney.

"Kindelan is the best hitter in the world, so I knew to be well prepared for him," Kuroki said. "But the pitches were a little high, so he hit them. He's not easy to get out."

The Cubans had rebounded nicely from their stunning loss to the Dutch by only allowing three runs in their four games since that day. Borges wouldn't divulge who his starting pitcher would be for the gold-medal contest, but it was widely expected that he would be sending righty Jose Ibar to the mound, who had dominated Team USA in pool play. The rest of the staff, including hard-throwing right handers Maels Rodriguez and Norge Vera and intimidating closer Pedro Luis Lazo, would also be available.

Japan would be forced to attempt to keep its streak of being the only team to win a medal in every Olympic baseball competition since 1984 (when baseball was still a demonstration sport) by sending ace righty Daisuke Matsuzaka to the mound in the bronze-medal game.

September 26, 2000 – Homebush Bay
SEMIFINAL # 2: USA (6-1) vs. KOREA (4-3)

Team USA and Korea line up for the introductions and starting lineups, prior to their semifinal game.

As Lasorda and his squad pulled up to Homebush Stadium in the team bus, the weather following the day game was not looking good. Forecasts called for intermittent showers all night, and the schedule had it that the game needed to be played, no matter what. The medal games were scheduled to be played the next day, and changes to an Olympic schedule wreak havoc on all kinds of ticketing and television broadcasting issues.

"We were mentally preparing for it to be a long night, and to deal with whatever was going to happen," said Team USA general manager Bob Watson. "The tension for all of us involved was already very high going into the game, so the potential for weather delays and rain was just going to make it worse."

Slated for a 7:30 p.m. (local time) first pitch, the Americans would be playing as the home team and situated in the third base dugout. The game began under ominous weather and a foreboding forecast that called for more rain as the evening progressed. A steady drizzle drifted through the cool evening air, in stark contrast to the warm, spring-like weather Sydney had enjoyed for much of these Olympics.

Oswalt took the mound for Team USA, to pitch in what would be the biggest game of his young life so far. And through two innings, both Oswalt and Chong looked just like they did when they had faced one another in pool play.

But in a scoreless game in the top of the third, Oswalt was finally touched up by the Korean offense. After allowing a leadoff walk to Sung-Ho Jang, shortstop Jin-Man Park, who was hitting just .130 entering the game, squared to bunt on the first pitch, then pulled back on the second pitch and lined a double to left field. Jang held up at third base, and Korea suddenly had a pair of runners in scoring position with no outs.

Jang gave Korea their first lead when he scored on a sacrifice fly by Soo-Keun Jung, and Park then scored on a double by Byung-Kyu Lee. Oswalt was able to escape further trouble by striking out Jong-Ho Park and retiring Seung-Yuop Lee on a long fly ball to right field (that just missed going over the fence for a home run). But the damage had been done, and the Americans trailed 2-0.

"That really gave me an uneasy feeling, because we weren't scoring against Chong, and things in the air just didn't feel right for us," said Seiler. "It certainly had me concerned."

Team USA finally answered back in the fourth off Chong, who had held them scoreless for 10 innings over two outings. Brad Wilkerson doubled to right field and moved to third on Mike Neill's ground out. After Ernie Young struck out, John Cotton broke out of an 0-for-14 slump with a first-pitch double to the gap in left-center field, scoring Wilkerson to make it 2-1.

"One of the biggest hits of my life, for sure," said Cotton. "Felt really good to come through for us in that situation, and get us on the scoreboard."

From there, Chong and Oswalt continued to match zeroes. American reliever Ryan Franklin came on to pitch in the seventh, and by that time, it was getting dangerously late for Team USA. Still trailing by a run, they had nine outs left to figure out a way to at least tie the score, or else their Gold-Medal dreams were over.

Chong seemed to still be in good control in the bottom of the seventh, when Mike Kinkade led off the inning by trying to surprise the Koreans, as he laid down a bunt up the third-base line. Hustling all the way, Kinkade was called safe at first base when Seung-Yuop Lee wasn't able to keep his foot on the bag while reaching for the throw. It was a bang-bang play at first base, but the call went the way of the United States, and they had their leadoff runner on.

At that point, Korean manager Euong-Yong Kim decided 98 pitches were enough for Chong and went to left-handed reliever Jin-Woo Song to face Doug Mientkiewicz, who batted left-handed. Doug battled the count and fouled off one 1-2 pitch before grounding the next one into right field for a single. Kinkade, attempting to take the extra base most likely due to the severity of his team's situation, rounded second and slid head-first into third base, just barely beating the throw from Korean right fielder Byung-Kyu Lee.

On the television replay, it had looked as if Kinkade's hand had slightly slipped off the base during the follow-through of his slide and that third baseman Dong-Joo Kim had tagged his arm while it was off the bag. But somehow, the third-base umpire missed seeing that, and kept with his original call of Kinkade being safe, much to the chagrin of Kim, who was arguing with the umpire as best he could.

When Marcus Jensen followed with an incredibly critical sacrifice fly ball to deep right-center field, Kinkade was able to tag up on the play and score the tying run.

"That was the first time in my life that I had ever seen a guy score a run after being out twice on the basepaths," said Mienkiewicz jokingly. "Arguably, he could have easily been called out at first base, but the call went our way. And then again at third, in which it had looked like he might have been out when he overslid the bag. Those calls going in our favor were just more signs that pointed to us being a team that was going to do something special. You just had a feeling like it was our time to shine."

Now with the score tied 2-2, Franklin went back to the mound and kept the game tied by keeping Korea off the scoreboard, giving his team a chance to take the lead in the bottom of the eighth. And that would become an inning that everybody in the Team USA contingent would never forget.

The bottom of the eighth ended up being one of the longest and most nerve-wracking, tense moments in USA Baseball history. With Chong out of the game, the Americans were now facing Korean reliever Seok-Jin Park. Brent Abernathy led off with a double to left field, a soft liner off the end of his bat that just landed fair down the line. It was a great start to the inning, as Team USA now had the potential go-ahead run at second base with nobody out.

Brad Wilkerson followed by failing on two bunt attempts, but succeeded in moving Abernathy over to third with one out, by hitting a ground ball to second base.

While all of this was happening, the weather had gotten worse, and rain had begun falling with more and more intensity. As left fielder Mike Neill stepped to the plate, the scene turned bizarre. Just before the first pitch, Korean catcher Sung-Heon Hong stood and asked for a timeout. So home-plate umpire Cesar Valdes of Cuba called time out while Park was in the midst of throwing a pitch. Neill then hit the pitch for a weak tapper back to the mound, but Valdes waved it off, much to Hong's hopping-mad dismay.

After that disputed pitch, a bolt of lightning struck beyond the left-field wall. First-base umpire Paul Begg of Australia jogged down the line, asking Valdes to delay the game. But Valdes waved him off and signaled for the game to continue, bringing a roar from the crowd.

To everyone's dismay, though, the count ran to 2-1 before

Valdes couldn't take it anymore. After wiping rainwater off his face, Valdes called for the official rain delay, with Abernathy just 90 feet away from scoring the potential winning run, in the bottom of the eighth inning.

The rain delay lasted exactly two hours.

"It was brutal, I couldn't sit still in the locker room. I had to do something, so I went and took some swings in the batting cage," said Neill. "It was raining, and you just didn't have a good feeling about the game. You're nervous, and that was the most tense game we played, in my opinion. For us to have gotten that far, if we were going to get a shot at beating Cuba in the gold-medal game, we had to win. At least if we got to the gold-medal game and got beat, that's what people probably expected of us. But if we had gotten beat by Korea, that would have been devastating. Just like the semifinal the year before against Mexico, the nerves were so high."

For Neill, he had two hours to contemplate going back up to the plate, with a chance to knock in the go-ahead run again in a semifinal game, just like he had done against Mexico in Winnipeg.

"Nobody was talking to me. All my teammates left me alone. So I just took some BP off the tee and kept to myself."

When play resumed, all of his batting practice off the tee was for naught. Neill was given an intentional walk, and Park followed by accidently hitting right fielder Ernie Young with a 2-2 pitch to load the bases, still with only one out. That brought up DH John Cotton. On a 1-1 pitch, Cotton hit a weak grounder to third baseman Dong-Joo Kim, and as Kim fielded the ball cleanly and threw home for the force out on Abernathy, Brent went out of the baseline and bulldozed the Korean catcher Sung-Heon Hong on the play. Valdes called Abernathy out for interference, making it an immediate double-play, because any time a runner interferes with a fielder, both the batter and the runner are out. It ended the Team USA threat and turned what looked like a golden opportunity to take a lead to the ninth inning into a squandered chance.

"That's the way I was taught to play," Abernathy said. "If I had the same situation, I probably would do the same thing again."

Added Lasorda, "I've never seen that play called like that before in my life, ever. But there's an old saying, 'If you stay around long enough, you'll see everything once,' and I saw plenty tonight."

Still tied after eight innings, Lasorda sent closer Todd Williams to the mound to pitch the top of the ninth, due to the fact that he had been warming up in case the Americans had scored. Williams, showing no signs of fear, calmly retired all three batters he faced, on a pair of strikeouts and a fly out.

Due up in the bottom of the ninth were Kinkade, Mientkiewicz, and Jensen, the same trio that had put together a rally to tie the score in the seventh. Park was still in the game for Korea, and he plunked Kinkade in the shoulder with a breaking ball, putting the winning run on base with nobody out.

Lasorda immediately inserted his fastest runner on the bench in Travis "Gookie" Dawkins, to pinch-run for Kinkade. And with Mientkiewicz at the plate, Lasorda played the baseball odds and signaled for him to lay down a sacrifice bunt in order to get the potential game-winner into scoring position.

Park, knowing that Dawkins also might attempt to steal second, wanted to keep him close, and threw over to first base twice. Mientkiewicz squared around to bunt, but took the first pitch for ball one. Then, still attempting to bunt, he took ball two.

"When we got the count to 2-0, Tommy put on the hit and run, and I fouled the pitch off," said Mientkiewicz. "So he put the hit and run on again." But this time, Park, anticipating that Dawkins would be running again, used a quick pickoff move to first and caught Gookie leaning the wrong way. He was out by a hair, despite Lasorda and first-base coach Reggie Smith's arguments with the umpire.

"I remember immediately thinking to myself, 'Okay, I'm

swinging away now. How have you elevated the ball against a sidearm pitcher before in your career? Let's get out in front of an off-speed pitch and see what happens.'"

As Lasorda and Smith spent a few minutes arguing with the first-base umpire over the critical pickoff call of Dawkins, Mientkiewicz took the moment to collect himself and his thoughts.

"I was thinking that I was still ahead on the count, and that I had gotten that big hit in the seventh, and right then, something just came over me, and the game slowed down. I've never had a two-week window in my life, the way those two weeks in Sydney were for me. No matter what I had, no matter what I saw in my mind or thought might happen, the game was slower than it had ever been in my entire life, my entire career. And I remember standing there in that at-bat thinking, 'I can see this guy's release point so clearly right now. I can see him releasing the ball to me.'"

As Mientkiewicz dug back into the batter's box to await the 2-1 pitch from Park, it was a moment he would never forget. "I remember seeing the pitch come up off his fingers, and the first thing I thought, the first instant when I saw the ball come out of his hand, was 'Game over. Just put a good swing on it, put a good swing on it, it's a change-up.' I remember being a little bit out in front of it, but I got a good part of the bat on it, and I remember running to first base thinking, 'Holy shit, that never happens. That never happens.'"

Mientkiewicz had launched the ball into the cloudy, dark night of Sydney Olympic Park. When it landed beyond the right-field fence, the Americans had won the game 3-2 and would be playing for the gold medal in Olympic baseball.

"I remember putting both arms in the air, and then taking the bat between my legs and throwing it up as far as I could, and not knowing where I threw it. I don't remember much after that. I do remember rounding third and looking at our dugout running out and jumping around, and seeing everybody pile on me when I got to home plate. And I remember everybody hugging me, and through all that pandemonium, Ben Sheets grabbed me and said, 'Dude, you just won us a fucking gold medal.' And I thought, 'If he's telling me that, then it's over.' We had Sheetsy going the next night, and he was going to win that game."

Mientkiewicz's homer ended a surreal game that featured a number of controversies and a two-hour rain delay. The victory, Team USA's fourth in its last at-bat in eight Olympic games, pushed Team USA (7-1) into the Gold-Medal game against Cuba (7-1) at 7:30 p.m. local time (4:30 a.m. Eastern in the USA) on Wednesday. Korea (4-4) would have to come back just a little more than 12 hours after its defeat to face Japan at 12:30 p.m. local time for the bronze medal.

"It's a bigger home run than last time, because of the stakes," said Mientkiewicz. "All I wanted to do was get on base, get a win, and go back to the Village, so I could get out of this soaking wet uniform. This park plays huge, so if it's not hit down the lines, it's not getting out of here. I've been lucky enough to get it down the line twice."

For Lasorda, the moment was unlike any he had experienced in his over 50 years in the game. "One second I was so angry that Gookie had gotten picked off first, and by the time I had gotten back to the dugout, Doug had hit that ball over the fence," said Lasorda. "And it was pure joy. Before his at-bat, Doug and I had a talk, and he said, 'Skip, I'll do whatever it takes for us to win the game.' He's never thought about his individual accomplishments this whole time, just of the team and winning."

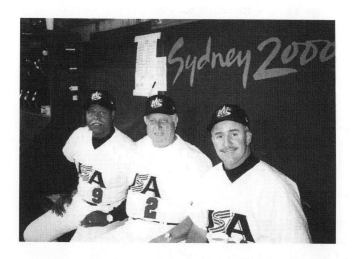

Team USA Manager Tommy Lasorda (center) with his coaches Reggie Smith (left) and Eddie Rodriguez (right), prior to the semifinal game vs. Korea.

DAVID FANUCCHI

```
Korea (4-4)                      USA (7-1)
              AB  R  H  BI                      AB  R  H  BI
Lee, BK rf    4   0  1  1        Abernathy 2b   4   0  1  0
Park, JH 2b   4   0  0  0        Wilkerson cf   3   1  1  0
Lee, SY 1b    4   0  0  0        Neill lf       3   0  0  0
Kim, DJ 3b    4   0  0  0        E. Young rf    3   0  0  0
Kim, KT dh    3   0  0  0        Cotton dh      4   0  1  1
Hong c        3   0  0  0        Kinkade 3b     2   1  1  0
Jang lf       2   1  0  0        Dawkins pr     0   0  0  0
Park, JM ss   3   1  1  0        Mientkiewicz 1b 3  1  2  1
Jung cf       2   0  1  1        Jensen c       2   0  0  1
Chong p       0   0  0  0        Everett ss     3   0  0  0
Song p        0   0  0  0        Oswalt p       0   0  0  0
Park, SJ p    0   0  0  0        Franklin p     0   0  0  0
                                 Williams p     0   0  0  0

Totals......  29  2  3  2        Totals......   27  3  6  3

Score by innings:                        R  H  E
---------------------------------------------
Korea                    002 000 000  -  2  3  0
USA                      000 100 101  -  3  6  1
---------------------------------------------
```

One out when the game ended.

E - Kinkade. LOB - Korea 2, USA 6. 2B - Lee, BK, Park, JM, Abernathy(6), Wilkerson(1), Cotton(2). HR - Mientkiewicz(2). SH - Jung, Jensen. SB - Jung. CS - Lee, BK, Wilkerson. K - Park, JH 2, Lee, SY 2, Kim, DJ, Jang 2, Park, JM, Neill, E. Young 2, Cotton, Jensen, Everett. BB - Jang, Neill, Kinkade, Mientkiewicz.

```
              IP   H  R  ER BB SO WP BK HP IBB AB BF Fly Gnd
Chong         6.1  3  2  2  2  6  0  0  1  0   21 24  4   8
Song          0.1  1  0  0  0  0  0  0  0  0    1  2  1   0
Park, SJ L 0-1 1.2 2  1  1  1  0  0  0  2  1    5  8  0   3

Oswalt        6.0  3  2  2  1  4  0  0  0  0   20 22 10   3
Franklin      2.0  0  0  0  0  2  0  0  0  0    6  6  1   3
Williams W 1-0 1.0 0  0  0  0  2  0  0  0  0    3  3  1   0
```

HBP - by Chong (Wilkerson), by Park, SJ (E. Young), by Park, SJ (Kinkade).

Umpires - Home:Valdes 1st:Begg 2nd:Bodaan 3rd:Castillo
Attendance: 14,002

The United States hadn't won the gold medal in either of the previous two Games in which it was a medal sport, finishing fourth in 1992 and third in 1996. Cuba won the championship in both Barcelona and Atlanta, and hadn't lost an Olympic game until the Netherlands pulled off an upset last week.

"After Doug hit that walk off homer, at worst, we knew we were going home with at least a silver medal, and if we had lost the next game, then we we're beat by the team that was expected to win, Cuba," said Neill. "So all the pressure was taken off of us, when he hit that home run. That's what Doug did, he gave us that. He lifted all that pressure, because if we had lost in that game, we would have failed to meet our expectations. We would have had to play for a bronze, and that's not why we went over there. I think that's why we all went crazy when he hit that bomb."

This was going to be the first time that the always highly anticipated USA vs. Cuba matchup was going to be played for Olympic gold. The Cubans had won 25 of the 28 games between the teams in major international competition.

"We didn't show Cuba our best game, the last time," Mientkiewicz said of Team USA's 6-1 loss earlier. "We wanted Cuba to win today. To be the best, you've got to beat the best, and until we do, we're still playing second fiddle."

With the adrenaline still pumping, Mienkiewicz and his teammates were finally able to get out of their rain-soaked jerseys and head back to the Athletes Village, just one win away from the ultimate. The next night, they would have the chance to write history.

"We got finished with the game and media obligations pretty late, and we were all really tired when we got back to the rooms," said Mientkiewicz. "So the next morning, all we really did was get up, and by the time we knew it, we were headed to the ballpark again. We didn't have time to think about it much, because we were doing so much other stuff. We all had an autograph session to sign a bunch of things for one another and USA Baseball. Leading up to the semifinal game, there wasn't much talking going on that day. Of all the games that we played there, that one was probably the most uptight we played. So I think the gold-medal game was actually the most relaxed we had felt the entire event. We felt like, 'Hey, let's do what we came here to do.' Yes, we wanted to win, of course. But there was never a doubt in my mind that we weren't going to win."

September 27, 2000 – Homebush Bay
<u>BRONZE-MEDAL GAME: KOREA (4-4) vs. JAPAN (4-4)</u>

Just 12 hours after suffering a heartbreaking 2-1 loss to the United States, the Koreans had to regroup for a day game that was to be played against their archrivals from Japan. It would remain to be seen how much energy the Koreans would be able to muster with a medal on the line.

For the third time in the 2000 Olympics, Japan sent 1999 Pacific League Rookie of the Year Daisuke Matsuzaka to the mound. And for the third time, Japan lost with him on the mound, falling 3-1 to Korea. It was the first time since the Olympics began staging baseball tournaments in 1984 that Japan had failed to medal. It became the first ever baseball medal for Korea.

Apparently, the Koreans had enough left in the tank to produce their second victory of the tournament against their biggest rival in Asia, and it completed an about-face in the event for a team that lost its starting catcher and top pitcher to injuries. But banged-up star first baseman Seung-Yuop Lee, who battled ankle and back problems during the Olympics, had the biggest hit of the tournament for his country.

In a tense pitchers' duel between Matsuzaka and Korean left-hander Dae-Sung Koo, Matsuzaka finally gave in when his defense betrayed him in the eighth inning. The game was scoreless when shortstop Jin-Man Park led off the bottom of the inning with a single. Center fielder Soo-Keun Jung sacrificed him to second, and Park advanced to third when

Japan second baseman Jun Heima booted right fielder Byung-Kyu Lee's ground ball.

With runners at the corners, Matsuzaka retired second baseman Jong-Ho Park on a flyout to shallow center field to bring Seung-Yuop Lee, Korea's home-run king, to the plate. Lee responded with a line-drive double to left-center field to drive in the game's first two runs. Third baseman Dong-Joo Kim, known as "The Rhino" in Korea for his stocky build, lined an RBI single to right to make it 3-0.

"I didn't sleep well last night," Lee said. "I was a little tired today and didn't have a lot of confidence. I expected a fastball, I waited for it, and that's what I hit."

Japan finally scored with one out in the ninth, as first baseman Nobuhiko Matsunaka doubled and scored on a single by DH Yukio Tanaka. Koo then struck out right fielder Jun Hirose looking and retired pinch-hitter Shinnosuke Abe on a routine grounder to second to end the game. Koo was thrilled to have won the bronze against the famed Matsuzaka.

"We thought he was very good, and we were nervous a bit at the beginning of the game," Koo said. "But as the game went on, we started thinking we could win. I don't know what else to say. I'm quite happy now."

September 27, 2000 – Homebush Bay
GOLD-MEDAL GAME: USA (7-1) vs. CUBA (7-1)

As Team USA came off the bus to enter the stadium for the gold-medal game, Lasorda led the way, with Sheets right behind him.

As the two teams warmed up and Homebush Bay Stadium filled up with a sold-out crowd full of anticipation, the atmosphere in the ballpark became electric. NBC Sports, which was broadcasting the Olympics back to the United States, was on hand with Bob Costas anchoring their pregame coverage from the field. This historic matchup on the baseball diamond had drawn a high priority on NBC's lineup and would be featured in their nightly live cut-ins and recapped the next day, when most Americans would be waking up to the news.

Lasorda, seemingly very calm prior to the big game, delivered a poignant but simple pre-game speech in the locker room, reminding his troops that they didn't come this far to lose. It was another gentle reminder Lasorda had mentioned to them over and over again, that they were playing for "the name on the front of their jersey, not the one on the back."

Lasorda delivers his pregame speech to Team USA in the locker room, just prior to the gold-medal game vs. Cuba.

From the very first pitch, the game took on a much different tone from the pool-play meeting between the two teams. After using ace Jose Contreras to beat Japan in the semifinals, Cuba surprisingly went with right hander Pedro Luis Lazo as its starter, instead of Jose Ibar. Lazo, who was a starter in Cuba's Serie Nacional, had been serving as the Cuban Olympic Team's closer in recent international competitions, and pitched the last two innings of Cuba's 6-1 victory in the two teams' first matchup in Sydney.

Lazo gave up Team USA's only run in that game, and he surrendered the first run in this one, in the top of the first inning. After striking out Brent Abernathy and Brad Wilkerson to start the contest, Lazo made what was his most critical mistake. When he left a 2-1 pitch to Mike Neill up and over the plate, Neill went with the pitch and blasted it out to left field and over the fence, for his tournament-best third home run. It gave Team USA an immediate 1-0 lead, and the entire tenor of the game changed at that moment. Any intimidation factor Cuba had expected to have over Team USA after winning the first meeting was now gone.

"I got ahead in the count 2-0, and he came in with a nice fastball, but I fouled it off. I remember thinking that was my pitch, and to be ready for another. I put a good swing on it when he came back with the same fastball, but the ball didn't carry very well in that little stadium. I didn't know if I could hit it out to the opposite field like that. So when it went over the wall, I was so pumped. I rounded the bases, and I remember yelling as I passed Omar Linares at third base, 'That's right, we came to play tonight, mother fucker!'"

For Lasorda, it was the perfect start. "That was a very big moment, Mike's home run really allowed us to relax," said Lasorda. "The minute he hit it, you felt a boost of confidence." And for Sheets, the one run meant a lot. "That first inning homer was huge, it allowed me to take the mound with a lead right away. It gave me a little room for error."

So as Sheets strode to the mound for what would become the biggest game of his life, for every decision that USA

Baseball had made to get Team USA to this point, the final result was in his hands.

"From Day One, we knew if we had one player we could build around, if we needed to have somebody who could win the gold medal for us, that player was Ben Sheets," said USA Baseball executive director Paul Seiler. "We didn't have the prettiest team, we didn't have a Ferrari. But if we did have one, it was Sheets."

"I was fired up. I knew it was an opportunity of a lifetime, and I was ready for it," said Sheets. "I didn't know for sure how the game was going to turn out, but when you're young, you think you're a lot better than you are. You think you're invincible. I just immersed myself into the situation. I knew I had a little edge, and I knew I was throwing the ball pretty well and that I felt good. So I was excited about our chances."

After retiring the first two hitters in the bottom of the first, Sheets gave up a single to Linares. But when he struck out first baseman Orestes Kindelan looking, the Americans had the lead after one full inning and never looked back.

"We had it set up a long time ago, that Ben was going to pitch this game," said Lasorda, "because we knew he was that good."

After giving up the homer to Neill but also getting the final out of the first, Lazo allowed a leadoff double to John Cotton in the second. And that would be it for Lazo. Cuba's manager Servio Borges decided to remove Lazo and bring in Jose Ibar, who escaped the jam. But it remained to be seen how critical that decision would be, not to start Ibar in the first place.

But on this night, it was Sheets who was electrifying the crowd. The Cuban bats were not making any noise, as they struggled to get any runners on base. Both pitchers posted zeroes in the second, third, and fourth innings, and the score remained 1-0 into the fifth.

Then in the top of the fifth, Team USA added to their lead, finally touching Ibar for some runs. When he walked Mientkiewicz to lead off the frame, catcher Pat Borders—who had battled back from his injured ankle to make the start catching Sheets behind home plate—then ripped a double to the right-center field gap, easily scoring Mientkiewicz to make it 2-0. Borders was then thrown out at third base on a bunt attempt by Adam Everett, but Abernathy followed with a base hit that put runners at the corners, with only one out.

Borges went to his bullpen again, but instead of choosing left-hander Omar Ajete to face the left-handed bats of Wilkerson and Neill, he went to his flame-throwing righty Maels Rodriguez. When Wilkerson worked out a walk, the bases were loaded for Neill. But this time, the Rhode Island native was unable to come through, as Rodriguez struck out Neill with a 100 mph fastball.

Now with two outs and the bases still loaded, Rodriguez was now facing Ernie Young. It was Young who had been hit in the back by an Ibar fastball in the pool-play game, which had started somewhat of an ugly back and forth of intimidation tactics.

"I was paying attention to how that inning unfolded, and I saw exactly how he was pitching to Brad (Wilkerson) and Mike (Neill)," said Young. "He was going right at them with his hard fastball. So I said to myself, 'Just relax, make him get the ball down in the zone and put a good swing on it.' And that's exactly what I did. It turned out to be a crucial hit in that part of the game, which gave us a little breathing room. I remember it like it was yesterday. I can still see that ball going right back up the middle."

Young had broken open the game with a two-run single that was smashed right back through the infield, a line drive that came within inches of Rodriguez's head. It was now 4-0, and Cuba had only 15 outs left to try and score four times.

"The way Sheetsy was pitching," said Abernathy, "there was no team in the world that was going to score four runs off of him."

"I had just been pounding the strike zone, letting them get themselves out," said Sheets. "But once we got four runs, I really just wanted to get back to the mound. I was in such a good rhythm. With Pat back there making things happen, it was pretty special. When I was warming up in the bullpen and I saw Pat come walk out there to catch me, it was a pretty calming feeling. Nothing against Marcus (Jensen), but Pat had been through the battles. That's why we had him on the team, and that's who I wanted catching that game for me."

Now staked to a commanding 4-0 lead, Sheets continued to dominate the Cuban hitters with an assortment of mid-90s fastballs and a curveball that was falling off the table. Sheets was able to go deep into this game, because he rarely went deep in the count. In his first start of the Olympics, Sheets threw 26 pitches in the first inning against Japan. But after three innings against Cuba on this night, he had thrown only 25.

Sheets was also getting plenty of defensive help. Mientkiewicz made a diving stop of a hard-hit Linares grounder in the fourth, and Everett was routinely handling every groundball anywhere near him. Third baseman Mike Kinkade, not known for his glove, handled a hard smash off the bat of Miguel Caldes, and Ernie Young ended the eighth inning by sliding to make a long, running catch in foul territory down the right-field line.

With Sheets in full command, the only question remaining was how long Lasorda would let him pitch. During Sheets's first two starts against Japan and Italy, Lasorda and pitching coach Phil Regan had stuck to the rule and pulled Sheets out of the game after he had extended past his allotted pitch count.

"All year in the minor leagues, my pitch-count max was set at 85, but for some reason when I had gotten to Australia, the Brewers had dropped it to 75," said Sheets. "So I was pretty disappointed about that, because I was hoping they'd bump it up to 90 or 100 for the Olympics. So I called the Brewers office back in Milwaukee from this little cell phone we had while we were training on the Gold Coast, and Dean Taylor bumped it back up to 90 for me."

Sheets had been moving through the Cuban lineup with

ease, but was approaching the 90 pitch limit in the eighth inning.

"I saw Bob Watson sitting behind home plate, when it was getting late in the game, and he stood up and hollered to me, and started throwing his hands out with the pitch count on Sheets," said Lasorda. "He wanted me to take him out. And I said, 'Sit down, Bull. I ain't taking this guy out of the game even if God tells me to. He's pitching all nine innings.'"

No pitch count or quality-control decision made by the Brewers was going to matter to Sheets either. This was his game.

"I don't know how many pitches I threw, but it couldn't have been much more than 90. Those were pretty quick innings, so I don't think Lasorda could have taken me off that mound," said Sheets. "Even if he'd come out to the mound to get me, it didn't matter, you know? Because I was living in the moment, man, and it was a special moment. You don't cheat yourself out of something like that. People might have said I shouldn't have stayed in the game, and that I hadn't thrown a complete game all season to that point. But that was something you never forget for the rest of your life, so there was no chance that I was coming out of that game, as long as we were ahead."

Sheets pitched comfortably with the early lead the entire game and was never out of control. His 84th pitch was clocked at 96 mph, and he touched 98 twice, as he showed major-league stuff against a battle-tested lineup.

Going to the bottom of the ninth with the 4-0 lead, the Cubans had only collected three singles—two by Linares and one by Oscar Macias—and they had not gotten any of those runners past first base all night. Sheets struck out pinch-hitter Javier Mendez leading off the ninth, then also fanned Luis Ulacia for his fifth strikeout of the game and the second out. That brought Yasser Gomez to the plate with one out to go, and the American dugout to the top steps, ready to celebrate.

Gomez connected on a looping line drive down the left-field line, but Mike Neill was there to slide and make a sno-cone catch of the ball for the final out. As Sheets saw the play, he turned toward home plate and fell to his knees, with both arms raised into the air, the iconic image that was plastered across every newspaper front page in America the next day. It was all over, and just as Sheets had predicted to Mientkiewicz the night before, the United States had just won the gold medal.

Sheets ended up needing only 103 pitches to go the distance. "I don't think you really know what just happened. That whole moment just came on so fast, and you don't realize how big of a moment that is, even looking back," said Sheets. "I had to get away from it before I realized how special it was. But what a great group of guys to share it with. What's so cool is that everybody had a part in that victory. It's easy looking at a picture of me on my knees, with my hands raised, to think it's all about me, but do you know how many great performances all of my teammates had to give, just to get us there? Each and every one of them did something to help us win that gold medal. It was incredible."

"I can't describe the feeling," said Abernathy, after clearing off the dogpile on the middle of the infield. "We came here to do one thing, win the gold, and nobody gave us a chance to do it. We proved everybody wrong."

"Everybody had set the Cubans as the standard for this sport," right fielder Ernie Young said. "But this is our sport. Baseball was started by us and it's played by us. And now we've won the gold medal. These were the best games of my life, and if I don't ever play again, I'll be happy I was able to play in this game tonight."

For Lasorda, it was the culmination of a career in baseball. "Well, you know when they said that the coaches don't get medals, I got my medal when I saw them put those gold medals around my players. I got my medal when they played the National Anthem. I got my medal when they not only played the National Anthem, but when they raised the American flag, that's when I started to cry. And when they played our National Anthem, I knew that we had done something. We had won for our country. I told people, even before I went over there, before I knew who we had on our team, how big this was going to be. I said, 'It's bigger than the World Series. It's bigger than the Los Angeles Dodgers.' And I have to say that it's the greatest thing that has ever happened to me."

Team USA celebrates on the field after the final out.

Just minutes after winning a gold medal, the American team huddled up for an emotional speech by several players.

DAVID FANUCCHI

```
USA 4 (8-1)                              Cuba 0 (7-2)
                 AB  R  H  RBI                            AB  R  H  RBI
Abernathy 2b     5   1  1  0             Ulacia lf        4   0  0  0
Wilkerson cf/rf  4   0  0  0             Gomez cf         4   0  0  0
Neill lf         5   1  2  1             Linares 3b       3   0  2  0
E. Young rf      4   0  2  2             Kindelan 1b      3   0  0  0
Sanders pr/cf    0   0  0  0             Pacheco dh       3   0  0  0
Cotton dh        3   0  1  0             Macias 2b        3   0  1  0
Burroughs ph/dh  1   0  0  0             Caldes rf        3   0  0  0
Kinkade 3b       4   0  0  0             Pestano c        2   0  0  0
Mientkiewicz 1b  3   1  0  0             Manrique ph/c    1   0  0  0
Borders c        3   0  2  1             Mesa ss          2   0  0  0
Everett ss       3   1  1  0             Mendez ph        1   0  0  0
Sheets p         0   0  0  0             Lazo p           0   0  0  0
                                         Ibar p           0   0  0  0
                                         Rodriguez p      0   0  0  0

Totals......     35  4  9  4             Totals......     29  0  3  0

Score by innings:                          R  H  E
-----------------------------------------------------
USA                       100 030 000  -   4  9  0
Cuba                      000 000 000  -   0  3  0
-----------------------------------------------------
```

DP - USA 1. LOB - USA 10, Cuba 2. 2B - Cotton(2), Borders(2). HR - Neill(3). CS - E. Young. Strikeouts - Abernathy 2, Wilkerson 3, Neill 3, Burroughs, Kinkade, Mientkiewicz, Everett, Ulacia, Gomez, Kindelan 2, Mendez. Walks - Wilkerson, E. Young, Mientkiewicz, Borders, Everett.

```
              IP   H  R  ER BB SO  WP BK HP IBB  AB BF  Fly Gnd
Sheets W 1-0  9.0  3  0  0  0  5   0  0  0  0    29 29   6  15

Lazo L 1-1    1.0  3  1  1  0  2   0  0  0  0     5  5   0   0
Ibar          3.1  2  3  3  2  3   0  0  0  0    12 14   1   6
Rodriguez     4.2  4  0  0  3  7   0  0  1  0    18 22   4   3
```

HBP - by Rodriguez (Cotton).

Umpires - Home:Rosario 1st:Koyama 2nd:Contreras 3rd:Castillo
Time: 2:37   Attendance: 14,107

MIRACLE ON GRASS

Team USA outfielder Brad Wilkerson is all smiles as he carries the American flag around the field, following his team's gold-medal triumph.

American players with their flowers and hardware, on the gold-medal stand.

Lasorda and Watson get choked up, as they watch their team receive gold medals.

Team USA acknowledges the crowd, their arms up in victory.

(L-R) MLB's Steve Cobb, USA Baseball's Paul Seiler, and Team USA Press Officer Dave Fanucchi, celebrating together that one special moment in time, with the Americans on the gold-medal stand in the background.

Mientkiewicz (upper left), Neill (left), and Sheets (right) show off their medals in the postgame media room, surrounding Lasorda.

Lasorda, Sheets, Neill and Mientkiewicz appeared on NBC's *The Today Show* with Matt Lauer.

Mike Neill holds up his gold medal and the ball he caught in left field for the final out of the game.

Following the game, in the bowels of Homebush Bay Stadium, International Baseball Federation secretary general John Ostermeyer of Australia took Paul Seiler's hand and congratulated him for a job well done.

Seiler, USA Baseball's executive director, had just watched the team of American minor leaguers he helped assemble beat Cuba 4-0 for the 2000 Olympic gold medal. He smiled at Ostermeyer and thanked him for his support in helping open the Olympics to professional players. The IBAF had ratified that decision on Sept. 21, 1996, a little more than four years before the Americans captured their first gold medal since baseball became a full-medal sport in 1992.

The 1999 Pan American Games in Winnipeg, Manitoba, gave the world a glimpse of what international baseball would look like with pros dotting the rosters. The Olympics proved the move a success.

"It was absolutely the best tournament in international baseball history," Seiler said. "There's no question, and I don't say that just because the United States won the gold."

The more than 245,000 fans who came to the tournament saw a string of upsets as pro players and wood bats leveled the playing field. The tournament proved a lot of things, first and foremost that the United States could bring together a team and staff of professionals and win an Olympic medal.

Seiler admitted his team wasn't a Dream Team, "but we got it done." And to a man, the American players said they enjoyed the experience of playing in the Olympics. They weren't the only pros who were impressed. Japanese first baseman Nobuhiko Matsunaka, said he would return to play in the Olympics if given the chance, despite his country's disappointing fourth-place finish.

"It's just a unique experience, and there's nothing like it anywhere else in the game," Seiler said. "When Pat Borders, a 12-year big-league veteran, tells you what a great time he's had and that it was one of his best experiences in baseball, that tells you we've done something right."

The cooperation among Major League Baseball, the MLB

Players Association, and USA Baseball was a major factor in Team USA's victory, but it had started in 1999 at the Pan Am Games. Seiler gave that team, coaching staff, and Selection Committee chairman Pat Gillick much of the credit for the success of the 2000 edition.

"When we got that last out, all I could think about was Buddy Bell, Jackie Moore, (Marcel) Lachemann, Pat Gillick, Mike Neill's hit (against Mexico), and the clutch pitching by J.C. Romero and Dan Wheeler," Seiler said. "I wanted to call Buddy and tell him he should have been on that medal stand for what he did. They factored into our success directly."

The 2004 Athens Games were on deck, and one thing would be certain: After beating Cuba for the gold, Team USA would have different players in four years, but would be the outright favorites.

"What this tournament proved about the Cubans is that they're human," Seiler said. "They've always been good, and if things stay the same there, they will still be very good in 2004. But I think we proved they can be beaten."

15

RETURNING HOME HEROES

In the immediate aftermath following the final out, Team USA players and coaches could be found running all over the Homebush Bay diamond, carrying American flags and hugging one another. It was a joyous celebration in which all of the USA Baseball contingent, including the men who had helped make it all possible—Seiler, Alderson, Watson, Cobb, and many others—flooded the field in front of the USA dugout.

"Such a special night, one that I'll never forget," said Alderson. "It ranks right up there with some of the greatest things I've ever accomplished in the game of baseball, for sure, including the World Series win with Oakland in '89. I was lucky enough to have my parents there with me that night in Australia, and was really proud that my dad was able to witness that game."

For Seiler, it was the outcome he had been longing for since the day he began working for USA Baseball as an intern back in Trenton, New Jersey in the early '80s.

"It was a pretty surreal moment, to see our guys up on the podium with gold medals, while the Cubans were standing next to them with silver," said Seiler. "To have come through in such a historic game, and to know that we had pulled it off, it really didn't sink in right away. I just tried to absorb every minute of that scene, because I knew how fleeting that was, and how difficult it would be to get back there again one day."

And for Watson, who had been an instrumental figure in the selection of both rosters, it was an emotional time. "Watching the guys receive their gold medals as I was standing next to Tommy, I could see it was bringing tears to his eyes," said Watson. "And to be able to hear our National Anthem played was just a thrill. I was so very proud to have been a part of that entire experience. At that moment, I couldn't help but get choked up as well."

For Bill Bavasi, who was watching intently from afar, he had come to the realization that he had missed something special. "What those kids did was so cool, it was a great life opportunity. My wife and I have talked about it a lot, that one of the greatest mistakes in my life was not just taking a chance and going to Australia," said Bavasi. "I should have said to anybody else I was committed to, 'Hey, I'm putting my life on hold for two weeks and I'm outta here.' Because looking back on it, there are a lot of things we go through in life that we wish we would have done differently. And if I'm being honest, that's my biggest mistake. Professionally, that's my biggest, not going with Team USA to Australia to experience the Olympics. But, having said that, it was still a terrific opportunity to work with that group, because I made some great friends that I'm going to have for life. So it's a really special thing to me as well."

As soon as the medal ceremony ended, the media interviews began, and the entire Team USA roster of players along with Lasorda filed into the press room to answer questions. Many were for Sheets, who had just pitched one of the greatest games in Olympic baseball history—if not the best—given the circumstances.

But Sheets was quick to erase the personal credit, and instead chose to shine the light on his teammates and the entire USA Baseball contingent. "That gold medal was about everybody we had, from the top all the way down to the players. What was so impressive to me was that we all became a true team," said Sheets. "It was a team in every sense of the word. From Tommy and Rod Dedeaux who was with us, to John Fierro our trainer, and all the way to our staff people like Paul Seiler and Steve Cohen, we were over there together and everybody got along, because we had one goal. None of us had ever been to the Olympics; we had baseball experience but not in that arena. We were all learning as we went along, and we just believed we could get it done! Every one of us just believing and hoping and thinking we could win, hoping we were the right guys to do it. So the victory meant the same to all of us. There were only 24 of us that got gold medals, but they could have given one out to everybody that had a role with our team. The ceremony was about the moment and what we'd done and what we accomplished, how we did it, and how special each and every game was."

The USA Baseball team's victory of Cuba became the story of the night worldwide, on that particular day of the 2000 Olympics. Even though ironically, another one of Team USA's biggest upsets had occurred during the gold-medal game being played that very same night.

Earlier that evening, American Greco-Roman wrestler Rulon Gardner had pulled off his own version of a shocking victory when he defeated Russian Alexsandr Karelin to win the gold medal. Karelin had been previously unbeaten in the past 13 years of international competition and had not given up in point in the last six years.

So although Gardner had claimed an amazing gold medal himself, it was Sheets's photo that ended up plastered across the front page of USA Today on September 28, 2000, with a headline that read "Gold Safe at Home."

Following the press conference at the baseball stadium, it was my job to escort Lasorda, Sheets, Neill, and Mientkiewicz to an appearance on NBC's *The Today Show* and a live interview with Matt Lauer. Because of the time difference, people in America were just waking up to the news that the Americans had won the gold medal in baseball. It was there that all four players proudly wore their gold medals around their necks, still in their dirty uniforms from the game, and signed autographs for the many fans who were surrounding the set.

The rest of the team headed back to the Athletes Village and began quite a party. USA Baseball administrators also filed back to their team hotel, for a little celebration that Cobb had arranged, prior to the game that night.

"I had ordered up some beverages and champagne to be placed on ice in one of our suites, with the idea that it would get used had we won the game," said Cobb. "Had we lost, I'm not sure what we would have done with it. But, it all turned out right, a lot like the entire trip. It was tremendous."

Back at the Village, as Team USA celebrated in their condos late into the night, they received a surprise visit. Several of the Cuban baseball players stopped by, not only to offer a small dose of congratulations, but to chat with the American baseball players that many of them respected.

It was a small gesture of peace now that the games had concluded, and both sides could put any animosity that may have still existed, to rest. Pat Borders—who had been steamrolled at home plate in the pool-play game, injuring his ankle—showed what a true professional he was when he gave away the catching gear he had used during the Games to the Cuban team. He understood that those players had far less access to quality equipment than he did, and therefore it was far more valuable to them.

American catcher Marcus Jensen did the same thing, and several other Team USA players as well as USA Baseball equipment manager Chris Gebeck gave the Cuban players as much of their gently used equipment that they could afford to do without, including bats, bags of practice baseballs, and helmets.

"It was nice to speak with them afterwards, without any hard feelings involved," said Team USA third-base coach Eddie Rodriguez. "I was able to speak to a few of the Cubans in Spanish, and one of their players told me that Fidel Castro had promised every player on their team each a brand-new car and a new house that they could live in with their families, if they had beaten us that night," said Rodriguez. "That was so shocking to hear, that they had lost much more than a baseball game. They had lost the chance for a better life."

The day after Cuba's 4-0 defeat at the hands of Team USA, the headline on the sports page of Gramma, the island's official newspaper, read, "Is it the End of the World?"

The loss was a major disappointment for millions of Cuban fans who were still groggy from getting up at 4:30 a.m. to watch the game. And it was a devastating defeat for the Cuban team that had dominated the international amateur game for more than three decades. The soul searching had begun as to what went wrong.

Clearly the addition of professionals to the tournament removed one advantage the Cubans had. Cuba could keep the same team of essentially pro players together year after year, while other powers such as Japan and the USA had usually sent college players to international tournaments.

But a more important reason for the decline of the Cuban dominance was that the same system that consistently produced outstanding players didn't offer many opportunities for them to advance on the island. That led Cuban authorities to rely on veterans to represent them each summer, because younger players often weren't improving or decided to defect.

While Orestes Kindelan was a dominant hitter in the 1992 and 1996 Games, his slower bat speed was evident in Sydney. Clearly age had caught up with Cuba, and a gold medal in Sydney only would have papered over cracks in their system.

As Cuban baseball officials regrouped to figure out how to best confront the world that was changing around them, fans throughout the island would be second-guessing those officials for years to come. Cuban fans questioned why their team's two best pitchers, right handers Jose Contreras and Norge Vera didn't face Team USA in the Gold-Medal game, and why left-hander Omar Ajete wasn't brought in to face the pair of left-handed USA hitters in the pivotal three-run fifth inning.

But even if the Cubans had started Contreras, it wouldn't have made much difference. This Cuban team couldn't score off Sheets, and there were no great clutch performances from Kindelan or Linares.

The Cubans had to scramble for runs in wins against Australia, Italy, Japan, and Korea, and they suffered an embarrassing 4-2 loss to the Netherlands that ended their 21-game Olympic winning streak.

"We lost in baseball and that hurts," Castro said. "But we will return, and then we will want to play a team of major leaguers, to see who wins."

Upon his return home to the United States, new American hero Ben Sheets was immediately summoned to Milwaukee, where the Brewers were playing their last ever game at the old County Stadium. In a special pregame ceremony along with famous Brewers and Milwaukee Braves of the past including Hank Aaron, Sheets threw out the first pitch in front of a sold-out crowd, and received a standing ovation.

"The Brewers called us and offered us a flight to Milwaukee to meet up with Ben, because we hadn't seen him yet and he hadn't had a chance to come home to Louisiana," said Betty Sheets, Ben's mother. "So I got my sister-in-law, my sister, and my girlfriends together, gave them some money, and told them to decorate my house. I wanted to have food, refreshments, and a big party when we got back. I wanted a homecoming, and they were all in charge of that."

Betty had even gone on Ben's word that he would pitch Team USA to a gold-medal victory. "When he called home from Australia and told us that he was pitching the gold medal game, I thought 'Well, we're gonna need a big banner in front of the house, because we're going to have ourselves a gold medalist.' So I went ahead and ordered one in red, white, and blue with stars all over it that said, 'Home of Olympic Gold Medalist Ben Sheets,' and a second one that read 'Proud parents of Olympic Gold Medalist Ben Sheets.' I put that one on the back of our truck and we started driving all over town with it."

When Sheets saw his parents in a suite at the Brewers game for the first time since becoming a national hero, all he could do was give them both a big hug. "We were all just so excited for him," said Betty, "and so very proud."

Sheets returned home to St. Amant, Louisiana the next day, and the hoopla didn't end there. His homecoming included a welcoming party at the airport full of fans waving American flags; a police escort to the St. Amant high school football game that day, where a massive crowd of his hometown supporters were on hand to greet him; and recognition at halftime on the middle of the field. It just happened to be the school's homecoming game, and Sheets was now their most famous alum.

"The people were just mobbing him, the whole time he had kids coming up to him, and they wanted him to autograph anything they had," said Betty Sheets. "He just continued to sign and sign and sign all night. Then after the game, he finally made it home to our house, and we had a big reception and a party for all our family and neighbors. We had the time of our lives."

As the American players all began to return home for the baseball off-season, most if not all were done playing for the year. The major-league playoffs had begun, and the New York Yankees wound up playing against the New York Mets in the 2000 World Series, which was dubbed the "Subway Series."

MLB Commissioner Bud Selig had invited every person involved with the USA Baseball Olympic Team to New York, along with the USA Softball Team that had also won the gold medal, for a night of recognition and celebration. Prior to Game Three of the World Series at Shea Stadium, both teams—with everyone wearing their USA Olympic Team jacket and their gold medal—stood along the second- and third-base lines and were introduced to the crowd, while the Yankees and Mets dotted the first and third base lines for the National Anthem, sung by N'Sync.

Then, Team USA Manager Tommy Lasorda threw out the ceremonial first pitch in recognition of him leading the charge to a historic victory for his country.

A month later, many of the USA Baseball players joined the rest of the USA Olympic Team at the White House, where they each got the opportunity to shake hands with President Bill Clinton, have their picture taken with him, and then take part in a team photo on the White House lawn.

And finally, near the end of the year, the United States Olympic Committee named the 2000 USA Baseball Olympic Team as their "Team of the Year." It was quite an honor, considering that several other teams had also won the gold medal in Sydney as well, including softball and men's basketball.

"What this group of players did for USA Baseball as an organization was give us that championship that we could hang our hat on," said Seiler. "In the history of Olympic baseball, it would have been a shame had the United States not won a gold medal at least once. With this team's victory, we can always say that we climbed to the top of the mountain and got it done, that we were the very best in the world for one moment in time."

Members of the 2000 USA Olympic Team visited the White House and met President Bill Clinton in November, 2000. (L-R) Todd Williams, Ernie Young, Mike Neill, Press Officer Dave Fanucchi, Marcus Jensen

16

SINCE WINNING IT ALL

As the ten-year anniversary of Team USA's stunning triumph over the Cubans in Sydney to capture the gold medal approached in 2010, it still undoubtedly remained the most significant victory in USA Baseball history.

Seiler and his staff were not able to reach the pinnacle of international baseball again in either the 2004 Games in Athens or the 2008 Games in Beijing.

In 2003, Team USA failed to qualify for the 2004 Athens Baseball event and a chance to defend the gold medal. That turned out to be as stunning a loss as the Americans' victory was in Sydney. At the Pan Am Qualifier that was being played in Panama, a group of minor-league professionals, including 2000 gold medalists Todd Williams and Ernie Young as well as future major-league stars Matt Holliday, Joe Mauer, Grady Sizemore, J.J. Hardy, and Ryan Madsen, lost a gut-wrenching 2-1 game in the do-or-die quarterfinals to the country that the USA had barely beaten in 1999: Mexico.

Cuba returned to form in the 2004 Games in Greece, capturing the gold medal, while Australia rose to the occasion and took home the silver medal and Japan captured the bronze.

Following the 2004 Games, it had been determined by the International Olympic Committee that the 2008 Olympics would be the last for the sports of baseball and softball. After many arguments and international politicking, IOC President Jacques Rogge and the Committee decided to add some new Olympic sports, and to make room, they needed to remove a few as well.

Most of the arguments for removing baseball centered around three key factors: 1) the sport could not figure out a way to bring the most elite-level athletes who play the game to the Olympics. Unlike USA Basketball, which brought a dream team of stars that would fill arenas and draw huge TV ratings, USA Baseball would never be in a position to bring a dream team of major leaguers with them, due to the fact that the games were in the summer, when MLB teams had a schedule of games to be played every day; 2) it was believed by many European sport leaders who dominate the IOC that baseball was not widely played enough around the world, and even though that wasn't true, not many countries in Europe were very good at it. Cuba, Japan, Korea, and the United States had dominated internationally for years, so the IOC believed that the competition was not well-rounded; and 3) the cost for host committees to build a baseball venue that would be used for two weeks, then likely unused for any reason after that, was a significant concern for cities around the world that wanted to bid on hosting the Games.

USA Baseball did rebound to qualify for the 2008 Olympic Games in Beijing, as Team USA traveled to China one last time looking to strike gold again. With a roster full of young minor leaguers such as Steven Strasburg, Jayson Nix, and Dexter Fowler, they opened with a tough 8-7 loss to Korea, but bounced right back to beat the Netherlands. They then dropped a 5-4 decision to Cuba before reaching the medal round with wins over Canada, China, Chinese Taipai (Taiwan), and Japan.

But they fell on the hard side of the draw and were beaten

by Cuba 10-2 in the semifinals. Coming back the next day, Team USA was able to secure an 8-4 victory over Japan to earn the bronze medal, while Korea went unbeaten in the event and pulled off their own shocker by stunning the Cubans 3-2, to capture their first Olympic gold medal in baseball, the last one that would ever be handed out.

Although no longer running a governing body for an Olympic sport, Paul Seiler remains the executive director and CEO of USA Baseball and is still heavily involved in the international baseball scene. Since 2006, Major League Baseball has adopted the USA Baseball organization and has helped with funding the programs that will help kids across America enjoy the game of baseball for years to come.

In addition, Major League Baseball has since begun their own major international competition that does allow for the biggest names in the game to represent their countries, the World Baseball Classic (WBC). Played every four years in March during the month of spring training, Japan won the inaugural event in 2006, beating Cuba in the finals. Team USA finished in a disappointing tie for sixth place after critical losses in the second round to Korea and Mexico, even though they had a roster that included the likes of Derek Jeter, Ken Griffey Jr., Mark Teixeira, Roger Clemens, and Alex Rodriguez.

In the 2009 WBC, Japan again captured the crown by beating Korea, while the United States fared a little bit better finishing fourth, losing in the semifinals to Japan, 9-4.

Then, in 2010, Seiler began to think about getting the 2000 USA Baseball gold medal team and staff together again for a reunion, as most of the players had retired from the game or were coaching. Many of the administrators and coaches were still involved in baseball in some capacity, so the offseason that year seemed like a good opportunity to try and reunite everyone.

Along with Steve Cobb's help in Arizona, Seiler invited the entire staff (including myself) and all 24 players and their spouses to a luxury resort in Scottsdale for a weekend getaway.

Tommy Lasorda was more than willing to attend, and it turned out to be a fantastic weekend, as everyone reminisced about the games played in Sydney and what those moments meant to them in their lives.

It was on that weekend that I got the idea to write this book. Listening to all of the people who were involved tell the story of what has happened since 2000, it gave me the motivation to re-create the story of what was such an important event to so many of us. I was only hoping I could do the story justice, and that readers would enjoy learning about it. I hope I have done that.

Where Are They Now?

Sandy Alderson remained in the Commissioner's Office of MLB for a few more years, before taking a front-office position with the San Diego Padres. He is currently the general manager of the New York Mets.

Bob Watson went on to become MLB's Vice President of Operations until he retired in 2010. He remains involved with USA Baseball in his spare time and resides in Houston, Texas.

Pat Gillick, after serving as the GM of the Seattle Mariners, moved on to the front office of the Philadelphia Phillies, and in the same capacity helped structure a club that won the 2008 World Series. He was inducted into the National Baseball Hall of Fame in 2011.

Bill Bavasi went on to become the general manager of the Seattle Mariners following Gillick's departure and spent four seasons there from 2004 to 2008. He is currently the special assistant to GM Walt Jocketty, for the Cincinnati Reds.

Steve Cobb remains in Scottsdale, Arizona as the executive director of the Arizona Fall League, MLB's premier proving ground for prospects looking to make a major-league roster the following spring training.

Steve Cohen is now a scout for the Philadelphia Phillies, working in the Southwest part of the country. He and his wife, Annette, live in The Woodlands, Texas.

Pat Courtney is now the director of public relations and communications for Major League Baseball.

Don Welke is a member of the scouting and player personnel department of the Texas Rangers, assisting GM Jon Daniels in putting together the rosters of two straight World Series teams in 2010 and 2011.

1999 USA Baseball Pan Am Team – Silver Medalists

After managing the Colorado Rockies (2000-2002) and Kansas City Royals (2003-2005) for three seasons each, Buddy Bell is now a special assistant with the Chicago White Sox.

Jackie Moore is now a bench coach for manager Ron Washington with the Texas Rangers and helped their club win back-to-back American League titles in 2010 and 2011.

Marcel Lachemann was Buddy Bell's pitching coach in Colorado before moving into the front office as an assistant to GM Dan O'Dowd from 2003 to 2011. He is currently the special assistant to the GM for the Los Angeles Angels of Anaheim. He also served as pitching coach for Team USA during the 2006 World Baseball Classic and the 2008 Beijing Olympics.

Ryan Anderson never reached the major leagues, and in fact only pitched one more season in the Mariners' farm system in 2000, going 5-8 with a 3.98 ERA and 146 strikeouts in 20 starts for triple-A Tacoma. After a series of injuries, his career came to an end in 2001. He is currently a professional chef and lives in Arizona.

Peter Bergeron batted .226 with 8 home runs and 56 RBIs in 308 games for the Montreal Expos, from 1999 to 2004.

Milton Bradley has bounced around the major leagues, playing for Montreal, Cleveland, the Los Angeles Dodgers, Oakland, San Diego, Texas, the Chicago Cubs, and Seattle. An All-Star with the Rangers in 2008, Bradley has hit over 125 career home runs in the majors, but has had disciplinary problems with several clubs that have prompted them to release or trade him. He did not appear on a major-league roster in 2012, after playing in 28 games for the Mariners in 2011.

Shawn Gilbert played in 51 games for the New York Mets, St. Louis Cardinals, and Los Angeles Dodgers from 1997 to 2000. He hit one home run and had three RBIs, collecting a total of seven base hits.

Charlie Greene got into three games for the Toronto Blue Jays in 2000 before playing three more seasons in the minors and retiring in 2004.

Jason Hardtke retired after the 2001 season he spent in the minors and never played another game in the majors after being with Team USA in Winnipeg. He had appeared in 67 games for the Mets and Cubs from 1996 to 1998.

David Holdridge never appeared in another game in either the major or minor leagues, after pitching in relief in one game for Team USA in Canada.

Adam Kennedy has remained in the major leagues since being called up by the St. Louis Cardinals after playing for Team USA in the Pan Ams. Traded to Anaheim in 2000, he was a member of the Angels' 2002 World Series Championship team and was an integral part of their club until 2006. He signed as a free agent again with the Cardinals in 2007 and has since played for Oakland, Washington, and Seattle. He recently finished the 2012 season as a member of the Los Angeles Dodgers.

Matt LeCroy played eight seasons in the majors with the Minnesota Twins and Washington Nationals, batting .260 with 60 home runs and 218 RBIs. He retired in 2008.

Mark Mulder spent the next nine seasons pitching in the major leagues from 2000 to 2008 for the Oakland A's and St. Louis Cardinals. He finished second in the American League Cy Young Award voting in 2001, when he went 21-8 with a 3.45 ERA in helping the A's reach the postseason. The two-time American League All-Star went 103-60 with a 4.18 ERA and compiled 834 strikeouts before retiring in 2009. He is currently an analyst for ESPN's *Baseball Tonight* show and resides in Scottsdale, Arizona with his wife and children.

Before joining Team USA for the Pan Am Games, Craig Paquette had already appeared in 426 major-league games with the Oakland A's, Kansas City Royals, and New York Mets. Then after the Pan Ams, he was called up by the St. Louis Cardinals for the rest of September of 1999. He played in 257 games for the Cards again over the next two years before spending 2002 to 2003 with the Detroit Tigers. Paquette ended up having a nice career over a total of 11 seasons in the majors, falling just one home run short of 100, and collecting 377 RBIs in over 800 games played.

John Patterson made it to the show in 2002 with the Arizona Diamondbacks and pitched in 23 games for them before being traded to the Montreal Expos in spring training of 2004. He then made 19 starts for Montreal in 2004 and had his best season in 2005, when the club moved to Washington, D.C. and became the Nationals. That year, he went 9-7 with a 3.13 ERA in 31 starts and 185 strikeouts. Arm injuries limited his productivity over the next two years, as he only made 15 more starts, retiring after the 2007 season with a career 18-25 record in the majors.

Brad Penny has enjoyed a very successful career and is still pitching today, having wrapped up the 2012 season working out of the bullpen for the San Francisco Giants. After starting both games that Team USA played against Cuba in the 1999 Pan Ams, Penny began the 2000 season as a rookie starter for the Florida Marlins. In 2003, he went 14-10 with a 4.13 ERA in 32 starts and helped the Marlins capture the 2003 World Series Championship when he won both Game 1 and Game 5 over the New York Yankees. Traded to the Los Angeles Dodgers in 2004, he spent the next five seasons on the West Coast, becoming a two-time NL All-Star. He has spent the past three years with the Boston Red Sox, St. Louis Cardinals, and Detroit Tigers, and has started over 330 games in his major-league career, with a 119-100 record.

Dave Roberts was called up by the Cleveland Indians after he returned home from Winnipeg; he played in 41 games for the Tribe that year. He appeared in 34 more games for

Cleveland over the next two seasons, before being traded to the Los Angeles Dodgers late in 2001. Roberts was a mainstay in the Dodgers outfield for both the 2002 and 2003 seasons before being traded to the Boston Red Sox at the trade deadline in July 2004. The Red Sox picked up the speedster who had stolen over 100 bases for LA, and the move paid off as the Red Sox attempted to advance deep in the postseason. During one of the most memorable American League Championship Series ever played, Roberts stole what most Bostonians consider the most important base in Red Sox history, and it has since become known simply as "The Steal."

With the Red Sox trailing the New York Yankees three games to none going into Game 4 at Fenway Park, the Red Sox were facing elimination in the bottom of the ninth inning, down 4-3. When Kevin Millar drew a leadoff walk from Yankees closer Mariano Rivera, Red Sox manager Terry Francona sent Roberts, who had not played in ten days, in to pinch-run. Rivera threw to first base three times (the last almost picked off Roberts), but on the next pitch, Roberts stole second base, just barely beating the throw. Bill Mueller then followed with a single, Roberts scored to tie the game, and the Sox went on to win in 12 innings. It started a comeback that saw Boston win each of the next three games against New York and produce a four-game sweep of the St. Louis Cardinals in the World Series, culminating in Boston's first World Series title since 1918. In 2006, the event was recognized as a Memorable Moment in Red Sox history by the Boston Red Sox Hall of Fame. Roberts retained lasting status as a hero in Boston, receiving standing ovations in Fenway Park every time he came up to bat for opposing teams later in his career. Having retired from playing in 2009, Roberts is currently the first-base coach for the San Diego Padres.

J.C. Romero has spent parts of every season since 1999 in the major leagues with Minnesota, the Los Angeles Angels, Boston, Philadelphia, Colorado, St. Louis, and Baltimore. Mostly a left-handed relief specialist, his best season was in 2002 with the Twins, when he went 9-2 with a 1.89 ERA and helped the Twins advance to the American League Championship Series. He also appeared in four games during the 2008 World Series for the Philadelphia Phillies and was the winning pitcher in two of the Phillies' four victories, as they won their first championship since 1980.

Scott Stewart made 214 relief appearances over the next four seasons for Montreal, Cleveland, and the Los Angeles Dodgers. He saved 17 games for the Expos in 2002 and finished playing in 2006.

After making three relief appearances for Team USA in Winnipeg, Derek Wallace appeared in eight games for the 1999 Kansas City Royals and never pitched again after suffering an arm injury.

Following his heroic performance for Team USA at the Pan Am Games, Dan Wheeler was named the 1999 USA Baseball Player of the Year. After three productive seasons working in the bullpen for the Tampa Bay Devil Rays, he was released following the 2001 season. He signed with Atlanta but spent the entire year in the minors before being released again and signing with the New York Mets. Wheeler was back in the big leagues for both 2003 and 2004 with the Mets, but was traded to the Houston Astros late in the 2004 campaign and helped the Astros to the 2004 National League Championship Series. He was also part of Houston's first and only National League pennant-winning team in 2005, when the Astros lost the World Series to the Chicago White Sox.

Wheeler made it back to the postseason again with the 2008 Devil Rays when they captured that franchise's only American League pennant to date, but lost to the Phillies in the World Series. By the end of the 2012 season, Wheeler was still pitching, ending the season with the triple-A club of the Cleveland Indians, the Columbus (Ohio) Clippers.

Jon Zuber spent the 2000 season playing for the triple-A team of the New York Yankees, then signed a contract with the Yokohama Bay Stars of the Japanese professional league. He returned back to the States in 2002 and played one final year in the minors for the Milwaukee Brewers.

2000 USA Baseball Olympic Team – Gold Medalists

Phil Regan served as the manager of the single-A West Michigan Whitecaps (Detroit Tigers) in 2002 and 2003 and managed various teams in the Venezuelan Winter League until 2009.

Eddie Rodriguez signed with the Arizona Diamondbacks following his stint with Team USA and was part of their memorable run to a World Series title in 2001. He later coached for the Montreal Expos and Washington Nationals and recently finished the 2012 season as the third-base coach for the Kansas City Royals.

Reggie Smith returned to USA Baseball service as the Team USA hitting coach for the 2007 IBAF Baseball World Cup in Taiwan, in which the United States won the Gold Medal with a 6-3 victory over Cuba, which qualified Team USA for the 2008 Olympic Games. Smith then also served as hitting coach for the bronze-medal-winning USA Baseball Olympic team in Beijing. He resides in Los Angeles, California and operates his own hitting school for Little Leaguers and amateur players.

Brent Abernatky reached the major leagues in 2001 and played parts of the next three seasons for the Tampa Bay Devil Rays before being acquired by the Kansas City Royals late in the 2003 season. He also played in 24 games for the Minnesota Twins in 2005 and finished his playing career in 2007 after two more years in the minors. Overall, he appeared in 232 major-league games with three clubs and batted .244 with eight homers and 79 RBIs. He currently works for a financial services company and resides in Fort Walton Beach, Florida with his wife, Allison, and daughters Emily (7) and Anna (5), while still driving the Mercedes-Benz he purchased with the jackpot he won on the Gold Coast of Australia.

Kurt Ainsworth reached the major leagues in 2011 with the San Francisco Giants, but only started two games. He appeared in six more games in 2002, picking up his first major-league win, and went 5-4 with a 3.82 ERA in 11 starts for the

Giants in 2003. The righty was traded to the Baltimore Orioles at the trade deadline in 2003, but only appeared in 10 games for the O's before he retired from pitching in 2005, due to elbow injuries. He went on to become the co-founder of Marucci Bats and currently works for the company in Baton Rouge, Louisiana.

Seemingly near the end of his career already when he became a gold medalist with Team USA in 2000, Pat Borders went on to play another six seasons of baseball, bouncing between the majors and the minor leagues. He saw action in the big leagues with the Seattle Mariners each season between 2001 and 2005 and spent his last year playing in the Dodgers' farm system in 2006. In over 17 seasons, he played in 1,099 major-league games. He resides with his family in Lake Wales, Florida.

As the youngest member of Team USA in Sydney, Sean Burroughs was just 19 years old when he had become an Olympic gold medalist. This came after he had played on a Little League World Championship team when he was 12. He reached the major leagues with the San Diego Padres in 2002 and had four productive seasons before being traded to the Tampa Bay Devil Rays in 2005. But his career fizzled in 2006, and he walked away from the game in 2007. For the next several years, Burroughs struggled with substance abuse. But he made a valiant comeback after attending the Team USA 10-year reunion in Scottsdale and made the roster of the 2011 Arizona Diamondbacks, appearing in 78 games. He remained playing for the Minnesota Twins in 2012.

John Cotton could be called the true "Crash Davis" of his time. Over his 15-year career, he played in 1,530 games in the minor leagues, without ever appearing in a single major-league game. After Sydney, Cotton played one more season in the minors with the Dodgers, Pirates, and Expos before finishing up his career with two seasons in the independent leagues. He has since retired and is now a fireman, living with his wife, Ronna, and son, Jackson, in Missouri City, Texas.

Travis Dawkins spent the entire 2001 season playing at

double-A Chattanooga in the Reds' farm system and then began the 2002 season at triple-A Louisville before being brought to the major leagues for 31 games with the Reds. He ended up with the Kansas City Royals in 2003 and played mostly at triple-A Omaha before getting a September call-up and appearing in three games for the Royals. He would go on to spend eight more seasons in the minors before retiring in 2012. He currently lives in Charlotte, North Carolina.

Following his stellar defensive effort in Sydney, Adam Everett carried that same solid work ethic to the major leagues. He broke through with the Astros late in the 2001 season and then became their everyday shortstop starting in 2003 and on through the 2007 campaign. Teammates with Dan Wheeler, he helped the Astros reach the World Series in 2005, as they captured their first National League title. He signed as a free agent with the Minnesota Twins in 2007 and then spent the next two seasons with the Detroit Tigers, before finishing up his career with the Cleveland Indians in 2011. He played in 880 major-league games and compiled an outstanding .976 fielding percentage to go with a career .242 batting average. He is now a minor-league instructor with the Indians.

Ryan Franklin's career blossomed after he performed so brilliantly in Australia, as he went on to spend the next 11 seasons in the major leagues with Seattle, Philadelphia, Cincinnati, and St. Louis. Working mostly as a starting pitcher for the Mariners, he won 35 games for them over a span of five years (2001-2005) and then became a relief pitcher in the National League. His best season was in 2009, when the Cardinals were utilizing Franklin as a closer. He went 4-3 with a 1.92 ERA and 38 saves and was named to the National League All-Star team. He retired following the 2011 season after pitching in 21 games for the Cardinals, but was placed on the injured reserve list during their run to the World Series title. He is now a special assistant to Cardinals GM John Mozeliak.

Chris George, better known to Lasorda as "Sandy," went

on to start 44 games for the Kansas City Royals over a span of four seasons from 2001 to 2004. He went 14-20 with a 6.48 ERA before spending the following eight seasons at the triple-A level with Florida, Toronto, Colorado, Boston, and Baltimore. He recently began the 2012 season with the Rochester Red Wings in the Orioles' farm system, but only appeared in four games before calling it a career. He lives with his wife, Brandi, sons Cooper and Logan, and daughter Sadie in Spring, Texas.

Shane Heams went 39-25 with a 3.85 ERA over 321 games in the minor leagues with Seattle, Detroit, Boston, and Colorado, and two seasons of independent ball in the Atlantic League. He never appeared in a major-league game and retired from pitching in 2006. He is currently the production manager at Mobis North America in Toledo, Ohio, and lives in Lambertville, Michigan with his wife, Miranda, daughter Anika, and son Hudson.

Marcus Jensen's best season in the majors also happened to be the year in which he helped Team USA win the gold medal. He played in 52 games for the Minnesota Twins that summer before being sent to the minors, and then on to the Olympics. Over the next two seasons, he did appear in the big leagues with Boston, Texas, and Milwaukee, and wrapped up his career after a full season at triple-A Columbus in the Yankees' farm system in 2003. He is now the manager of the rookie-level team of the Oakland A's in the Arizona League and lives in Scottsdale.

Mike Kinkade went on to appear in 61 games for the 2001 Baltimore Orioles before signing as a free agent with the Dodgers in 2002. In Los Angeles, he batted .255 with seven homers and 25 RBIs in over 100 games in a two-year span, before playing four more years at the triple-A level with Cleveland, Florida, the Chicago Cubs, the New York Yankees, and Seattle. He retired from playing in 2009 and is now a minor-league instructor for the Seattle Mariners. He lives with his wife, Michelle, and sons Kameron, Konner, and KJ in Pullman, Washington.

When Rick Krivda ended up as Team USA's only left-handed starting pitcher in Australia, he had already appeared in 72 major-league games for the Orioles, Indians, and Reds from 1995 to 1998. After compiling a record of 11-16 with a 5.57 ERA in over 250 innings pitched, he never appeared in another major-league game. Upon returning from Sydney, Krivda played his final season in the minors in 2001 for triple-A Memphis in the St. Louis Cardinals' farm system and went 4-6 in 13 starts.

In 2001, Doug Mientkiewicz was awarded the starting first-base job for the Twins and responded by batting .306 with fifteen home runs and 74 RBIs (all career highs) while earning the American League Gold Glove Award for the top defensive first baseman. His numbers dipped a bit in 2002; however, he helped the Twins reach the postseason (for the first time in his career) and hit two home runs in the 2002 American League Division Series against the Oakland A's.

Then, at the 2004 trade deadline, Mientkiewicz was picked up by the Boston Red Sox and proved to be a valuable addition as the Red Sox surged to within three games of the Yankees by the end of the season and took the AL wild card by seven games over Oakland. Mientkiewicz then went 4-for-10 in the postseason and recorded the final out when Cardinals shortstop Edgar Rentería grounded back to pitcher Keith Foulke, who trotted toward first base and underhanded the ball to Mientkiewicz at the bag to complete Boston's four-game sweep of the 2004 World Series, ending the Curse of the Bambino.

Mientkiewicz went on to play for the New York Mets in 2005, the Kansas City Royals in 2006, the New York Yankees in 2007, the Pittsburgh Pirates in 2008, and finally the Los Angeles Dodgers in 2009, reuniting with his manager in Sydney, Tommy Lasorda, who was still in the LA front office. Doug is currently a hitting instructor in the Dodgers' farm system and the hitting coach of the rookie-level Ogden Raptors in the Pioneer League. He resides with his wife, Jodi, and son, Steel, in Islamorada, Florida.

Arguably, Roy Oswalt went on to have the most successful major-league career of any of the 24 gold medalists from Team USA in 2000. He made his major-league debut with the Houston Astros in 2001 and went 14-3 with a 2.73 ERA, finishing second in the Rookie of the Year voting to Albert Pujols.

Oswalt would become a mainstay in the Astros' starting rotation for the next 10 years and became a back-to-back 20-game winner in 2004 and 2005. He helped the Astros to their first World Series appearance in 2005 and was named the Most Valuable Player of the 2005 National League Championship Series in the Astros win over St. Louis, when he went 2-0 with a 1.29 ERA. He was the winning pitcher in both Game Two and Game Six (beating 1999 USA Pan Am Team member Mark Mulder, who started both of those games for the Cardinals), clinching the series for the Astros in St. Louis with seven strong innings of work, allowing just one run on three hits in a 7-1 victory.

When he left the Astros in 2010, his victory total (143) and strikeout total (1,593) was second in franchise history only to Joe Niekro (144) and Nolan Ryan (1,866). He was a three-time All-Star, selected from 2005 to 2007, and was later traded to the Philadelphia Phillies at the trade deadline in 2010.

After two more seasons with the Phillies in which he helped them reach the playoffs both years, Oswalt's career strikeout total was among the top 100 pitchers of all time. He was still pitching in the major leagues for the Texas Rangers, at the end of the 2012 campaign.

Jon Rauch became another pitcher who had great success in the majors and was still active near the end of the 2012 season. The *Baseball America* Minor League Player of the Year in 2000, Rauch made his debut with the Chicago White Sox in 2002, and at six feet, 11 inches tall, he became the tallest pitcher in major-league baseball history. But he returned to the minors for one year before being brought back up with the White Sox again in 2004. Then in July of that year, he was traded to the Montreal Expos and picked up three victories in nine games for them that season. On August 13, 2004, Rauch hit a home run against the Houston Astros off Roger Clemens, making him the tallest man to ever hit a home run in MLB history.

When the Expos moved to Washington, D.C. in 2005, Rauch became the winning pitcher in the first game ever played at the new Nationals Park. In D.C., his career began to flourish, as he stayed in the Nationals' bullpen for the next four years, making a career-high 88 appearances in 2007. He later pitched for Arizona, Minnesota, and Toronto, before spending the 2012 season with the New York Mets. He has recorded 61 saves in over 500 relief appearances in the majors, going 42-38 with a 3.74 ERA.

After Anthony Sanders returned home to Arizona to spend the offseason with his brand-new baby boy, he returned with the Mariners in 2001 and broke camp with the major-league team. In Seattle, he played in nine games, going 3-for-19 with a pair of doubles before being granted free agency in late April. He decided to head back overseas and signed a contract with the Yokohama Bay Stars of the Japanese League. He later returned to America, played four more seasons, all at the triple-A level for Cincinnati, the Chicago White Sox, Toronto, and Colorado, and one last season in the Mexican League in 2006, before calling it a career. He is now a minor-league coach with the Colorado Rockies and still lives in Tucson with his wife, Claudia, and sons Logan (who was born while Sanders was in Sydney), Marcus, and Troy.

Bobby Seay managed to put together a nice major-league career of eight seasons pitching in relief for Tampa Bay, Colorado, and Detroit from 2001 to 2009. His best season was in 2007, when he went 3-0 with a 2.33 ERA in 58 appearances for the Tigers. Overall, he won 11 games in the majors—all in relief—and finished pitching after the 2009 campaign.

After appearing in 10 games for the 1998 Montreal Expos, and eight more for the 2000 Boston Red Sox before joining Team USA's bullpen in Sydney, Tim Young never reached the major leagues again. He pitched the 2001 season for the Hiroshima Toyo Carp in Japan and then spent three more years at the triple-A level in the American minor leagues with five different organizations.

Todd Williams spent another seven years pitching in both the majors and the minor leagues. He went on to appear in 15 games for the 2001 New York Yankees, but his best years came in 2004 to 2007 with the Baltimore Orioles, when he won nine games as a valuable reliever in 177 appearances and picked up two saves. In the 2003 season, Williams was again selected by USA Baseball to play for Team USA at the Olympic qualifying event, this time in Panama City, Panama.

Down in Panama, Williams only appeared in one game, and pitched one shutout inning. That's because the Americans cruised to easy victories over Nicaragua, Columbia, Panama, and Brazil, before being shockingly upset by Mexico in the quarterfinals and eliminated from the tournament, failing to qualify for the Athens Games and a chance to defend the gold medal they had won in Sydney. Williams retired from pitching after the 2007 season and currently lives in Tampa, Florida.

Brad Wilkerson made his major-league debut with the Montreal Expos on July 12, 2001 and appeared in 38 games in left field, recording his first major-league hit off Greg Maddux and his first major-league home run off Jason Marquis.

In 2002, he hit 20 home runs, an Expos rookie record, and was named Rookie of the Year by The Sporting News. His most productive season came in 2004, when he posted career highs in homers (32), hits (146), doubles (39), runs (112), walks (106), slugging percentage (.498), and OPS (.872), and hitting .255 with 67 RBIs. Also that year, he hit the last home run in Expos history and appeared once more in a Montreal Expos uniform during the MLB Japan All-Star Series shortly after the 2004 regular season. The Expos were to become the Washington Nationals for the 2005 season, prompting some to refer to Wilkerson as "The Last Expo."

Wilkerson opened the 2005 season as the regular center fielder and leadoff hitter for the new Washington Nationals.

Then on April 6, 2005, against Philadelphia, in their second game after moving from Montreal, Wilkerson hit for the cycle and later that season hit the first grand slam home run by a Nationals player.

After being traded to the Texas Rangers, his time there was highlighted by a three-homer game. He played one more season in Texas, split the 2008 season with Seattle and Toronto, and hung up his cleats after attempting to make the Boston Red Sox in 2009. Wilkerson was inducted into the University of Florida Athletic Hall of Fame as a "Gator Great" in 2010 and was also inducted into the National College Baseball Hall of Fame in 2012. He lives in Florida with his wife, Dana, and children Ella, Ava, and Max.

Ernie Young played all or part of eight seasons in the majors for the Oakland A's, Kansas City Royals, Arizona Diamondbacks, Detroit Tigers, and Cleveland Indians. He also played one season in Japan for the Yokohama Bay Stars in 2002. In his major-league career, Young played in 288 games, had 179 hits, 27 home runs, 90 RBIs, 10 stolen bases, and a .225 batting average.

During the 2003 season, Young joined his fellow gold medalist Todd Williams on the 2003 USA Baseball Olympic qualifying team in Panama and led the team in hitting with a .455 batting average over the five games played.

Later in his career back down in the minors, Young hit his 300th career minor-league home run in 2006, while playing for the Charlotte Knights, the triple-A affiliate of the Indians. At the time of his retirement after the 2007 season, Young was the active minor-league home-runs king, with 319.

He became the hitting coach on the Chicago White Sox's rookie-level Great Falls Voyagers, then was named the manager of the Kannapolis Intimidators for the 2009 season. He later moved on to manage the West Michigan Whitecaps, the class A affiliate of the Detroit Tigers, where he was still working as of the 2012 season. Young is a member of the USA Baseball Board of Directors as an at-large athlete and also serves as an Executive Committee Member for the

International Baseball Federation (IBAF) as a Recent Athlete.

Seiler tabbed Young as his manager of the 2011 USA Baseball World Cup Team that won the bronze medal in the event played back in Panama City and the United States team in the 2011 Pan Am Games, which won the silver medal (losing a heartbreaker to Canada in the gold-medal game 2-1, after beating Cuba in the semifinals, 12-10). Young currently spends his offseason at his home in Scottsdale, Arizona with his wife, Kim, and has three children: Aubrey, Miranda, and Elijah (who was born during the 2000 Olympic Games, while Ernie was in Sydney).

Mike Neill admittedly calls his time with Team USA in both 1999 and 2000 the peak of his career and the highlight of his life in baseball. He went on to play the 2001 season with the triple-A Pawtucket Red Sox, batting .245 in 67 games. But he never again made it back to the majors and ended his playing career in 2002. He is currently a financial advisor and lives in Philadelphia.

"My goal was always to be a long-term major-league player. But because of a couple of injuries, or maybe I just wasn't quite good enough, that didn't work out," said Neill. "But I have a gold medal, and to be a part of that group of guys twice, with the Pan Ams and the Olympics playing for the United States, it was something you dream of. It was just an incredible experience that I will treasure the rest of your life. There's no other way to describe it. That was an unbelievable team, an unbelievable run, and I was just really fortunate to be a part of it."

Coming out of spring training in 2001, Ben Sheets had been promoted to the Milwaukee Brewers' starting rotation. His first two starts resulted in losses, but he won his next four, while pitching to a 1.73 ERA. In his ninth career start, he tossed his first complete-game shutout, giving up just five hits against the St. Louis Cardinals. Bothered by lower back problems later in the year, he finished with a record of 11-10 with a 4.76 ERA.

Sheets became a front-line starter for the Brewers over the

next eight seasons and was named to the National League All-Star team four times. Some of his career highlights include a game on June 13, 2004, when he struck out three batters on nine pitches in the third inning of a 5-4 loss to the Houston Astros, becoming the 26th National League pitcher and the 35th pitcher in major-league history to accomplish the nine-strike/three-strikeout half-inning.

Also during the 2004 season, he struck out 18 batters in game against the Atlanta Braves, shattering the franchise record of 14, set by Moose Haas in 1978. He was also selected to start the 2008 All-Star Game for the National League at Yankee Stadium, against Cliff Lee of the Cleveland Indians. He pitched two scoreless innings and did not factor in the decision of a game that ended up being won by the American League, 4-3 in 15 innings.

With Milwaukee, Sheets ended up with an overall record of 86-83 with a 3.72 ERA and a Brewers franchise record 1,206 strikeouts over eight seasons. He spent the 2009 season rehabbing his elbow after having surgery to repair a torn flexor tendon, then signed a one-year, $10 million contract with the Oakland A's in 2010. Sheets got the Opening Day start, going five innings and allowing three runs (two earned) on four hits while striking out three, receiving a no-decision in a game the A's lost in the bottom of the ninth. His season ended with Sheets going 4-9 in 20 starts, when he would miss the latter part of the season again due to a torn flexor in his right elbow.

Sheets sat out the 2011 season and began coaching his sons in Little League baseball. But the itch to pitch returned again, and Sheets attempted a comeback with the Atlanta Braves, signing with the team two months into the 2012 season. In July, the Braves announced that they had called Sheets up from the minors, and he made his first start in nearly two years on July 15 against the New York Mets. Sheets pitched six scoreless innings, giving up two hits and striking out five to earn the win.

After his second start also resulted in a six-inning shutout performance, Sheets reiterated that he has always had the fire to compete. "If you asked me if I'm surprised I haven't given up a run yet, yeah I am. But I'm not surprised I'm getting people out. I wouldn't have come back if I didn't think I could get people out." His most recent attempt with the Braves lasted nine starts, in which he went 4-4 with a 3.45 ERA and helped Atlanta remain in the 2012 playoff chase.

Sheets still lives in Louisiana with his wife, Julie, and sons Seaver and Miller. He operates his own USSSA travel ball club called Sheets Baseball, with Seaver being one of his starting pitchers.

And his mom, Betty, still beams with pride when talking about her son's special time in Sydney. "While Ben was playing in the major leagues, he kept the gold medal at our house. My husband and I run a water well business, and so we would have customers and friends come into our office and look at all of the pictures of Ben on the walls," said Betty. "And they would see Ben on his knees with his arms in the air, and they'd ask, 'Do you have the gold medal?' and I'd say, 'Yes, I do.' So I would bring it out, and we used to take everybody's picture with the gold medal. So we would just spread our joy as much as we could."

And there's no questioning how proud the entire Sheets family is of their Olympic champion.

"On our Christmas tree this year, I bought these special frames that you can hang on a tree that hold pictures of my kids when they were little, and all my grandkids. And one of the pictures that I put on the tree this year in memory of the Olympics, was my mother, my husband's mother, and my aunt, and they're holding Ben's gold medal. I did it in black and white and framed it and put it up on our Christmas tree. That's what it has meant to our family. I think Ben will go down in history being known as an Olympic gold medalist, and hopefully—even after I'm gone—my great-grandkids will be reading about him for years to come."

Tommy Lasorda is the special assistant to the president of the Los Angeles Dodgers and remains retired from managing. In 2009, he marked his sixth decade in one capacity or another with the Brooklyn/Los Angeles Dodgers organization, the longest non-continuous (he played one season with the Kansas City Athletics) tenure anyone has had with the team, edging Dodger broadcaster Vin Scully by a single season. He and his wife, Jo, celebrated their 60th wedding anniversary in 2010 and have resided in Fullerton, California, for more than 50 years. Lasorda remains the only person in history to have been the manager of both a World Series Championship team and an Olympic gold medal team.

 Baseball Team
Games of the XXVIIth Olympiad
Sydney, Australia

Top row (L-R): Fanucchi, E. Young, Williams, Sabathia, Rauch, Jensen, Seay, White, Dawkins
Third row (L-R): Mientkiewicz, Abernathy, Neill, Coolbaugh, Ainsworth, Kinkade, Borders, Gilbert
Second row (L-R): Sanders, Oswalt, Heams, Sheets, Cotton, Wilkerson, Everett, T. Young
Front row (L-R): Gebeck, Regan, Rodriguez, Lasorda, Smith, Fierro, Behrens

ACKNOWLEDGMENTS

As a journalism major coming out of college, I always had it in the back of my mind that one day, I'd love to write a book. But I had no idea what it would ever be about, and I didn't have a particular subject that I could focus on. It certainly wasn't ever going to be a fictional book, being that I just don't have the imagination it would take to accomplish that. What I did know was that I had the ability to tell a good story, which is what I've tried to do for you with this narrative nonfiction piece.

Which leads to the first group of people whom I'd like to thank most of all—the players, coaches, and administrators involved with both the 1999 USA Baseball Pan Am Team and the 2000 USA Baseball Olympic Team. They provided for me the most important thing—an actual story to write about.

Among this group, I need to start at the top, with USA Baseball CEO Paul Seiler. A tremendous friend who has given me so many opportunities in my career and has always stuck by my side, it was such an honor to be a part of this Olympic journey with him. I will forever be grateful for the role I was given as the Press Officer for both of these teams in Winnipeg and Sydney, because those experiences gave me the foundation for a career in sports and led me to so many other fantastic moments in my life. Paul, I still to this day cherish all the time I spent at USA Baseball, being able to witness you and your lovely wife, Wendi, build such a strong and beautiful family.

I would be remiss if I did not also acknowledge the man who gave me my first full-time job and hired me to work for USA Baseball, Dan O'Brien. And among my other co-workers from the USAB office back then, I must also thank Eric Campbell, Steve Cohen, Ray Darwin, Jake Fehling, Miki Partridge, David Perkins, and Jeff Singer, for all of their support and friendship during my seven years as Director of Communications.

In addition, Seiler, Fehling, and Perkins have all been a tremendous help to me and incredibly patient as I've gone about the process of collecting data and information for this book and asked them lots of questions about our marketing plan. Their unwavering support for this project is what I needed in order to think that this would make any sense for me to actually do.

A second man who has been equally important in encouraging me throughout my career and getting me to the finish line of this book would be Steve Cobb of Major League Baseball. Along with Seiler, he and Cobb have been the two biggest influencers in my career in professional sports.

Back when I was a young intern in the office of the triple-A Phoenix Firebirds, Cobb gave me my first opportunity to work for the Arizona Fall League in 1994. He then hired me back again in 1995, and for a third time in 1998, after my two-year stint with the St. Louis Cardinals came to an end. Without his confidence in my ability and loyalty as a friend, I certainly would never have been in the right place to be offered a position with USA Baseball in 1999.

The fact that we were able to work together again with both of these two USA teams was a bonus, and such great fun. Being that Steve arguably knew this whole story as well as I did, having his support for my book project and being able to lean on him for advice was invaluable to me. Steve, being invited to stay in your gorgeous home in Scottsdale as I went about my business of interviewing players and coaches during spring training was a typical gesture of your uncommon kindness. I thank your lovely wife, Laura, for her hospitality, and I cannot forget your amazing assistant, Joan McGrath, who has always been one of my biggest fans.

Then of course there are numerous other baseball front-office men who were so kind to me with their time and patience during the interview process. Those would include Sandy Alderson, Bill Bavasi, Pat Gillick, Dean Taylor, Bob Watson, and Don Welke.

There are the coaches who gave me exceptional insight and were raw with their memories and feelings, including Buddy Bell, Dick Cooke, Jackie Moore, Tommy Lasorda, and Eddie Rodriguez. Also the medical staff of both teams: Dr. Fred Dicke, Trainer John Fierro, and Dr. Angelo Mattalino; and the MLB Scouting Bureau folks, mainly Jerry Kelley, Frank Marcos, and Jim Walton.

No doubt that the players themselves all had a major impact on this story and were nothing but gracious in sharing their thoughts with me: Brent Abernathy, Marcus Jensen, Doug Mientkiewicz, Mark Mulder, Mike Neill, Ben Sheets (an extra thanks for his hospitality at the Paradise Bayou Lodge and for the warmth shown by Betty and Arnold Sheets during my overnight stay), Ernie Young, Dan Wheeler, and Todd Williams.

There is the Media Relations staff related to Major League Baseball and its 30 clubs, that allowed me the access I needed. That list includes Mike Swanson and Dina Blevins of the Royals, Colin Gunderson of the Dodgers, Rob Butcher of the Reds, John Blake and Rich Rice of the Rangers, Bart Swain of the Indians, June Napoli of the Mets, Scott Reifort of the White Sox, and from the MLB Commissioner's Office, Pat Courtney. Pat, it was a pleasure working the Sydney media with you by my side, and I thank you for your enthusiasm behind this idea, as well as the willingness to help promote it. I also need to thank Brian Bartow of the Cardinals, for giving me an opportunity to learn the ropes in the big leagues.

A friend and colleague who writes for MLB.com, who gave me great advice about the book-writing world and the overall process: Barry Bloom. Barry, I appreciate you steering me in the right direction over dinner at Don and Charlie's.

I need to also acknowledge the fantastic and lifelong friends I made in both Winnipeg and Sydney who were working alongside me at the United States Olympic Committee and their Communications Team: Cecil Bleiker, Bob Condron, Nick Inzerello, Brett Johnson, Melissa Minker, Darryl Seibel, and my Sydney Press Officer condo roommate, Randy Walker.

Other friends I'd like to thank for offering layers of support and guidance throughout my career: Mike Baca, Chris Corso, Roger Hacker, Brian Hudson, Anthony Passarelli, and Coach Ritch Price.

I need to be up front about the fact that I borrowed a good amount of information from my friend John Manuel of *Baseball America*, who was there with us every step of the way in both Winnipeg and Sydney and chronicled this story better than anyone, in true time while it was happening. I referred to his archived literature for details and quotes, especially during the chapters about the games played in Sydney and information regarding the opposing Olympic teams. I cannot thank him and *Baseball America* magazine enough for granting me the permission to utilize that critical information. Other authors at *Baseball America* whom I need to credit include Jim Callis, Ken Daley, Wayne Graczyk, Milton Jamial, Will Lingo, Bruce Miles, Alan Schwarz, and Thomas St. John.

I could not have written the book at all without the unbelievable assistance of Sabrina Rood, who took on my project like it was her own: first transcribing hours of audio and putting it onto paper and then editing my first draft as well as the final version. Sabrina, I am forever grateful for your hard work and dedication in helping me come up with a finished product.

Of course, none of this would have been possible without the amazing support of my wife, Jessica. After having her encourage me numerous times over the course of our marriage to write a book, I finally took her advice. Once I began the project, I don't think she was fully prepared for the amount of time I spent locked in my office. But nonetheless, she got through all the lonely nights. Jessica, your love and support, and that of our two beautiful daughters, Emma and Grace, means everything to me.

I need to credit my younger brother, Steven, with whom I spent so many days after grade school playing whiffle ball and stick ball in the street in front of our home in Cupertino. It was then that I developed my love for the game of baseball, which in turn ended up being a strong enough passion for me to pursue a career in. Steven, I have enjoyed sharing with you in being a lifelong fan of the San Francisco Giants (including their 2010 World Series title at Game 5 in person with you in Arlington, TX) since our time as kids in the Bay Area, and I thank you and your wife, Heather, along with my nieces, Madeline and Olivia, for your support.

I want to thank all of my family and friends—our group that we hang out with all the time here in Houston, my wife's side of the family in New York, and my relatives and friends in Northern California—along with some in particular who have always been among my loudest cheerleaders: Jackie and Ron Burns, Bruce and Barbara Dunlop, Jason and Michelle Jester, Karol and Walter Scally, Kevin, Alison, Zach and Ben Schreiber, and Craig and Karin Waugh (BTD's biggest fans).

Last but not least, I need to thank my parents, Larry and Sue Fanucchi, for the values they taught me and the dedication it took on their part to see that I received my education and a college degree. In an example of how much they enjoyed supporting me and being a part of my career, both of my parents traveled to Canada for the Pan Am Games and were there in the stands cheering on the red, white, and blue as very proud Americans. And I was so proud to have them there with me as part of this journey. We had such a great time celebrating in Winnipeg after Team USA had clinched an Olympic berth.

I will never forget the excitement level in Dad's voice when he called my archaic cell phone in Sydney during the gold medal game vs. Cuba (in the middle of the night back in Arizona no less), after he had seen on the internet that Team USA had taken a 1-0 lead. Nor will I forget how excited Mom was to see me come walking off the airplane back in Tucson, after I had been a part of something so spectacular.

Mom and Dad, I hope you enjoy reading the book so much that it brings back some of the thrill, just like those moments did over a decade ago.

Lastly, I hope I've provided some interesting reading and a couple of exciting moments for each and every one of you readers. I thank you for taking the time out of your life that you spent with this story. That is an honor of mine that I do not take for granted.

My parents, Larry and Sue Fanucchi, with me in Winnipeg, Canada at the 1999 Pan Am Games

ABOUT THE AUTHOR

David Fanucchi was born in Burlingame, California and was raised in the small San Francisco Bay Area suburb of Cupertino, near San Jose. A 1988 graduate of Monta Vista High School, Fanucchi attended De Anza Junior College for two years to play on the Dons' golf team before transferring to California State University, Chico in 1990.

After graduating from Chico State in 1993 with a degree in journalism, Fanucchi has spent the last 20 years working in various media relations and communications capacities for both amateur and professional sports teams and organizations. Most notably, Fanucchi was the Director of Communications for USA Baseball from 1999 to 2006. It was then that he worked as the official Team USA Press Officer for the 1999 USA Baseball Pan Am Team and the 2000 USA Baseball Olympic Team. He was inducted into the Chico State Public Relations Department Hall of Fame in 2009.

Currently, Fanucchi is the President of his own sports-business public relations firm, Gold Medal PR. He resides in Houston, Texas with his wife, Jessica, and daughters Emma (8) and Grace (6). This is his first published book.

Made in the USA
Charleston, SC
10 November 2012